LIVING WITH DRUGS

Living with Drugs

SIXTH EDITION

Michael Gossop

Now in its sixth edition, Living with Drugs continues to be a well-respected and indispensable overview of drugs and drug taking. Michael Gossop has updated this new edition to take account of the changes in drug use and in social responses to drug problems that have occurred since the previous edition, published in 2000.

Written in an accessible style and providing a balanced perspective, the book is ideal for psychologists, nurses, social workers, and for anyone with an interest in this complex, ever-present and emotive issue.

Living with Drugs
Sixth Edition

MICHAEL GOSSOP
Maudsley Hospital/Institute of Psychiatry, Kings College London, UK

ASHGATE

Published by
Ashgate Publishing Limited
Gower House
Croft Road
Aldershot
Hampshire GU11 3HR
England

Ashgate Publishing Company
Suite 420
101 Cherry Street
Burlington, VT 05401-4405
USA

Ashgate website: http://www.ashgate.com

British Library Cataloguing in Publication Data
Gossop, Michael, 1948-
    Living with drugs. - 6th ed.
    1. Drugs - Physiological effect 2. Drug abuse 3. Narcotic habit
    I. Title
    615.7

Library of Congress Cataloging-in-Publication Data
Gossop, Michael, 1948-
    Living with drugs / by Michael Gossop. --6th ed.
        p. cm.
    Includes bibliographical references and index.
    ISBN-13: 978-0-7546-4917-5 1. Substance abuse--Dictionaries. 2. Substance abuse--Popular works. I. Title.

    RC564.29.G67 2007
    362.29--dc22

2006032976

ISBN: 978-0-7546-4917-5 (Hbk)
ISBN: 978-0-7546-4919-9 (Pbk)

Printed and bound in Great Britain by MPG Books Ltd, Bodmin, Cornwall.

Contents

Preface to the Sixth Edition

It is easy to look at 'the drug problem' through today's eyes only. But this gives, at best, a partial, and at worst, a seriously distorted view of drugs and drug taking. The use of drugs, like everything else, has a context and a history. And it is both dynamic and constantly changing.

Not surprisingly, there have been many changes since the first edition of *Living with Drugs* was written. There have been changes in the types of drug problems that cause most concern. Some of these have their roots in earlier patterns of drug taking. Others appeared unpredictably and without clear links to existing patterns of use. What has not changed is the vast economic influence of the legal and illegal drugs trade. The alcohol and tobacco industries continue to prosper and to feed the national governments who derive taxes from them. The global trade in illegal drugs continues to expand, and is estimated (United Nations, 1998) as being worth about $400 billion per year (almost twice the size of the market in motor vehicles).

In the UK, as well as in many other countries, the use of heroin has increased greatly during the past 25 years. Patterns of heroin use have also changed. At one time, heroin was taken almost exclusively by injection. Many heroin users in the UK as well as in Asia now take heroin by smoking. Many former Soviet-bloc and Eastern European countries have developed serious heroin problems, and other countries, such as Thailand, Pakistan and India, have suffered from explosive increases in heroin problems which have caused serious imbalances and stresses within the social, political and health care systems of those countries.

New types of drug taking have appeared and caused consternation. The rapid increase in the use of crack cocaine and its associated problems has produced concern (at times verging upon hysteria). The development of crack cocaine use in the UK and in other European countries has taken a different path from that in the US, where the use of crack cocaine and a variety of associated problems forced themselves onto the country's attention during the 1980s and caused a great deal of social and political agitation. In Europe, despite many warnings to the contrary by US commentators, there was no sudden increase in the use of cocaine or any dramatic appearance of problems linked to the use of crack cocaine. However, the fact that the US's problems were not immediately translated into European countries tended to disguise what has been a more gradual expansion of cocaine use.

The main European entry points for the trafficking of cocaine are Spain and the Netherlands, and cocaine trafficking within Europe is now well established and increasing. Spain currently has the highest prevalence of cocaine use in Europe. The UK was among the first of the European countries where the availability and use of cocaine became widespread, and estimates for 2002/3 suggest that as many as 700,000 people may have used cocaine in the previous year. A fairly accurate indicator of the increased availability of the drug is that the street price for a gram of cocaine in Europe has fallen steadily since 1990. Street prices in 2002 were about half those of 1990. In the US, street prices have fallen even more, and in 2002 they were about one-third of the levels in 1990. Worldwide estimates suggest that there may be about 13 million users of cocaine.

Some of the earlier complacency about the relatively benign effects of cocaine use was linked to the use of cocaine powder and the fact that it was often taken by snorting. Crack cocaine smoking has been associated with more problems and with more serious problems. However, many of the problems that are attributed to crack are in fact caused by poverty and inflamed by social alienation. This is true, for example, of a great deal of the crime and violence that has been associated with crack in the US. A considered political response to such drug problems should include action against poverty and urban alienation. Attempts to isolate drug problems from their social context are doomed to failure.

Ecstasy appeared and established itself as a popular and fashionable dance drug among young people during the late 1980s. It also reawakened the same sort of outrage that was directed against cannabis and LSD during the 1960s. Indeed, the social history of ecstasy has many similarities to that of LSD: both had a dormant period after development, a brief flirtation with psychotherapy, and then both established strong links with the music and hedonism of a youth culture.

The use of cannabis continues to wax and wane. For several years it ceased to be a fashionable drug among young people in the UK, though it retained many ageing users. More recently it appears to have regained its appeal for younger drug users, and its use has now become virtually normalized for many people. The British Crime Survey (2002/3) showed that cannabis was the most widely used of the illegal drugs with about 3 million people having used it in the previous year, and more than a quarter of 20–24-year-olds having used it. During recent years, a shadow has appeared over the use of cannabis with the revival of the ancient belief that cannabis causes madness among its users.

It remains disappointing that the UK has failed to correct its profoundly flawed drugs laws. In the previous editions of *Living with Drugs* I argued strongly against the nonsense of wasting resources upon chasing, arresting and, too often, expensively and pointlessly locking people up in prison for using cannabis. Even after the recent reclassification of cannabis, it continues to be illegal and still attracts the same legal sanctions as more dangerous drugs. Cannabis users may still be criminalized and imprisoned because of their use of this drug.

The UK and US enthusiasm for imprisonment as a solution to social problems is peculiar. There is a growing divide in the approach to criminal justice between the US and UK on one side and most Western European countries on the other. The increasingly harsh approach of the UK and the US is characterized by the greater use of imprisonment which is reflected in the ever-increasing prison populations of those countries. The US now has a prison population of more than one million people, and the number of people imprisoned in the UK every year increased from about 20,000 in 1950 to 40,000 in 1970, then to over 75,000 in 2005. Up to three-quarters of those in prison are there because of drug-related problems. Increasing use has been made of rigid and often disproportionate sentencing rules such as minimum sentencing, or making punishments more onerous or degrading through the wearing of distinctive clothing and other forms of public shaming. The average length of sentences for drug offences has increased from about 2 years in 1984 to about three and a half years in 2004. Less attention is paid to individuality in sentencing, more sparing use of imprisonment, effective rehabilitative interventions or respect for the dignity of prisoners as citizens.

It is possible to learn a lot about a society by the ways in which it deals with offending behaviours. Prisons are a reflection of the society in which they exist. Winston Churchill said that the responses of society towards crime were an 'unfailing test' of civilization, and Nelson Mandela said no one truly knows a nation until they have been inside its jails. A crude test of the role of prisons is to ask whether we would be happy for our relatives to be held in them. It was Friedrich Nietzsche (improbably) who wrote, 'Mistrust those in whom the urge to punish is strong'.

Without doubt the most dramatic impact on the drugs scene over the past decades has been caused by the arrival of HIV infection and AIDS. The first cases of AIDS among drug injectors in Europe were reported in 1984 (two years after the publication of the first edition of *Living with Drugs*). The experience of Edinburgh is, perhaps, one of the best-known accounts of HIV in Britain. Edinburgh was doubly unfortunate to experience an increase in the numbers of people who were injecting drugs just before the threat of HIV was identified. This led to a large number of inexperienced drug injectors with a ready supply of good quality heroin but with restricted access to clean injecting equipment and little or no contact with services which might advise them or respond to their needs. Worse still, some of the existing local responses and attitudes to drug taking made the problems worse. This was certainly true of the anti-drug campaign which restricted the availability of needles and syringes. This was one of the main factors leading to drug users sharing injecting equipment and therefore to the very high rates of HIV infection.

HIV infection has not spread evenly either within or across countries. At the time of writing this sixth edition, rates of HIV infection among drug injectors in Britain remain relatively low. Some countries have experienced a much more rapid spread of the virus and are faced with extremely serious problems. Since the break-up of the former Soviet Union, there has been a huge increase in drug injection problems in several of the post-Soviet countries. Russia, for example, is now estimated to have at least three million drug injectors, with at least 650,000 drug injectors in Ukraine. This increase in injection drug use has been accompanied by the appalling threat of HIV infection, and HIV/AIDS has established itself as a grave public health threat throughout much of Eastern Europe. In many of these countries, the HIV epidemic is already largely out of control and is rapidly accelerating. HIV incidence rates in some post-Soviet countries are now among the highest in the world.

One of the pragmatic measures that has since been adopted in many countries to reduce the harm associated with injecting drugs involves making clean needles and syringes available to drug users. This has sometimes been done by supplying injecting equipment from pharmacies on a commercial basis, or through free exchange schemes. Needles and syringes have been made available through dispensing machines and in several countries the use of bleach has been recommended and provided as a back-up to the provision of clean equipment.

The urgent need to respond to the threat of HIV and AIDS has radically altered the drugs agenda. The rhetoric of the US and some other countries may continue to promote the discredited ideals of the 'war against drugs' and 'zero tolerance', but living with drugs has now become an imperative. Throwing drug takers into prison seldom deters them from using drugs (either in prison or after leaving prison). Simply putting drug takers in prison in order to punish them does not make the problem go away. Some people are introduced to drugs (including injected drugs) for the first time while in prison. Drug injectors who may carry HIV or hepatitis infections may continue to inject drugs and to share needles in prison. It is dangerously counterproductive for society to aggravate the already serious threat of HIV by creating its own sumps of infection.

AIDS has produced many changes in national responses to drug problems. Some of these have been welcome. It is good that there has been an increased awareness that it is both acceptable and desirable to reduce the harm that drug users may suffer as a result of their drug taking. Concern about AIDS has also increased political willingness to provide money to support drug treatment and support services. It is a great pity that it has taken such a tragic development to produce these changes.

Living with Drugs, as the title indicates, is about drugs – the different kinds of drugs, the reasons why people take drugs, the ways in which people have used drugs, and some of the difficulties associated with drugs. It is also about the ordinariness of drug taking. Where drugs are presented as if they were something peculiarly alien and unusually dangerous, it becomes difficult to hold a sensible discussion about them. Since most of the 'information' we receive about drugs and drug taking comes from television and newspapers it is unfortunate that the mass media have failed so dismally to give an accurate portrayal of these issues. Media coverage of drug taking is generally characterized by inaccuracy, exaggeration and sensationalism. Television coverage in particular has often been irresponsible in peddling misinformation about drugs. If drugs could sue for misrepresentation, defamation and libel, they would have done so.

This book tries to put drug taking in a more balanced perspective. It looks at the full spectrum of drugs, and shows how drug taking is something that almost everyone does. People who drink tea and coffee are drug takers. Cigarette smokers are drug takers. Beer, wine and whisky are drugs just as surely as heroin and cocaine are drugs. Nor is this a clever play on words. Alcohol, that most domesticated drug, is a very powerful intoxicant. It can produce dramatic changes in people's behaviour and it can cause many different sorts of illness and health damage, including cancers and brain damage. The social costs of alcohol are massively greater than those of all the illegal drugs put together. Cigarette smoking is also an ordinary form of drug taking that kills vastly greater numbers of people each year than are killed by every one of the illegal drugs.

Nonetheless, it would be wrong to take the message of *Living with Drugs* to be simply that alcohol or cigarettes are more dangerous than the illegal drugs, or that all drugs are equally dangerous (or equally safe). It is true that the number of casualties of cigarettes and alcohol is much greater than that of illegal drug use. But the number of cigarette smokers and drinkers is also much greater. A considered assessment of the risks (as well as the benefits) of drug use requires a more detailed and a more complex analysis. Each of the drugs discussed in this book tends to vary along many different dimensions. The hazards of use may include risks to the physical and psychological health of the users, the social penalties incurred by use or abuse, and the risk of dependence. In addition, the effects of drugs may be directly linked to the drug or indirectly related to behavioural patterns of use or to social consequences of use. Different drugs cannot simply be compared on some broad, generalized scale of safe/dangerous or good/bad.

The analysis of risk is a complicated business. Some element of risk is involved in every single aspect of human behaviour. A proper understanding of the risks of drug taking depends upon the understanding that there is no such thing as behaviour with zero risk, absolute safety. Our perceptions and judgement of risk are also dependent upon our preconceptions, beliefs and values. Some risks are greater than they seem. Other risks are less than they seem. And it is a peculiarity of human psychology to underestimate common events and activities which carry relatively high risk and to overestimate others which have an extremely low risk. The risk of dying from a lightning strike are infinitesimally small (about 10 million to one) yet many people are frightened of this remote possibility. The risk of dying from a smoking-related disease is very high, yet few smokers are as worried by this risk as they should be. Our cities are managed for the convenience of a metal life-form which runs on wheels and expels poisonous gases. In the course of the 20th century, the motor car has killed off 25 million of us. But despite this appalling fact, few of us seriously view it as a threat.

When we assess the risks of drugs, and if comparisons between drugs are attempted, it is best to attempt to do so at a specific level. Some drugs appear to carry greater risks of dependence than others. Some drugs can be used in ways which carry greater or lesser physical risks to the user. Some drugs carry serious health hazards however they are used. Some drugs carry moderate health risks but, because they are widely used, the extent of the damage associated with them is widely felt. Other drugs are more hazardous but, because they are used by only a comparatively small number of people, the extent of the damage is less clearly seen. More commonly, different drugs are perceived to be dangerous or not because of the socially accepted image that is attached to them.

One reason why this message has taken so long to be accepted is that it does not suit the requirements of the mass media. The need for big headlines, catchy soundbites and, particularly, scare stories, does not fit easily with the task of communicating complex issues. And the desire to report instant quick-fix cures does not make it attractive to provide responsible coverage of less dramatic but more effective responses and interventions. There is a rough hierarchy of irresponsibility within the media, with television and tabloid newspapers at the lowest and worst level, the 'serious' newspapers at a marginally higher level, and with only the radio coverage approaching competence. Somewhere there must be a strong PhD thesis to be written about this topic of drugs in the media.

Living with Drugs is a book about the fact that drug taking in one form or another is with us to stay. Campaigns to rid the world of drugs are misconceived and utterly futile. A drug-free society may not even be desirable. But in any case, an illegal drug trade which is worth hundreds of billions of dollars is a powerful testimony to the massive and pervasive demand for drugs. Drug taking is here to stay and this book is about how we must learn to manage our drug taking, to make more sensible decisions about our use of drugs in order to reduce the risks of drug taking and to try to avoid the many sorts of harm that drugs can cause. *Living with Drugs* is about living with drugs.

Michael Gossop
National Addiction Centre
Maudsley Hospital
London
June 2006

Author's Apologia

The words that we use to talk about drug taking confront us with a terminological minefield. Unfortunately, many of these terms are central to the discussion. For example, the word *addiction* is strongly disliked by many because of its 'excess meaning' and in particular for the implications that it is believed to carry of physical processes or forces outside the control of the individual which compel them to act in certain ways. My own view is that the word is not without its uses precisely because it does still capture something of the flavour of the compulsion to use drugs that is at the heart of what we mean by this problem.

But I do not believe that an addiction is understandable merely as a physical process (though some of its underlying foundations are unquestionably physiological) or that addictive behaviour is literally uncontrollable (though the addictions are characterized by an impairment of control). An addiction seems to be most sensibly viewed as a learned psychological process (perhaps as an over-learned habit). There are those who take exception to the use of the word *alcoholism*. There is a lobby which objects to the use of the term *syndrome* in talking about dependence because of its medical connotations. The World Health Organization, for reasons of its own, objects to *addiction* but encourages the much nastier (in my opinion) *narcotics* (a word which either has no meaning or else has an inaccurate meaning). The term *addict* is regarded by some as pejorative, and at least one scientific journal refuses to accept articles containing such words as *addict* on the grounds that they are likely to perpetuate negative stereotypes. *Abuse* and *misuse* also create consternation. Some authors insist that methadone should not be called an opiate but is more correctly described by the uglier term *opioid*.

My own preferences for certain terms will no doubt become clear to the reader. As far as possible I have tried to avoid getting bogged down in terminological issues. That is not to say that I think these issues are unimportant. Many of them are both important and interesting. But one cannot please all the readers all the time, and I would rather have tried to look at the issues of drugs and drug taking than at the language which we use to talk about them.

Acknowledgements

I would like to be able to thank by name the very many people who have helped in so many ways while I was writing the several editions of this book. If they are not named here, I offer my apologies. They include Mark Brutton; Roy Johnson of the National Council on Alcoholism; Malcolm Lader, Griffith Edwards, John Strang and Martin Jarvis at the National Addiction Centre; Alex Irving of the Transport and Road Research Laboratory; Douglas Davies of the Department of Theology at Nottingham University; Hans Eysenck at the Institute of Psychiatry; Roy Robertson at the Edinburgh Drug Addiction Study; Amanda Sandford at ASH; and my Australian colleagues Robert Ali and David Watts (at the Drug and Alcohol Services Council, Adelaide) and Maggie Brady (at the Australian Institute of Aboriginal and Torres Islander Studies). I would like to thank John Witton, formerly of the Institute for the Study of Drug Dependence, and currently at the National Addiction Centre, for his help with all editions of this book, and especially for his advice about the cannabis chapter; also Susanne Schaaf of infoSekta, Zurich; Bill Saunders, formerly of Curtin University in Perth, Western Australia; and Gillian Tober at the Leeds Addiction Unit for their many suggestions and contributions to the book since it first appeared. I am grateful to the climbers Joe Tasker and Alan Rouse for talking to me about their experiences. Finally, I would like to remember two friends who have died since *Living with Drugs* was first published. I would like to acknowledge the help and support that I received during my visits to Pakistan from my friend Don McIntosh who was so tragically killed in an air crash in Thailand in 1991. I would also like to remember my friend James Hunt, the former World Champion Grand Prix driver who helped me put together the material for Chapter 12 by describing his experiences of racing Formula One Grand Prix cars. James died at his home in London in 1993.

Chapter 1

The Chemistry of Everyday Life

Every society has its own drugs. People have always used drugs to alter their states of consciousness, eagerly seeking out whatever naturally occurring substances can be used as drugs, and wherever possible deliberately cultivating them. Every part of the Earth that is capable of producing drugs has been used for this purpose, and even where the land is not available, other technologies have been invented to support the production of drugs. Vast areas of Europe are covered by vines. The cannabis plant flourishes in Africa and Asia; and from the Middle East down through Asia the opium poppy grows – both in its wild state and under cultivation. In the cooler, wetter climate of the British Isles some of the best arable land in the country is turned over to the production of that most English narcotic, the hop. In the colder countries of northern Europe where the winters are long and the growing seasons are short, spirits are distilled. In the Americas there are plantations of the coca plant, tobacco and cactuses containing mescaline, and throughout the world there are mushrooms containing other hallucinogenic drugs. The only people with no traditional drug of their own would appear to be the Inuit, who live in a land so bleak and uncompromising that it does not permit the cultivation of any intoxicant.

Drugs play an important part in the lives of every one of us. Drug taking is an almost universal phenomenon, and in the statistical sense of the term it is the person who does not take drugs who is abnormal. Many readers are likely to react against any suggestion that they are drug takers, to see it as some sort of accusation. The comfortable but quite mistaken orthodoxy insists that the 'normal' people who make up the majority of our society do not use drugs: set in sharp contrast to this sober normality are the 'abnormal' minority who do.

The term 'drug taking' conjures up an image of syringes, needles, heroin and all the paraphernalia of the junkie dropout. It is surrounded by all manner of sinister implications which reinforce the view that the use of drugs is a strange, deviant and inexplicable form of behaviour – possibly even a symptom of mental illness. We have been encouraged to regard the junkies who are such a conspicuous part of the city centres and urban wastelands of New York, London, Amsterdam and Zurich as some sort of alien breed. Consequently, we are tempted to feel that our own use of cigarettes, of alcohol, of sleeping tablets or of tranquillizers is quite different from their use of heroin. But are the two sorts of drug taking really so dissimilar?

The emotional reaction that is so common whenever drugs and drug taking are mentioned is quite unwarranted, and it presents a serious obstacle to our efforts to understand this issue. Tea and tobacco contain drugs (caffeine and nicotine). Alcohol

Living with Drugs

is a drug; heroin and cocaine are drugs. All are drugs in the same sense of the term, though that does not mean that all drugs are the same or that there are no differences in the risks associated with using these different substances.

Dictionaries are particularly unhelpful in clarifying precisely what we mean by the word 'drug'. There are few satisfactory definitions of any of the terms that are used in this area. The traditional definitions of a drug tend to emphasize the chemical properties and the medical values of a specific substance. In *Butterworth's Medical Dictionary*, for instance, a drug is defined as 'any chemical substance, synthetic or extracted from plant or animal tissue and of known or unknown composition, which is used as a medicament to prevent or cure disease'. This definition is hardly adequate for the actual way in which doctors use drugs, much less for the purposes of the present discussion. Here we are concerned most especially with the psychological (psychoactive) effects of drugs.

It is extraordinary that so little attention has been paid to the mind-altering properties of drugs. Throughout history, men and women have made strenuous efforts to discover and to invent substances and techniques which will help them change their psychological states. Another definition of drugs is needed which does cover their psychoactive effects. A psychoactive drug may therefore be seen as any chemical substance, whether of natural or synthetic origin, which can be used to alter perception, mood or other psychological states.

As definitions go, this is reasonably acceptable. The difficulty with trying to provide a definition of drugs is that drugs have no intrinsic property that sets them apart from other substances. Certainly, there is no objective characteristic which can be used to distinguish them from non-drugs. People have become drunk on water which they were told was gin; they have swallowed salt tablets and shown clear signs of sedation; they have smoked inert material which they have been told was cannabis and become stoned. Should these otherwise inert chemicals therefore be classified as drugs? Certainly, they were able to produce a definite psychological effect on the person who took them. In the final analysis, the concept of a 'drug' is a social artifact. What we regard as a drug depends as much upon its social meaning and the way in which people use it as upon its pharmacological or physiological properties.

An important part of what is generally called the drugs problem is the set of attitudes that society maintains towards drugs and drug taking. Much of the damage that is associated with drug taking is a result of mistaken laws and policies, and of hypocritical and self-deluding attitudes. We live in a society which tries to reconcile its disapproval of the use of drugs for non-medical purposes with the fact that vast amounts of psychoactive drugs are consumed in this way. The term 'drug taker' is used as a condemnation, as a way of identifying someone who is involved in a strange and deviant form of behaviour. There is a continuing reluctance to face up to the fact that drugs and drug takers are a part of our everyday life. Many people find it too threatening to acknowledge this, including a sizeable number of scientists, doctors and other 'experts'. Society is not made up of drug takers and non-users. We all take drugs in one way or another. The essence of the drugs problem seems to be that other people sometimes decide to take different drugs for different reasons.

When people are faced with inconsistencies of this sort, they frequently use psychological defence mechanisms in an attempt to reconcile the conflict. One of the most common of these defence mechanisms is called 'denial'. In order to resolve their conflict people deny that their own use of alcohol, tobacco or whatever else it might be has anything in common with the illicit drugs that are used by the people they like to think of as 'drug takers'. The general reluctance to recognize that tea, coffee, alcohol and tobacco really are drugs is a reflection of a widespread, completely irrational, fear of drugs. Of course, this is not to deny that many people are badly damaged by the way they use drugs. But the generalized fear of drugs is misplaced. There are sensible as well as stupid ways to use drugs. It is a reasonable expectation that no drug should be considered completely safe; and even the least dangerous of drugs can be used in a way that is likely to be damaging to the person who is taking it. But since there is no chance that people will stop using drugs, it is imperative that we try to understand what sort of process drug taking really is. We can only do this if we re-examine some of the basic misunderstandings that surround the whole issue. At the very centre of the muddled thinking is this refusal to acknowledge that we are all drug takers.

As a continuation of this basic misconception, society clings to the notion that some of the substances we use are 'good' drugs whereas others are 'bad' drugs. LSD is a 'bad' drug. Heroin and crack cocaine are, supposedly, the worst of the 'bad' drugs. Prozac, Librium and Valium are 'good' drugs: alcohol tends to be classed as a 'good' drug even though we are becoming increasingly aware of the risks that can be associated with its misuse; and tobacco has fallen fairly rapidly from the 'good' towards the very 'bad' category. Some substances escape the 'drug' classification altogether and are regarded as non-drugs – like tea and coffee. Sometimes the 'good/bad' distinction becomes synonymous with that of 'safe/dangerous'. Society would like to believe that our good drugs are all safe, or at least comparatively safe, whereas the bad drugs should all have sinister and dangerous effects. In this way, scientific questions about the actual effects of a particular drug become entangled with issues of personal morality and subjective beliefs. This has led to some quite absurd pronouncements on the part of otherwise respected scientists and physicians: the need to justify their belief in the badness of certain drugs seems to have been so powerful that they have lost the ability to think straight on those matters. By presenting personal opinions and moral views in the guise of incontrovertible scientific fact they have done more than anyone to perpetuate the myths and misconceptions about drug taking.

These 'good/bad' and 'safe/dangerous' classifications vary from time to time, and from culture to culture. The decline and fall of smoking, for example, has taken place within the lifetime of this book. During the 1960s young people seemed to be turning to drugs in a quite unprecedented manner. LSD and cannabis were taken by millions of people. During the latter part of the decade and into the 1970s, other more sinister names such as methedrine, barbiturates and heroin began to be heard more often. The reaction of the press and of the mass media was one of righteous indignation. It seemed as if some completely new form of evil had suddenly descended upon the world.

A similar response was provoked by the appearance of crack cocaine in the US. One of the first newspaper references to this was in the *Los Angeles Times* in November 1984. Soon after this, America began to experience increasing levels of social problems associated with crack, and the drug served as a convenient focus for President Reagan's 'war on drugs'. In a nationally televised address to the nation the president claimed that cocaine was 'killing a whole generation of our children' and 'tearing our country apart'. Words like 'plague' and 'crisis' had become standard terminology for discussion of the use of smokeable cocaine.

The Americans lost no time in passing on the message and in telling the UK that what America has today the rest of the world gets tomorrow. The UK's news media saw the emperor's new clothes and duly discovered non-existent horrors in 'the crack of doom' which threatened our cities (*Daily Star*), 'an epidemic of the killer drug crack' (*Cambridge Evening News*) and 'crack highway to oblivion' (*Liverpool Echo*). More appropriate headlines might have been 'Newspapers Overdose on Outrage'. Few better examples could ever be found of the sort of moral panic which is so regularly provoked by drug taking. These drug scares do not deter people from taking drugs. If anything they are likely to advertise and promote the behaviour that they claim to be preventing. The frequency of teenage suicides goes up after news reports about them, and in a piece entitled 'How to Launch a Nationwide Drug Menace', Brecher tells of how exaggerated newspaper reports and televised police raids starting in 1960 actually functioned as promotion and advertising for glue sniffing.

The term 'Bohemian' is often used to refer to someone who acts and dresses in an unconventional way. Few people know much about the original group of Bohemians except indirectly through Puccini's opera *La Bohème*. The Bohemians belonged to Paris of the 1840s. Like the hippies of a later age, the young men let their hair grow long, and they dressed in a manner which seemed shocking to their middle-class critics. They espoused unconventional, non-materialistic philosophies, lived in comparative poverty and flaunted their unconventional patterns of sexual behaviour. As with the hippies, drugs played an important part in their lifestyle. As well as drinking large amounts of alcohol, they horrified the public by their enthusiasm for a particular stimulant which they consumed in large quantities. A medical textbook published in 1909 by Sir T. Clifford Allbutt and Dr Humphrey Rolleston warned against the excessive use of this drug: 'The sufferer is tremulous and loses his self command; he is subject to fits of agitation and depression. He loses colour and has a haggard appearance … As with other such agents, a renewed dose of the poison gives temporary relief, but at the cost of future misery.' This drug which so shocked public opinion was coffee.

A reversal of roles of a different sort has taken place with regard to opiates such as heroin and morphine. Few people nowadays would hesitate in naming them as the most dangerous of drugs. Yet, in the US, it seems to have been a common medical practice during the early part of the 20th century to treat alcoholics by prescribing morphine for them.

Drug Taking – A Wider Perspective

It is impossible to be certain how long people have been using drugs to change their states of consciousness; certainly the systematic use of drugs dates back many thousands of years. It seems likely that the earliest drugs to be used would have been those that occur naturally. About 4,000 plants are known to yield psychoactive drugs, but only about 40 of these have been regularly used for their intoxicating effects. Interestingly, very few seem to have been known in the Old World. Prior to the voyages of exploration, Europe had comparatively little choice in its drugs. There was no tea, no coffee, no tobacco, little opium, little or no cannabis and virtually no hallucinogens ... only alcohol. As a result, alcohol had to fill a very wide range of functions. It was used as a social beverage, as a tranquillizer, as a sedative, as a stimulant and as an intoxicant to produce drunkenness and delirium. Alcohol became the European drug and it is still the dominant drug in European and Western culture.

The voyages of exploration that opened up the Americas revealed a wide range of psychoactive drugs hitherto quite unknown in the Old World. The first voyage of Christopher Columbus discovered people on Hispaniola and Cuba who smoked cigars, and in Central and South America there was an abundance of psychoactive substances. The explorers brought these home with them. Strangely enough, the one drug that seems to have been largely unknown to the Native American peoples was alcohol. In return for showing such drugs as tobacco, peyote and cocaine to the European explorers, they were introduced to alcohol.

The general reluctance to use psychoactive drugs (and particularly drugs with hallucinogenic properties) that was built into European society at this time cannot be entirely explained in terms of the absence of the drugs themselves. Mescaline, peyote and cocaine may have been unknown in the Old World, but other drugs were available. Hallucinogenic mushrooms grow widely throughout northern Europe and there are various common substances which can be used to induce altered states of consciousness. Cannabis had been introduced into Europe with the Muslim occupation of Spain more than a thousand years ago, and although there was little interest in it as a psychoactive drug, it was being regularly cultivated for hemp fibre by the 17th century. So drugs were available, had there been a sufficient desire to use them.

This tendency to resist using drugs other than alcohol may have owed much to the dominant cultural influence of the Christian Church. Despite a distinctly secular attitude towards certain pleasures of the flesh, the use of drugs (other than alcohol) to modify states of consciousness has been consistently reviled by the Church. This may have been because of their links with other, more 'primitive', religions. Alternatively, it may have been because dramatically altered states of consciousness were thought of in terms of possession – usually possession by devils. Consequently, knowledge about the uses of drugs remained in the hands of various closed groups: apothecaries, alchemists, physicians and a few individuals who involved themselves with such esoteric practices as witchcraft.

Although many of the things that seem to have found their way into the witches' cauldron were probably there for their psychological significance, others contained powerful drugs. Bufotenine, for instance, is a highly toxic drug secreted by the toad. It is related to psilocybin (a drug which is found in certain hallucinogenic mushrooms) and to LSD. It is also related to an extremely important brain chemical called serotonin from which it was first isolated. However, the toxic effects of bufotenine were known for centuries before its chemical discovery.

In 1670, the Professor of Medicine at Leipzig noted that 'Toads aroused to the point of fury are venomous', and the following suggestion is contained in a medieval recipe for poisoners: 'Place a toad in a sack with a little salt and shake well. Use the salt for giving to men.' This procedure could be guaranteed to provoke fury in even the most placid of toads, and was apparently useful for slow and chronic poisonings.

Nor was the life of the South American toad made any happier by the existence of an ancient Maya drink of heated mead into which a live toad was dropped at the last minute. Again, this was not done out of a desire to invent the cocktail olive but for the hallucinogenic drug in the toad's skin. A bizarre modern counterpart has been reported in connection with the South American cane toad (now also available in Australia). In the US, a University of Florida student described the process of toadlicking: 'Picking them up is easy because they have dry skin, and that's usually enough to get them mad so they slime. Then all you've got to do is lick the head a couple of times and you're on the way' (reported in *The Guardian*, 11 July 1990). The high is described as being similar to that of LSD.

Plants containing henbane and belladonna have also been used in the manufacture of salves and potions for witchcraft. Henbane contains scopolamine, and has been known for thousands of years to produce hallucinations and delirium. In the 13th century Bishop Albertus Magnus described how henbane was used to conjure up demons; under its influence people routinely described and believed in their visions of hell. Similarly, the thornapple, or devil's apple, which contains atropine, was said to be a major ingredient in the witches' Sabbath. Under the influence of these and other drugs, the witches flew through the night on their medieval trips. The ignorant and the superstitious mistook the hallucinations for reality, and it suited the Church to discourage the use of psychoactive drugs through their supposed link with the devil.

Of the naturally occurring drugs, those that have had most influence upon our thinking about drugs have been opium and its derivatives, notably heroin and morphine. The word 'opium' is derived from a Greek word meaning juice, and the substance itself is derived from the oriental poppy. This annual plant produces white or purplish flowers. If a cut is made into the fruit capsule shortly before the flowers fall, opium oozes out in the form of a sticky solution.

One of the first references to opium is probably to be found in Homer's *Odyssey*,[1] where Helen of Troy was presented with a gift of a drug called 'nepenthe' by the king of Egypt. By the second century AD, opium had established itself as a valuable aid to contemporary medicine. The Roman physician Galen recommended the drug theriaca, whose principal component is opium, as a treatment for many conditions, including headaches, deafness, epilepsy and jaundice, as well as 'melancholy and all pestilences'. The use of opium spread from Asia Minor through Persia to India and China. It was not, however, until the second half of the 18th century that opium smoking became an established habit in the Far East, though it was probably first introduced to China by Arab traders as early as the 8th century.

England, too, has consumed its fair share of opium. Byron, Shelley, Keats, Lamb and Scott all took it, and William Wilberforce, George Crabbe, Thomas De Quincey and Samuel Taylor Coleridge became addicted to it. But its use was not confined to poets, writers and philosophers. It was often used instead of alcohol in the marshy Fenland areas of Cambridgeshire, Lincolnshire, Huntingdonshire and Norfolk. For most of the 19th century, the Fens were an unhealthy area in which to live: they were one of the main areas of the country in which malaria was endemic, and ague and rheumatic complaints were also particularly widespread. Opium was undoubtedly a useful folk remedy for such disorders, but its use was not restricted to such medical problems. Poppy-head tea was often given to fractious children to calm them down, and opium was also used for recreational purposes. At the time, virtually no distinction seems to have been made between the social and the medical uses of the drug.

One custom was to drink beer with a piece of opium dissolved in it. Indeed, this custom became so well established that brewers and publicans produced opium beer in order to meet the popular taste – much to the surprise and inconvenience of travellers to the area. In 1850, Charles Kingsley described how on market days in Cambridge 'you will see the little boxes, doozens and doozens, a'rcady on the counter; and never a venture man's wife goo by, that what calls in for her pennord o' elevation'. In such a dreary, foggy and unhealthy place, drugs could well provide some diversion. Another commentator at the time (one Dr Rayleigh Vicars) observed that for many people 'their colourless lives are temporarily heightened by the passing dreamland visions afforded them by the baneful poppy'.

The use of laudanum (a tincture of opium in alcohol) was also very common in England at the time and contemporary reports suggest that it may have been particularly common among women. Some women built up what would now be

---

1   There is some doubt about when Homer lived: estimates vary between 1050 and 850 BC.

considered enormous habits; in one case, a woman was reported to be using a daily amount of 96 grains of the drug! This is about one hundred times greater than the amount used by most heroin addicts today. The regular use of opium was generally seen as quite normal and it appears to have provoked no marked concern.

Alcohol is one of our most extensively used drugs. Even the most primitive peoples have used it, and its history stretches back into prehistoric times. Neolithic man knew how to make alcoholic drinks through the fermentation of cereals, and Stone Age beer jugs have been found. By 2000 BC, there were taverns in Mesopotamia. It is sometimes suggested that the Australian Aborigines did not have their own intoxicants prior to the arrival of the European settlers. However, the Tasmanian Aborigines knew how to tap a species of gum tree so that the sap ran down into a stone-lined hole, where it was left to undergo a process of natural fermentation. The end product was a crude but evidently quite effective intoxicant. Aborigines also used other mind-altering substances such as the indigenous tobaccos and a drug called pituri which was mixed with ash and chewed.

There are also cases of animals which have learned the pleasures of alcohol intoxication. Dogs and horses have been known to acquire their masters' taste for alcoholic beverages, and the chimpanzee will also drink them. In fact, chimpanzees seem to have clear preferences for certain drinks: sherry and port are preferred to Italian and German wines, and spirits are particularly unattractive. Bees and wasps become uncoordinated and temporarily grounded after eating fermenting fruit. However, the most impressive example of alcohol intoxication in the animal kingdom is probably that of the East African elephants which seek and eat fermenting mangoes and other fruits; as a result they become overexcited, drunk and boisterous. Most drunks are worth avoiding. Fortunately, few of us ever encounter a drunk of the size and temperament of the African elephant.

The doubtful honour of being the first person ever to have his drink problem recorded goes to Noah. Genesis 9:20–21 records that 'Noah began to be an husband man, and he planted a vineyard: and he drank of the wine, and was drunken; and he was uncovered within his tent'. Noah's sons were ashamed of this display of naked drunkenness, but his intemperance seems to have had little effect upon his health since he lived for 950 years.

Other records of the uses and abuses of alcohol have been found in ancient Egypt. Carvings have been discovered on the walls of the tombs of Beni-Hassen, which relate to the drinking habits of the Egyptian people 4,000 years ago. Some of the carvings illustrate the methods of cultivating and gathering grapes, and the operation of wine presses. Other pictures show parties at which people appear to have had too much to drink. Some of the revellers are attempting to stand on their heads. At the end of the proceedings, men are being carried home on the heads of their slaves. In the midst of such revelries, there were voices advocating moderation. One Egyptian papyrus carried the warning: 'Make not thyself helpless drinking in the beer shop … Falling down, thy limbs will be broken, and no one will give thee a hand to help thee up.'

In ancient Greece, Dionysus (or Bacchus) was the god of wine. Through the use of wine he was able to free the soul of all impediments of the flesh. The Greeks, however, appear to have used alcohol in moderation, and water was usually mixed with wine to reduce the strength of the drink. Plato took an especially strong line on drinking. For instance, he considered that it was barbaric to drink undiluted wine; and in *The Republic* he advocated that no one under the age of 30 should be permitted to drink wine at all. After that age it should be used only to relieve the infirmities of the flesh. It is odd that one of the few examples of immoderate drinking amongst the ancient Greeks should also have involved one of their heroes: Alexander the Great. On his death, Seneca wrote, 'invincible by the toils of prodigious marches, by all the dangers of sieges and combats, by the most violent extremes of heat and cold, here he lies, conquered by his intemperance, and struck to earth by the fatal cup of Hercules'.

It is the Greeks who gave us the symposium – the word as well as the event. My own experiences of these events has been mixed, with moods varying between attentive interest and terminal boredom. There must be many students who sit through the symposia so thoughtfully provided for them in their universities and colleges who would be amused to learn that a symposium was originally a drinking party in which alcohol played a central part in livening the conversation.

The Ancient Romans had a much more robust attitude towards drinking, and excessive drinking was widespread, particularly during the late years of the Roman Empire. Indeed, the practice of drinking vast amounts of wine became a common affair, with people trying to outdrink each other at all-night banquets. By the first century AD, the Emperor Domitian was so alarmed by the widespread drunkenness in Rome that he ordered half the vineyards to be destroyed, and prohibited the planting of any more without his imperial licence.

The discovery of distillation, and therefore of spirits, is a more recent event. It seems to have occurred about a thousand years ago, though the first coherent description of the process was made by Albertus Magnus in the 13th century. Some physicians and pharmacologists are ever-optimistic about discovering new 'wonder drugs'. This is as true now as it was in the Middle Ages, when the alchemists were so impressed by this amazing new drug. The distilled alcohol was credited with remarkable properties. It was thought to be an antidote to senility, hence its title, aqua vitae, water of life.

Drunkenness existed long before man knew how to distil alcohol, but in their powerful distilled form spirits were a convenient and concentrated source of drunkenness. As the process of distillation became more efficient, spirits became cheaper and more widely available. In 18th-century England, the consumption of gin had reached epic proportions. Gin houses were everywhere. They advertised their delights by hanging out signs announcing that their customers could become drunk for a penny, and dead drunk for twopence. Among the added attractions, the floors of the cellars were covered with straw where those drinkers who had achieved total insensibility could be left until they were capable of rejoining the drinking.

This amenity was provided free. By 1736 the situation had deteriorated to such an extent that Parliament introduced drastic new measures in the form of the Gin Act. This imposed severe restrictions on the sale of spirits and aroused considerable excitement both for and against the Act. This culminated in a series of riots and civil disturbances. In 1743, the Act was repealed.

Tea, coffee, cocoa and chocolate are such familiar domestic substances that most people find it hard to take seriously any suggestion that they are also drugs. Yet there is no doubt that tea and coffee are psychoactive drugs: both contain caffeine and tannin. Cocoa and chocolate also contain caffeine. Caffeine is one of a class of chemicals known as the xanthines, which produce a stimulant effect on the central nervous system and on the heart. Caffeine is among the drugs that have been deliberately used for its stimulant effects by athletes: it is listed as a banned drug by the International Olympic Committee because of its effects upon performance.

Like any other drug, caffeine can be used wisely, or it can be used foolishly. People who take excessive amounts of caffeine through their consumption of tea and coffee can experience various unpleasant side effects as a result. More often than not, they fail to recognize these as toxic effects. A dose of 200 milligrams of caffeine per day (about two cups of coffee) is usually considered large enough to have pharmacological effects which are clinically significant. It has been known for a long time that over-consumption of tea and coffee can lead to headaches and mental irritability. What is less well known is at what level of consumption a person is taking an excessive amount of caffeine. Some estimates suggest that anyone who is taking more than 600 milligrams a day (five or six cups of coffee, or nine to ten cups of tea) may be running a health risk. At such levels caffeine can produce headaches, insomnia, dizziness, trembling, diarrhoea, breathlessness and anxiety symptoms. Caffeine also has various toxic effects on the heart: these can include palpitations, rapid pulse or irregular pulse rate, and when consumed in sufficiently large amounts it can lead to increased blood pressure. Many people who have found themselves suffering from these side effects of excessive caffeine consumption must have reached for one of the common proprietary tablets used to relieve such problems. Surprisingly, some of these contain yet more caffeine, and may therefore aggravate the headache even further.

There has been some disagreement about the amounts of caffeine contained in tea or coffee. The most popular belief is that coffee contains more caffeine than tea. Several authorities suggest that coffee, as it is usually prepared, may be two or three times as strong as tea in this respect. Others have asserted that the two are approximately of equal strength. When translated into everyday terms, of course, these arguments are beside the point, since people make each drink to their own taste. An approximate comparison of the relative amounts of caffeine in various popular drinks is shown in Table 1.1.

Table 1.1 The relative caffeine content of different drinks

Brewed coffee	100–150 mg per cup
Instant coffee	85–100 mg per cup
Decaffeinated coffee	2–4 mg per cup
Tea	60–75 mg per cup
Cola drinks	40–60 mg per glass

In the US, as in many other Western countries, coffee is drunk in large quantities: the coffee break has become an established pattern of working life for many people. Cola drinks are popular among young people in all countries, and the consumption of soft drinks containing caffeine in the US has more than doubled since 1960. In the UK, tea drinking is a ritual component of everyday life. Every one of us must have heard it said at some time or other that 'I couldn't get started properly in the morning without a drink of tea/coffee', or that 'I don't know how I would get through the day without it.'

One US survey of a group of housewives found that 26 per cent drank more than five cups of coffee every day. Even those who drank only one or two cups a day almost invariably drank a cup in the morning. When asked why, a surprisingly high proportion gave reasons that showed they were aware of its drug effects: 46 per cent said that 'it helps to wake you up', 42 per cent said that 'it gets you going in the morning', and about a quarter either said that it 'gives you a lift' or that it 'stimulates you'. What is even more impressive is that nearly a third of these housewives described themselves as being dependent upon their morning coffee. When asked what would happen if they were not able to obtain their usual drink, those who drank five or more cups per day described exactly the sort of symptoms that make up the caffeine withdrawal syndrome: headache, irritability, loss of efficiency at certain tasks, nervousness and restlessness. These withdrawal symptoms tend to appear about 12–16 hours after the last dose of caffeine and they may last for up to a week. People joke about being 'addicted' to their drink of tea or coffee. For some it is a joke; for others, the dependence is a fact.

Another more recent study of the use of tea and coffee in Canada produced the same sort of result – about one-third of the Canadian population may be regarded as being dependent on the caffeine provided in tea and coffee. The proportion is probably about the same in most other Western countries and in many other countries throughout the world. In 2005, the population of the UK drank two and a half billion cups of coffee. But as if in confirmation of the national stereotype, we drank six billion cups of tea.

Tea, coffee and the other caffeine-containing drinks are drugs in the full sense of the term. People become dependent upon them so that they are psychologically uncomfortable if deprived of their drink. Heavier users also experience withdrawal symptoms in the absence of their drug. Whether or not one chooses to regard this dependence as a bad thing depends upon one's initial attitude towards dependence itself. Tea and coffee are comparatively cheap, freely and legally available, and their use carries no social stigma (with the exception of one or two religious groups). The main problems associated with the use of this drug are probably the result of using it in excessive quantities. However, there are unanswered questions about the health risks associated with caffeine. The threat of heart disease linked to increased blood pressure is one area of concern and there are also worries about the possible effects of caffeine consumption by pregnant women upon the development of unborn children.

As well as the side effects that have already been mentioned, each of the caffeine-containing drinks can lead to restlessness and disturbed sleep. This runs against the popular belief in the effectiveness of chocolate as a 'nightcap' to help you to sleep. When it is taken in very large quantities, caffeine is a poison. It can produce convulsions like those of epileptic fits, and finally leads to death through respiratory failure. It is hardly likely, though, that any of us would take an unintentional fatal overdose. To do so would involve drinking between 70 and 100 cups of coffee at a single sitting. Any such achievement would indicate considerable determination.

Chapter 2

The Effects of Drugs

In Xanadu did Kubla Khan
A stately pleasure-dome decree:
Where Alph, the sacred river, ran
Through caverns measureless to man
Down to a sunless sea.
…
I would build that dome in air,
That sunny dome! Those caves of ice!
And all who heard should see them there,
And all should cry, Beware! Beware!
His flashing eyes, his floating hair!
Weave a circle round him thrice,
And close your eyes with holy dread,
For he on honey-dew hath fed,
And drunk the milk of Paradise.

Opium is traditionally the drug of dreams, and these lines from Coleridge's *Kubla Khan* were inspired by opium: the rhythm of the poem reflects something of the hypnotic quality of the drug itself. There is also an intriguing allusion to opium within the poem. Coleridge had an extensive knowledge of the classics and as a lifelong opium addict he can hardly have failed to notice the references to the drug in classical literature. In the Aeneid, Virgil writes of *Humida mella soperiferumque papaver* ('the narcotic poppy with honey-dew'; Book IV, line 486).

Coleridge described how, after drinking laudanum, he fell into a drug-induced trance in which he seemed to compose two or three hundred lines of poetry. The images rose up before him as if he were the passive observer. When he awoke, he began to write them down, but was interrupted by a visitor. After returning to his writing, he found he was left with only the vaguest recollection of his original vision and could remember no more than a few scattered lines and images. Coleridge did not publish *Kubla Khan* for almost 20 years after it was written, and then only on the urging of Byron. This was probably because of his doubts about the worth of what he rather dismissively described as 'a psychological curiosity'.

The suggestion that *Kubla Khan* was inspired by opium produced intense feelings in literary circles. To some romantics, the notion that this entrancing vision could have been inspired by the drug of dreams was very appealing. Others were just as strongly offended by the idea. One recent biography, for instance, utterly rejects Coleridge's own account of how the poem was inspired, preferring instead to talk of writing poetry as 'a labour as hard and exhausting as road building'.[1] This same puritan reinterpretation of Coleridge's own account of the poem's origins asserts that, far from contributing to Coleridge's poetry, opium was directly responsible for extinguishing it.

In fact, Coleridge and his puritan critics share the same misconception. Opium was not the source of his poetry, nor did it lead to the death of his muse. The effects of a drug depend largely upon the psychology of the person who has taken it. Had Coleridge not experienced that particular drug reverie of which he spoke, he might never have been inspired to write *Kubla Khan*. At the same time, the vision itself, and more particularly the translation of that experience into lines of poetry afterwards, owed more to the personality and talent of Coleridge than it did to any drug. It is patently absurd to claim that anyone can produce great poetry merely by taking drugs, though some drug takers have been convinced of the depth of their artistic vision when intoxicated.

The way in which a drug affects the user and their behaviour is likely to depend as much upon the psychological characteristics of the individual (their personality, how they believe the drug will affect them, their emotional state, and so on), as upon the chemical properties of the drug itself. The idea that specific drugs have fixed and predictable effects which are the same from person to person is extremely widespread, but it remains a fallacy. In the particular case of the psychoactive drugs, such effects are the exception rather than the rule.

Few people have difficulty in understanding that different people react in different ways after drinking alcohol. Thinking of other drugs, they often forget how much the psychology of the individual can influence the drug effects. The biochemistry of a drug is only one of a wide range of factors that interact to produce the final effects. These depend to a certain extent upon the basic personality structure of the person who took it. Reactions to alcohol (and to other sedative drugs such as the barbiturates), for instance, seem to depend upon whether the drinker is an introvert or an extravert. The typical extravert is sociable, likes parties, has many friends and prefers the company of others to being alone. They look for excitement and enjoy taking chances. The typical introvert is a quiet, retiring sort of person who is reserved and reticent except with their close friends. They tend to plan ahead rather than act impulsively, and are reliable and usually rather pessimistic. Introverts seem to be comparatively resistant to the effects of alcohol, whereas extraverts succumb to its intoxicating influence much more readily. The opposite is true of stimulant drugs like amphetamine or caffeine. Introverts react most strongly to these drugs and extraverts least.

---

1   Molly Lefebure (1974), *Samuel Taylor Coleridge. A Bondage of Opium*, London: Gollancz.

One way of demonstrating this involves giving a sedative such as a barbiturate to groups of subjects who differ in their levels of introversion/extraversion. This has been done in several experiments, and it has been found that the amount of a sedative necessary to produce a given level of sedation varies considerably between introverts and extraverts. A standard dose of the drug that is sufficient to sedate more than 95 per cent of the most extraverted subjects will sedate fewer than 10 per cent of the introverted subjects.

Because of the way drugs are classified (in this case, either as stimulants or as sedatives), the way they relate to personality and behaviour is often misunderstood. It is assumed that any drug which is classified as a stimulant will make the person who takes it more impulsive and excitable, whereas sedative drugs will make them quieter and less excitable: roughly speaking, that stimulants will make the user more extraverted, and sedatives will make them more introverted. In fact, the opposite is nearer to the truth. The physiological action of stimulants generally makes the user more introverted and sedatives make the person more extraverted.

In practice, the extraverting effects of sedative drugs are already well-known. Alcohol is widely used for precisely this purpose at social gatherings such as parties. At most parties, the extraverted behaviour of the guests can be directly linked to the amount of drink that has been consumed. Drunkenness is a chemical equivalent of extreme extraversion. There is, of course, a limit to this effect. In very large quantities the sedative effects of alcohol have a disruptive effect on behaviour, and finally it produces unconsciousness.

Although the introverting effects of stimulants are less well-known, these drugs have been used in psychiatry for some years, mainly in the treatment of hyperactive children. More than 20 million prescriptions for such drugs were issued in 2000 to children with hyperactive or attention disorders. This represents an increase of 70 per cent on the number of prescriptions in 1995.

Superficially, it might seem strange that stimulant drugs have been used to calm impulsive, irritable and intractable children. The paradox, however, is more apparent than real, provided one reminds oneself that drugs such as the amphetamines and methylphenidate (Ritalin, an amphetamine-like stimulant) can have an introverting effect upon behaviour. Usually, between 60 and 90 per cent of hyperactive children show some improvement after being given stimulants. Unfortunately, the treatment seems to be effective only for as long as the child continues to take the drugs. Many of those who show a marked improvement while on the medication fail to maintain these gains when the drug is withdrawn. In the long term, it seems that children who have been given this form of drug treatment do no better than those who have not. And while they are taking the drugs, the children are frequently approached to sell or trade their medications so that they can be used for less medical purposes.

The User's Beliefs about Drugs

Taking a drug is not a psychologically neutral event. Whether it is prescribed by a physician, bought over the counter of the local chemist or obtained through illegal sources, the user will almost certainly have clear ideas about how and when it is appropriate to use the drug, and about the ways in which it is likely to affect his or her thoughts, feelings and behaviour. Even in those rare cases where users have no knowledge of the drug they have taken, they actively search for reasonable explanations about how the drug might be affecting them. These psychological and social influences are generated by the users themselves, by what they have been told by others, and by the immediate social circumstances in which the drug is taken; and these influences are powerful enough to alter a user's response to the pharmacological effects of the drug itself.

One study which demonstrates this was carried out at the University of Stockholm. The subjects who had volunteered to take part were divided into three groups. The first received a fairly large dose of one of the most common of the sleeping tablets currently being prescribed (200 milligrams of pentobarbital) and were told that this would make them feel sleepy. The subjects in the second group were given the same sedative drug but the experimenter told them that they did not know what sort of effect it would have. Those in the third group were not given any drug at all, merely a capsule containing a pharmacologically inert powder, but they were given the same explanation as the first group – that this was a sleeping tablet that would make them feel tired and drowsy. As predicted, those who were given the active drug together with the information that this would make them feel sleepy showed the greatest response. However, the direct drug effects alone were no more powerful than the experimenter's suggestions alone: both produced the same amount of drowsiness.

The physiological actions of drugs are not sufficient to produce the sort of psychological changes associated with the use of psychoactive drugs (for example, euphoria). Before this can happen, the user must attach a psychological 'label' to the way they feel (though this labelling seldom occurs at a conscious level). One of the best-known investigations of this labelling process was carried out by the US psychologists Stanley Schachter and Jerome Singer (1962). In their ingenious study, the student volunteers were led to believe that they were taking part in a psychology experiment concerned with vision. The subjects were given an injection of adrenaline, a hormone produced in the central nervous system which causes a wide range of physiological changes in the body but no consistent psychological effects. One group was given an accurate description of the effects of the drug: that they might have a sensation of their heart beating faster, and experience some hand tremor and a warm and flushed feeling in the face. They were reassured that these effects would last only for a short time. Another group was given a misleading description of how the drug would affect them. They were told that it would cause numbness in the feet, itching sensations and a slight headache.

In the second part of the experiment, the subjects were asked individually to go to a waiting room to let the drug take effect before the start of the visual tests. In the waiting room was another 'subject' waiting for the visual tests. In fact, this other subject was really an actor who was part of the experiment. While the two were together in the waiting room, the actor started to behave in a most peculiar fashion, running about the room playing basketball with a scrap of paper and a waste paper basket, making paper aeroplanes and throwing them around the room, and generally behaving in an exuberant and excitable manner.

The experiment was designed to investigate the ways in which emotional states (such as euphoria) are produced, and the real interest of the experimenters was to find out how the subjects behaved in the waiting room. The two groups in the experiment received the same drug and were exposed to the same unusual behaviour in the waiting room. They differed only in one respect. The first group already knew how the drug would affect them; the second group did not. The results show that the people who had been misled about how the drug would affect them were more likely to be influenced by, and to imitate, the actor's behaviour: they too were inclined to become euphoric and excited.

The same experiment was then repeated, but with three groups. One received an injection of adrenaline plus an explanation of how it would affect them; the second group was given the drug but with no explanation of its effects; and a third was given a placebo injection. The subjects were then taken one at a time to the waiting room. This time the actor's performance was one of irritation and anger. Again, those who knew that their altered physiological state was due to the adrenaline were least affected by the actor's behaviour. Those who had been given the drug but no explanation of how it would affect them were more likely to become angry and irritable. The placebo group were less influenced by the events in the waiting room than those who had been given the drug but no description of its physiological effects, but more so than those who had received the drug plus an accurate description.

In this experiment, there are two factors at work. On the one hand, there is the physiological arousal (heart beating faster, tremor and so on) caused by the drug itself, and on the other, there are the expectations and beliefs that the person has about their state of arousal. When people do not understand why they feel the way they do, they seem to relate their feelings to the particular situation in which they find themselves. It is as if the subjects who did not know how the drug would affect them had said to themselves, 'I feel strange. My heart is racing and I am trembling. Therefore I must feel angry/happy like the other person in the experiment.' Those who already knew how the adrenaline would affect them were uninfluenced by the actor's behaviour because they could attribute their altered physiological state to the drug.

The beliefs, attitudes and expectations of the drug taker are no less important outside the laboratory. In what has since established itself as one of the classic studies of cannabis smokers, Howard Becker (1953) looked at the ways in which a person learns how to get stoned on the drug. The first time someone tries cannabis, they do not usually get high. Sometimes the user feels a little strange, but is not sure how to interpret the changes they experience. Sometimes the effects are perceived as being physically unpleasant and the novice may actually be sick. Sometimes users may claim, rather indignantly, that they do not feel any different at all. When this happens they may decide that the whole business of smoking cannabis is simply not worthwhile; or they may be worried by their failure to experience any euphoric effects and ask others about it. In such conversations they will be made aware of specific details of their experience with the drug which they may not have noticed before, or which they had noticed but failed to identify as a part of being stoned. So the next time they try cannabis they will be better prepared to know when they are stoned.

Novices must learn the details of how it feels to be stoned, and acquire the necessary concepts to be able to identify and describe how they feel after smoking cannabis. Before that, the effects of the drug are sufficiently ambiguous for them not to know how they feel (as in the results of those experiments where the subjects did not know which drug they had taken). Inexperienced drug takers sometimes become confused and frightened by their early experiments with drugs. They may be so alarmed by the changes in their state of consciousness that they become convinced at the time that they are going insane. Yet the same alterations and distortions of consciousness which so frighten the novice may be regarded by the experienced drug taker as extremely pleasurable. Nor is there anything unique about cannabis in this respect. Drugs such as heroin also require an initial period during which the novice learns how to interpret their effects. Most people find their first experience of heroin unpleasant, and many are sick. In one study where a group of non-addicts were given either a small injection of heroin or a placebo, the placebo was reported to be more pleasurable than heroin. One can go through a whole list of drugs making the same point. Most children experimenting with their first cigarette find it a nauseous experience. Similarly, most people find their first taste of alcohol far from appealing. In order to become a regular drug user it is necessary to learn how to enjoy the effects.

After people have learnt how to experience the effects of a drug, their beliefs and expectations about that drug may lead them to react as if they were intoxicated when they had not taken a drug at all. In one study of experienced cannabis smokers, the subjects were given cigarettes containing either cannabis or a placebo preparation of cannabis material from which the active drug had been artificially removed. Although the average level of intoxication reported after smoking the placebo was lower than for cannabis, some of the subjects felt just as intoxicated on the placebo as on the active drug. The more experienced cannabis users were the most likely to get stoned on the placebo, whereas those who had had least experience with cannabis were better able to differentiate between the drug and the placebo.

The Placebo Effect

Fillet of a fenny snake,
In the cauldron boil and bake;
Eye of newt, and toe of frog,
Wool of bat, and tongue of dog,
Adder's fork, and blind worm's sting,
Lizard's leg, and howlet's wing,
For a charm of pow'rful trouble,
Like a hellbroth boil and bubble. (*Macbeth*, IV, i, 12–19)

Because psychological factors play such a large part in determining how people respond to drugs, it is possible for them to react as if they had taken a drug even when no such drug has been used. This is, of course, the placebo effect (that is, those psychological and physiological changes produced by the placebo). Conventional definitions of a placebo usually emphasize that it should be a pharmacologically inert substance: starch, talc and sugar powder are often used in making up placebos. These 'dummy' tablets may be thought of as 'pure' placebos in the sense that they have no pharmacological effects, but it is too restrictive to think of a placebo only as a completely inert preparation. 'Pure' placebos are not used very often except in controlled experiments; for most practical purposes it is the 'impure' placebo that is more important. This is any medicine or treatment which is prescribed because either the doctor or the patient, or both, believe that it works, but which really has no specific effects upon the condition being treated. Many pharmacologically active drugs are used for their placebo effect in this way.

Placebos belong to that twilight world of medical science that has never quite been able to claim respectability. This is a pity, because the placebo effect is both interesting and important. It is important in practical terms because it is a major therapeutic influence (albeit an unacknowledged one) in many medical treatments. It is important in theoretical terms because it highlights the psychological component of the response to drugs. It can also lead to clinical improvements which can be mistakenly attributed to direct drug effects. In one of the successful trials of Prozac, the patients given dummy pills showed substantial improvements after receiving the placebo treatment only.

A special case of this phenomenon is placebo analgesia, which the belief that one is receiving an effective analgesic can reduce pain. The experience of pain arises from both physiological and psychological factors, including beliefs and expectations. Thus, placebo treatments that have no intrinsic pharmacological effects may produce analgesia by altering expectations. An important piece of evidence that the placebo effect is real and not just 'imagined' is that it can be reversed by the opioid antagonist drug, naltrexone. Also, neuroimaging studies have shown that placebo analgesia is related both to decreased brain activity in pain-sensitive brain regions, and to increased activity during anticipation of pain in the prefrontal cortex, providing further hard evidence that placebos alter the experience of pain.

All manner of extraordinary organic and inorganic substances, including almost every conceivable form of human and animal excretion, have been used as medicines at one time or another. Crocodile dung, the teeth of pigs, hooves of asses, eunuch fat, lozenges of dried vipers, powders made from precious stones, brick dust, fur, feathers, hair, human sweat, earthworms and spiders have all taken their place among the tools of the physician: by comparison, the witches' brew described in *Macbeth* seems positively benign. In these enlightened times, few physicians would place much confidence in such esoteric preparations. On the other hand, it has been suggested that as many as one-third of all prescriptions issued by UK and US doctors may be for drugs which have no specific pharmacological effects upon the condition being treated (that is, they are placebos).

To many people, the placebo carries rather derisory connotations which may, in part, be due to the idea that doctors use placebos as a harmless method of humouring demanding or difficult patients. Undoubtedly this does happen. But, more often, placebos are not prescribed deliberately to deceive the patient, but with both the doctor and the patient believing them to be an effective medicine. Far from being the omniscient, detached scientists who know what 'really' has therapeutic value and who sometimes use placebos just to keep the patient quiet, many physicians unwittingly use valueless drugs because their personal experience tells them wrongly that they are 'getting results'.

In ancient Egypt, the physicians who prescribed crocodile dung did so not merely to have a cynical laugh at the patient's expense; nor is it entirely plausible to believe that they carried on using this unusual medication in the absence of any improvement by their patients. In the same way, patients have been purged, poisoned, punctured, blistered, bled, leeched, heated, frozen, sweated and shocked. Treatments which were administered so confidently have turned out to be either ineffective or dangerous, or both. One can only assume that the physicians' faith in their remedies was strong enough to establish in the patient the hope and expectation that they would lead to improvement. As a result, both the patient and the physician would interpret the symptoms more optimistically after the medicine had been taken, and in many cases there would indeed be a marked improvement in the patient's condition. Nor should the reader suppose that the problems which respond favourably to placebos are imaginary or 'only psychological'. Severe post-operative pain, chest pain associated with coronary heart disease, multiple sclerosis, diabetes, radiation sickness, stomach ulcers, toothache, seasickness, arthritis and the common cold are just a few of the disorders in which placebos have produced a therapeutic improvement. Across a wide range of problems, the proportion of patients who improve after receiving a placebo averages out at about 35 per cent.

Placebo responses can be more powerful than those to active drugs. The psychological response to a drug may also profoundly alter or even reverse the direct drug effects, and, as with active drugs, placebos can produce unwanted side effects.

Headache, nausea, dryness of the mouth, drowsiness and tiredness have all been reported by people who have taken a placebo. In some cases there have been major toxic reactions. After being given a placebo containing sugar powder, one patient complained of extreme weakness, palpitations of the heart and nausea; another developed a widespread skin rash (which disappeared after they stopped taking the placebo). There are even cases in which people have become addicted to placebos, and in the *Journal of the American Medical Association* (1955) an editorial warned that 'When withdrawing a placebo on which a patient has become dependent it will not help him to be told that it was only a placebo.' It is difficult to imagine a more convincing illustration of the essentially psychological nature of drug dependence than an addiction to placebos.

Nor should it be imagined that an addiction to placebos is necessarily trivial. Many active drugs are used inappropriately because the user wrongly attributes the placebo effect associated with taking the drug to the drug itself. Pain-relieving (analgesic) drugs such as aspirin and paracetamol are the world's most widely used drugs. They are also the most widely misused drugs. They are seldom taken under medical supervision, and generally they are unwittingly used for the placebo effect that goes with them. For example, they are regularly taken to suppress the symptoms of the common cold, yet aspirin has no effect upon viruses or bacteria; they are also taken to help the user to get to sleep, though their sedative properties are minimal. The inhabitants of the US consume more than 9,000 tons of aspirin each year (the equivalent of about 44 million tablets every day). A study of blood donors in Connecticut found that 37 per cent of the people who gave blood had recently taken aspirin. These drugs are at least as popular in the UK, whose population swallows a yearly supply of some 2,000 tons of analgesics (about 4,300 million tablets) and where there are more than a million people who use them regularly each day. One criterion for identifying analgesic abuse is the consumption of more than one kilo (2.2lb) of the drug in a six-month period. On this basis, it has been estimated that there may be as many as a quarter of a million analgesic abusers in the UK. The heaviest user of such drugs that I have seen was a 42-year-old woman who was obviously as dependent upon them as any junkie is upon their heroin. She was using between two and three hundred aspirin tablets per week.

This form of drug abuse is encouraged by the misconception that these tablets are not really 'drugs' at all, and that they can be used as often as one likes without ill effects. This is not so. Some 7,000 patients each year are admitted to UK hospitals for aspirin-induced gastrointestinal bleeding (usually associated with stomach ulcers). Heavy use of these drugs can also cause kidney damage, and they are one of the most common causes of accidental death among children. Such extensive misuse of these drugs reflects a deeper need to obtain instant chemical relief from each and every one of the aches and pains that are part of living.

The placebo effect can be observed in another eternal preoccupation, the search for a reliable aphrodisiac. Papyri from ancient Egypt have been found with instructions for preparing 'erotic potions', and the Greeks too wrote at length on this subject (as in the *Medea* of Euripides). There is even a reference to the subject in the Bible (Genesis 30:14–16), where Leah used the mandrake to 'lie with' Jacob. The mandrake holds a position of unrivalled importance in European witchcraft because of its magical properties. It was said, for instance, to utter such unearthly shrieks when pulled from the ground that whoever heard them might die. Early Christians thought it was created by God as an experiment before He created man in the Garden of Eden, and Machiavelli was sufficiently impressed by its erotic powers to write a comedy in its honour (*La Mandragola*). Despite all this, the mandrake has no chemical properties that would make it a useful aphrodisiac, though its major components (scopolamine, atropine and hyoscamine) could produce distortions of consciousness that might render the user more susceptible to persuasion. In this century, scopolamine has been used in interrogation procedures as a 'truth drug'.

In Western societies, the truffle and the oyster have a current reputation as aphrodisiac foods. Sadly, neither contains anything which is remotely likely to fire the passions. The constituents of the oyster are water (76–89 per cent), carbohydrates (3.7–9.6 per cent), mineral salts (0.9–3 per cent), proteins (8–11 per cent) and fat (1.2–2.5 per cent). When subjected to this sort of chemical analysis, the truffle proved to be even less sexy: 77 per cent water, 13.5 per cent carbohydrates, and the remainder fat, albumen and salts. Few of the other reputed aphrodisiacs do much better. Even the humble potato was once regarded as an especially useful erotic stimulant.

The aphrodisiac effect of these foods and drugs is without any physiochemical basis, though it is some testimony to the fact that they are not completely useless that these and other substances have been so persistently used in seductions. The reasons for this are psychological. The aphrodisiac is really a special sort of placebo. A good meal in relaxed surroundings can be a most effective means of turning the thoughts towards other sensual pleasures. This can be assisted by that least arcane of the seducer's devices – alcohol.

Candy
Is dandy
But liquor
Is quicker. (Ogden Nash)

However, even the effects of alcohol are indirect. It does not provoke sexual desire directly so much as remove the customary restraints on such behaviour. The would-be Lothario might do well to remember Shakespeare's warning about alcohol: 'it provokes the desire, but it takes away the performance' (*Macbeth*, IV, iii, 29–30).

Spanish fly is a quite different kind of aphrodisiac in that its physiological effects are supposed to work directly upon the genitals. The drug is prepared from a beautiful sheen-covered beetle found in southern Europe which is dried and heated until it disintegrates into a fine powder. This contains a drug called cantharidin which causes acute irritation of the gastrointestinal system and an inflammation of the urinary tract. This provides some sort of genital stimulation which can be perceived as sexual desire. The use of Spanish fly is not to be recommended, as it carries a number of dangers.

In recent years, vitamin E and ginseng have established themselves in some quarters as fashionable drugs. Claims about their effectiveness have been typically extravagant, and if one were to believe everything that has been said about them there would be few ills left to mankind. Vitamin E is ideally suited to the commercial exploitation of those in search of a panacea since it can be taken in enormous doses without producing any toxic effects. On the other hand, it has no beneficial effect either. It has been promoted and used for every imaginable disorder, from acne to cancer, from baldness to coronary heart disease. As a drug in search of an illness, it is the latest example of the age-old fallacy that health, happiness and sexual fulfilment are all available in tablet form. Ginseng also fulfils this need, though it is a more potent drug than vitamin E. It has been known and used in China for thousands of years, and in traditional Chinese medicine its effects are explained in terms of harmonizing the balance of yin and yang forces in the five bodily systems. It seems to act as a mild stimulant drug, much like coffee, and it may also possess anti-inflammatory properties. Predictably, both vitamin E and ginseng have been hailed as aphrodisiacs (few substances have not).

During the past few years, the latest discovery to have aroused the enthusiasm of the seekers after chemical aids to sexual stimulation is Viagra. This drug can be taken by a man prior to anticipated sexual activity and it provides a direct chemical action which makes erections easier to obtain and easier to maintain. The drug is effective from 25 minutes after taking it for up to four hours. The arrival of this drug has provoked an astonishing (or perhaps not) interest. Although it is a prescription-only medicine, it is advertised across the Internet and a black market in the drug developed almost immediately after its introduction. But despite the mass enthusiasm for the drug, and despite its effectiveness, it is still not, strictly speaking, an aphrodisiac. It does not create desire. It makes best use of existing desire and sexual stimulation to make the best use of the male physical equipment for sex.

In the end, there is little evidence to show the existence of any such beast as the reliable aphrodisiac. Sexual desire is too capricious to respond obediently and automatically to the demands of a drug.

Mechanisms of Drug Action

The significance of psychological factors in determining how someone will react to a psychoactive drug has been vastly underestimated. However, it would be just as seriously misleading to give too much weight to psychological factors. Drugs are chemical agents which are capable of producing rapid and powerful effects. Anyone who drinks a large amount of alcohol or who takes too much heroin will be affected by the chemistry of these drugs whatever their beliefs.

The psychology of the user, the social setting in which he or she takes drugs and the specific pharmacological properties of the drug all influence how the user finally responds to the drug. Sometimes the psychological factors are most important (as with the placebo effect), sometimes social factors are the most powerful influence, and sometimes the pharmacology of the drug plays the most important role (especially at high-dose levels). The emphasis given in this chapter to the psychology of the drug taker is intended to serve as an antidote to the more orthodox view that the effects of drugs are intrinsic properties of those substances. It is a grave mistake to imagine that we can understand the ways in which people respond to psychoactive drugs simply as a consequence of physiological reactions to a chemical substance. Nonetheless, psychoactive drugs do have powerful effects upon the brain and bodily systems of the drug taker, and some of these effects are very interesting in their own right.

One group of people who have exploited the physiological effects of drugs are those athletes who have sought to obtain a chemical advantage over their competitors. The first reports of doping in sport appeared in 1865, among swimmers in the Amsterdam Canal Races, and stimulants such as caffeine and cocaine were also known to be used by cyclists during the 19th century. In 1955, urine testing among cyclists in the Tour de France showed positive results for five cyclists, and by 1962 the issue was sufficiently well recognized for the International Olympic Committee to pass a resolution against doping. In 1967, the death of the cyclist Tommy Simpson during the Tour de France was televised across the world. Subsequent tests showed that he had taken amphetamine and methamphetamine. The association between doping and cycling came back to haunt the Tour de France in a major way during the 1998 tour when the athletic significance of the event was overtaken by the chemical activities of the cyclists, their teams and their medical support services.

Various drugs have been used in sport. These include stimulants (such as the amphetamines, caffeine, cocaine and ephedrine) to reduce fatigue and increase competitiveness or aggression, and opiates (including codeine and morphine) to reduce responsiveness to pain. Drugs known as beta blockers are sometimes used to reduce the physiological symptoms such as shaking hands or pounding heart that are associated with nervousness. These drugs are useful in sports requiring a steady hand such as target shooting, archery and snooker. They are also useful in events where nervousness might be expected, such as ski jumping, bobsleigh or free-style skiing.

For many years, the drugs which were most often used in sport were the steroids. These drugs are properly known as androgenic anabolic steroids and they are similar in chemical structure to the naturally occurring male hormone, testosterone. Androgenic means promoting the development of male characteristics, and anabolic means stimulating the development of muscle tissue. In sports where strength, stamina and physical bulk are important attributes, steroids are frequently misused. The use of steroids began with body builders and weightlifters in the late 1950s and has since spread to many other sports. The laboratory results after the 1988 Olympic

Games in Seoul confirmed doping among athletes in the pentathlon (two positive results), weightlifting (five positives), athletics, wrestling and judo.

In the US, the National Football League has admitted that as many as 6 per cent of the NFL players tested positive for steroids in 1987/88. Other commentators have suggested that professional American football players are among the most frequent misusers of steroids and that the actual rate of use is much higher. One former advisor to the NFL suggested that up to 25 per cent of players take steroids.

The steroids are sometimes known as 'training drugs' because of their uses in helping sportsmen and women to train harder and for longer, to increase muscle strength and to increase their competitiveness. One internationally successful athletics coach has stated that the use of steroids gives a top-class sprinter about an extra metre of pace over 100 metres. Steroids are used both by 'stacking' (several different types of anabolic steroid being used at the same time) and by 'cycling' (alternating the use of several types and using high doses). The most serious risk of using these drugs is liver damage leading to jaundice, liver failure and liver cancer. Steroids also cause sexual problems, including reduced sperm production, sterility and shrinking of the testicles among men, and a range of problems such as changes in the sexual organs, hair loss, and growth of facial hair among women. Steroids can also cause behavioural changes. It is especially unfortunate that women and adolescents, two of the groups of athletes who are most likely to derive performance benefits from steroids, are also at greatest risk from the side effects. Women will undergo masculinization with hair growth on the face and body, irreversible voice changes and disturbances to the menstrual cycle: adolescent males may experience stunted growth and sexual development.

In recent years, and largely as a result of attempts by the authorities to regulate it, doping in sport has become extremely sophisticated. Indeed, it has become so sophisticated as to push at the limits of the definitions of what constitutes a drug. Many of the procedures and substances currently being used are not drugs in the simple sense of chemicals which are exogenous to (made or formed outside) the body. Naturally occurring hormones are being used. Human growth hormones are currently misused by American football players because there is no effective test for them. EPO (erythropoietin) is another hormone, produced mainly in the kidneys. It is normally produced when the body is stressed through heart disease, respiratory disease or anaemia, and leads to increased production of red cells in the blood. The value of this to the athlete is that the extra red cells increase the oxygen-carrying capacity of the blood, providing extra oxygen to the muscles and giving an immediate improvement in performance. The specific benefit is that runners do not slow down in races over long distances. Runners over 10km may show improvements of over a minute in their times. These improvements may be retained for up to two weeks.

Another way of achieving the same effect is through blood doping. Blood doping involves the injection of blood or blood products containing red blood cells. Because this can be done by giving an infusion of the athlete's own blood, this is virtually impossible to detect. The effects of blood doping are the same as those of using EPO:

elevated haemoglobin concentrations, increased aerobic capacity and increased endurance. A major risk of using EPO or blood doping is that of left ventricular heart failure and stroke, and there have been numerous cases of suspicious early deaths among athletes. EPO has been found to be extremely useful in tests of extreme endurance such as the Tour de France, and the revelations surrounding the extent to which this form of doping was being used by cyclists created a massive scandal during the 1998 Tour. At least 12 Dutch cyclists are known to have died between 1987 and 1991, and, in 1998, the Olympic gold medallist sprinter Florence Griffith-Joyner died suddenly, at the age of 38. Other risks of doping in sport are related to injection procedures. An injection, whether it is blood or any other substance, carries the same risks of infection as for the heroin injector.

The manner in which people take psychoactive drugs can have a powerful influence upon the effects experienced by the user. For instance, a drug which is taken by intravenous injection will have a more rapid and more powerful impact upon the user than one which is swallowed and absorbed through the stomach. Smoking is also a very effective way of taking drugs. Nicotine, for example, is rapidly absorbed through the lungs to reach the brain within a few seconds. It takes only seven seconds for nicotine in the lungs to reach the brain, compared with 14 seconds for blood to flow from arm to brain after an intravenous injection.

The route by which a drug is taken can also have an influence upon the development of dependence. In general, those who take cocaine by sniffing it appear to be at lower risk of becoming dependent than those who smoke it. Those who take tobacco as snuff do not appear to become as dependent upon the habit as cigarette smokers. Similarly, heroin smokers appear to be at lower risk of dependence than those who inject it. This lower dependence risk seems to be related to the route by which the drug is taken and, although the precise mechanism underlying this is not known, it may be due to the user's response to the intensity or the speed of changes brought about by drug concentrations in the bloodstream.

The neurophysiology of drugs has always had a special fascination for some scientists, and this has been an active field of research during the past decade or so. The history of such research has many roots. During the 1950s a young psychologist at McGill University in Canada was interested in the way in which particular areas of the brain affected learning. To test one of his ideas, he planned to apply an extremely small electric current to the brain of his laboratory animals. At that time, the technique of implanting electrodes in the brain was still extremely crude and unreliable, and through an accident one of the electrodes was implanted in an entirely different area of the brain from the one originally intended. As a result, the animal did not show the expected alerting response to the electrical stimulation, and many other scientists might have simply removed the animal and continued with the experiment. Dr Olds, however, was intrigued by the fact that the rat seemed to be interested in the part of the cage where it had received the electrical stimulation. After it had been given a few more tastes of the brain stimulation, the rat never left that part of the cage. It seemed as if it were waiting for more.

Later, when the experiment was systematically repeated, it was found that animals which had the opportunity of administering their own dose of electrical stimulation would press a lever repeatedly in order to obtain it. Some animals would deliver more than a hundred doses per minute and, if left to their own devices, they would maintain this pace for hour after hour. This only happened when the electrodes were located in a specific part of the brain – in what is called the limbic system. The functions of this area of the brain are not well understood, but it is known to play an important part in regulating the emotions. Olds' experiments represented a remarkable discovery. Never before had there been any suggestion that electrical stimulation of the brain could be pleasurable. And there seemed little doubt that the experimental animals enjoyed the experience. Animals that had not received any electrical stimulation for several days would jump out of the experimenter's hands into the test apparatus in their eagerness for more. On the rare occasions when this electrical stimulation has been tried with human subjects, it has produced feelings of euphoria and sexual pleasure. One female subject experienced repetitive orgasms after five to ten minutes of such stimulation. Not surprisingly, these areas of the brain rapidly became known as 'the pleasure centres'.

This research generated considerable excitement. To many people, it reawakened the ancient fear that others could take control of one's own mind. In his *Profiles of the Future*, Arthur C. Clarke spoke of the possibility that it could lead to 'the electronic possession of human robots' and commented that this research may turn out to have more far-reaching consequences than the early work of the nuclear physicists: 'the possibilities here, for good and evil, are so obvious that there is no point in exaggerating or discounting them'.

These early experiments fired the enthusiasm of some researchers who thought that stimulation of the pleasure centres could offer a neurophysiological explanation of drug taking. After a drug enters the bloodstream it is rapidly absorbed into the brain, and several proponents of this view of drug taking have suggested that many of the psychoactive drugs act directly on the pleasure centres of the brain. With repeated use these drugs were said to swamp the brain's ability to respond to other pleasurable forms of stimulation and the person's capacity to experience pleasure at all, except through the use of higher and higher doses of drugs. This account has a certain superficial plausibility, and it may contain some element of truth, but it has a number of serious weaknesses as an explanation of drug taking. It conveniently chooses to ignore those aspects of drug taking that cannot be explained in physiological terms. For instance, if psychoactive drugs stimulate the pleasure centres of the brain directly, this suggests that the drug experience should be one of unambiguous pleasure; and if the experimental studies are correct, it should be almost irresistible in its attractions. Yet many people find their first experience with drugs to be distinctly unpleasant: only later do they learn to enjoy the effects. Similarly, the vast majority of those who have used drugs on several occasions never become addicted to them; and even among drug addicts, very few people compulsively fill themselves with the maximum amount of drugs even when they have more than enough for their immediate needs, and eventually a sizeable number of addicts stop using drugs.

These features of drug taking are seldom recognized because they do not fit neatly into a physiological explanation. The reader may recall the legend of Procrustes, the robber who waylaid travellers and tied them to a bed. If they were longer than the bed he chopped off the offending limbs, and if they were too short he stretched them until bed and traveller were the same length.

In the middle of the 1970s, the flagging interest in possible relationships between brain mechanisms and drug effects was revived by the identification of chemical substances in the brain which had a remarkable biochemical similarity to morphine. The resemblance seemed so close that these substances were named 'endorphins', an abbreviation for endogenous (natural) morphine. Throughout the central nervous system, there are specific receptors programmed to react to these endorphins.

Such chemicals may be produced by the brain as a natural defence against pain. For instance, there have been several observations that endorphins are released in greater quantities during childbirth, and that this could account for the reduced sensitivity to pain at such times. It has been reported that the release of endorphins is often found after acupuncture intended to relieve pain. It has also been argued that endorphins could provide a neurochemical basis for that curious phenomenon, the placebo effect. The existence of these chemicals and of receptors in the brain programmed to react both to them and to drugs such as heroin and cocaine would appear to have great significance for our understanding of opiate addiction. Under normal circumstances the endorphins probably maintain the balance of the nerve impulses in the brain which respond to pain and stress. The opiate drugs, however, are more powerful than their naturally occurring counterparts. As a result, the opiates overwhelm the body's natural chemicals and take over the control of these pain-inhibiting mechanisms. With repeated use, the drugs may reduce the body's sensitivity to the natural chemicals, or even reduce its capacity to produce such chemicals. The body then becomes dependent upon its outside supply of drugs in order to function normally, and when the opiates are withdrawn, the body's natural responses are inadequate.

One of the most fundamental questions at the heart of the paradox of addiction is how the transition from drug use to drug dependence involves also a transition from behaviour which is consciously controlled and intended to achieve pleasurable effects, to a more automatic form of behaviour consisting primarily of learned habits. Many people are initially motivated to start taking drugs because they enjoy the effects, because their friends are doing it, or for a whole range of other psychosocial reasons. But in drug addiction, the motivation to take drugs (*wanting*) may become dissociated from the subjectively pleasurable effects of drugs (*liking*).

How do the initially voluntary choices about drug taking become compulsive? And how does the person come to find it so extremely difficult to control or stop their use of drugs? Research into addictive behaviour needs to explain how the addictions are often characterized by an increasing separation between the need for drugs and their pleasurable effects. With the development of an addiction drugs become pathologically wanted ('craved') even though the user may find that they are getting less and less pleasure from the drugs. It is a common observation in the treatment of people with addiction disorders that they report they are miserable, their life is in ruins, and that they are desperate to give up taking drugs. In short, they are often bewildered by the intensity of their compulsive behaviour.

Research into another brain neurochemical called dopamine has revived interest in the possibility that a common brain mechanism may be involved in pleasure and reward. It is now well accepted that most (or all) of the potentially addictive drugs lead to increases in the concentration of the dopamine in a specific region known as the nucleus accumbens towards the front of the brain.

There are many different hypotheses about how dopamine leads to reward and to the development of addictive behaviours. One interesting suggestion arising from recent neurobiological research is that the dopamine systems of the brain play a particular role in relation to the 'wanting' component of motivation. In this research model, addiction is seen primarily as a motivational disorder linked to sensitization of the dopamine brain systems. Research has shown that with the repeated use of drugs, a number of changes occur in the brain that make the reward systems hypersensitive (sensitized) to the effects of drugs. The sensitized brain systems appear to play a central role in determining those aspects of reward that lead to the experiences of 'wanting' and 'needing'.

However, even at the neurochemical level, more than dopamine is involved in reward and sensitization. The release of glutamate into the brain is also an important contributor to the reward systems that underlie drug taking. Studies of such neurochemicals and their effects are of immense scientific interest and are increasingly being used to account for some of the phenomena of addiction. But it would also be a mistake to elevate neurophysiological descriptions of brain processes into a complete explanation of the addictive disorders. The recent enthusiasm by some experts for talking about addiction as a 'brain disease' can easily be misunderstood. Even the effects of neural sensitization are manifested through complex forms of human behaviour which are modified by psychological, social and environmental factors.

Another fascinating recent scientific development is the search for anti-drug vaccines. This represents a unique approach to the pharmacotherapy of drug addiction. Vaccines have now been prepared which are targeted at a range of drugs including nicotine, cannabis, cocaine, methamphetamine and heroin. Antibody therapies can be provided either by active or passive immunization, and they are designed to prevent drugs from entering the central nervous system (CNS). An anti-cocaine vaccine, for instance, has been developed by linking it to a carrier protein derived from cholera B. The cocaine vaccine is designed to prevent cocaine and a subsequent release of dopamine from reaching the brain, in order to reduce any drug reinforcement effect. Because the antibodies remain primarily in the circulatory system, they have no apparent side effects upon the central nervous system.

It remains to be seen how effective such vaccines will turn out to be. Some of the first studies on anti-drug vaccines were developed for treating heroin addiction. This research was abandoned because of the ease with which drug users could simply switch to other opiates which were not covered by the heroin-specific vaccination. This will be a problem for other drug-specific immunization treatments such as the cocaine vaccine. The cocaine vaccine may also be less effective for crack smokers because smoking delivers the drug to the brain so rapidly that the vaccine may not have time to intercept and block the cocaine. It is possible that the anti-nicotine vaccines may prove more effective than cocaine vaccines because the antibody levels needed for blocking nicotine effects are a thousand times lower for nicotine than cocaine. A further challenge to the effectiveness of these treatments is that the currently available vaccines are short-acting and require booster injections at regular intervals. But assuming these problems could be overcome, what of the ethical difficulties? For instance, would it be ethically acceptable to immunize children against future drug use?

Chapter 3

The Social Context

The Vietnam War (1959–1975) was the longest military conflict in US history, and the war held many unpleasant surprises for the Americans. Not least among these was the widespread use of drugs by US troops. By 1970, almost every enlisted man in Vietnam was being approached by someone offering him heroin – usually within the first few weeks of his arrival in the country. One soldier described how his first offer of heroin came, as he was leaving the plane on which he had arrived in Vietnam, from a soldier preparing to board the same plane to return home. By 1971, it had been estimated that almost half of the enlisted men serving in Vietnam had taken opiates (mainly heroin) on at least one occasion. Most of those who used opiates used them repeatedly and over a long period, and most of the troops who used drugs while in Vietnam used more than one type. Amphetamines and barbiturates were both widely used, and some estimates suggest that more than three-quarters of the troops in Vietnam smoked cannabis. As many as 20 per cent of the troops reported that they had been addicted to opiates. This was a cause of considerable alarm to both the military and civilian authorities. At a time when the defence of South-East Asia against the communist menace was felt to be essential for the maintenance of the American way of life, it was not reassuring to hear that a substantial proportion of the fighting troops were using heroin. Nor was there much comfort in the thought that tens of thousands of heroin addicts might soon be discharged from their duties in the killing zones of Vietnam onto the streets of the US.

Even more shocking were certain revelations about the behaviour of the troops in Vietnam (many of these were so unpalatable to the Americans at home that they were not believed). In 1968, there occurred what the official inquiry was later to refer to as the 'unusual events' of My Lai; these included individual and group acts of murder, rape, sodomy, maiming and assault on non-combatants, almost all of whom were women, children and old people. The number of deaths was never clearly established, but may have exceeded 400. Other 'unusual events' of the war which understandably caused a great deal of concern were 'fragging' attacks, in which officers who tried too zealously to force their men to engage the enemy were killed with fragmentation grenades. The number of reported fragging attacks increased sharply, from 126 in 1969 to 333 in 1971. There were occasions on which helicopter pilots reported being deliberately fired upon by US troops, and the number of men who deserted also reflected the growing problems within the army at that time. The desertion rate more than quadrupled between 1966 and 1972, rising from 16 per cent to 65 per cent. The overall situation was such that a former officer described the army in Vietnam as being 'in a state of approaching collapse, with individual units avoiding or having refused combat, murdering their officers and non-commissioned officers … and dispirited where not near mutinous'.

There was some speculation that these various incidents and atrocities could have been the result of drug taking. There is no evidence to support this. It makes more sense to regard the extensive drug taking as a symptom of the breakdown of morale combined with an increased awareness and use of drugs in all sections of US society during that period. However, it remains one of the darkest ironies of the American involvement in Vietnam that the heroin sold to the troops was flown into the country in planes paid for by the US government. Unlike almost everything else that the Vietnamese sold to the Americans, this heroin was of excellent quality. This was one of the real presents from Indochina to America, and from Nixon and his predecessors to the men of the US army.

Since the illicit heroin available on the streets of the US was many times more expensive than in Vietnam and much less pure, there was a certain amount of trepidation about the chances that the new addicts would become seriously involved in crime. The government set up a special screening system to try to identify and detoxify the addicted soldiers before their return to the US. Those whose drug use was detected were obliged to remain behind for a brief period during which they were withdrawn from drugs before they were sent home.

It must have surprised everyone that, when these men returned to the US, only a small minority of them became re-addicted. After their discharge from the army, only 7 per cent used any opiate drugs, and less than 1 per cent felt that they had been addicted to drugs since their return. Even among those who said that they had been addicted to opiates in Vietnam, less than 10 per cent said that their addiction had continued beyond their return. Compared with the usual civilian statistics about opiate addiction, these figures are remarkably low: one might have predicted that many more of the men would have had serious problems relating to the use of opiates. The low re-addiction figures are also surprising in view of the extensive psychological readjustment problems experienced by many of the returning soldiers. Post-traumatic stress syndrome was increasingly recognized among these men.

What happened in Vietnam and afterwards conflicts with several popular beliefs about drug addiction. It is usually assumed that heroin addiction is an inevitable consequence of using the drug, and that, once it has taken hold, it is virtually impossible for the user to rid himself of the habit. The Vietnam experience shows that neither of these beliefs is true. Of the troops who used heroin, many did not become addicted. But even of those who were addicted in Vietnam, the vast majority were able to cast off their addiction when they returned home.

This curious episode in the history of drug taking is a good example of the ways in which changes in social circumstances can have a powerful effect upon the way people use drugs. The young men who served in Vietnam were removed from their normal social environment and from many of its usual social and moral restraints. For many of them it was a confusing, chaotic and often extremely frightening experience, and the chances of physical escape were remote except through the hazardous possibilities of self-inflicted injury. As a form of inward desertion, drugs represented a way of altering the nature of subjective reality itself, and for the US serviceman drugs were cheap and very freely available.

There are a number of separate influences at work here, each of which affects the likelihood of drug taking. During the Vietnam War, these combined to provide the conditions in which drug taking was most likely to occur. Psychologically, the experience of suddenly being removed from a safe, familiar environment to a strange, foreign and extremely threatening one increases the pressure upon the individual to take drugs. Drugs are a useful means of coping with the mixture of fear, physical tiredness and boredom that is such a familiar feature of military life during a war. Socially, the tour of duty in Vietnam was characterized by a removal of many of the usual social and moral restraints that reduce the likelihood of drug taking. The soldiers themselves were inclined to regard their tour of duty as something separated from 'real life' and there were various social pressures to take drugs simply because so many others were using them. Last but not least, there was the physical availability of all kinds of drugs. It is difficult to imagine conditions more likely to promote their widespread use.

But the same unusual combination of factors which led to so much drug taking in Vietnam is also the key to understanding why such a high proportion of addicts managed to break the habit after going back to the US. With their return, the effectiveness of all three of these influences was reduced, and as a result, the pressures to go on using drugs were correspondingly less. In order to understand the ways in which people use drugs, we need to look beyond the immediate intoxicating effects, and take account of what it means to use drugs in any particular social setting. In Vietnam, the social and psychological influences acted together in a unique manner. Although this does not happen very often, there are other interesting (though less striking) examples of how social factors can influence the ways in which drugs are used.

Availability is such an obvious social determinant of drug taking that it is often overlooked. In its simplest form the availability hypothesis states that, the greater the availability of a drug in a society, the more people are likely to use it, and the more they are likely to run into problems with it. This hypothesis applies to all drugs. Because sociocultural factors will also have an effect, the precise manner in which different societies respond to the availability of drugs will vary. In addition, there are several different dimensions to the concept of 'availability'. The physical availability of the drug is the most obvious of these, but there is also psychological availability (whether the individual's background, personality, beliefs, and so on serve to increase or decrease their interest in using particular drugs), economic availability (whether or not the use of particular drugs is affordable) and social availability (the extent to which the use of a drug is permitted, encouraged or discouraged by other people whose opinions and behaviour are important to the individual user). The circumstances of the enlisted soldier in Vietnam ensured that heroin was readily available in all of these different ways.

The development of heroin problems in Pakistan provides an interesting national case study demonstrating the impact of changes in the availability of heroin. During the 1970s, Pakistan had no problem with heroin. Heroin was only available in very small amounts at high cost in Karachi or other major cities, and the only heroin users in the country were a handful of people who had acquired the habit during their international travels. After the Shah's regime was overturned by Khomeini in 1980, Iran drove its own heroin manufacturers out of the country and many of them fled to areas in Afghanistan and northern Pakistan, taking with them their technology for converting opium into heroin.

The local farmers and tribesmen of Pakistan rapidly appreciated the financial implications of this new technology and from 1980 began to grow large quantities of opium poppies which were then turned into heroin. The area of heaviest cultivation and refining activity was the North West Frontier Province, much of which was under the control of fiercely independent local tribes which have defended their activities from government interference and, not least, from drug-enforcement activities. The development of the new heroin industry was aided by the collaboration of millions of refugees who fled from neighbouring Afghanistan to escape the escalating war against the Soviet occupation. Within a few years, Pakistan had become one of the world's major heroin producers and exporters and in 1988 the country's opium crop was estimated to be more than 200 metric tons.

Prior to the arrival of heroin, many young men in Pakistan smoked hashish; with the arrival of the new powdered drug, many of them also began to smoke heroin. The heroin was physically available, psychologically available, socially available (within the immediate local subcultures if not within the mainstream Islamic society), and economically available (the drug was available in such quantities that prices were low and the local distribution networks virtually guaranteed that heroin could also be obtained through 'leakage').

This combination of availability factors led to an explosive growth in the number of heroin users, so that, by 1982, estimates of the number of heroin users in Pakistan were as high as 100,000. This rate of increase continued for some years; by 1984, it was estimated that there were more than 50,000 heroin addicts in Karachi alone, and in 1988 national estimates suggested that there might be as many as 700,000 addicts in a country of 100 million people.

The previous chapter showed how our beliefs, attitudes and expectations about drugs can have a powerful influence upon how they affect us. These attitudes and beliefs are not entirely personal, something insulated from the society in which we live. We learn about drugs from other people, from reading books and newspapers, or from watching the television. In a study of the presentation of cigarette smoking in 20 of the most successful films for each year between 1960 and 1990, smokers tended to be successful, attractive, white males. Smoking was presented as a way of relieving feelings of stress. Interestingly, although the prevalence of smoking by the main characters fell with the passing years, it remained nearly three times as common on screen as in real life.

The way we think about drugs reflects our understanding of the social world around us, and as a result the social context influences three central aspects of drug taking. It influences what is defined as a drug and what is not; it influences the way a person behaves after taking a drug; and it influences their subjective experience of the drug effects. We cannot hope to understand the complexities of drug taking by studying either the drugs or those who take them in isolation from the social context.

One variation on this theme is the question of what happens to drug taking when it is taken out of its usual social context. Khat is a perennial shrub, the leaves of which can be chewed to deliver a mild stimulant drug (cathinone). Khat is chewed in several north African countries, including Somalia. In a study of Somalian refugees living in London, we found that the majority had increased their consumption of khat and, unlike their experience when in Somalia, a number of users were experiencing moderate, and occasionally severe, problems of dependence. Several users also reported problems associated with stimulant abuse, such as insomnia, anxiety symptoms, paranoid ideation and panic attacks. It seems likely that the increased consumption and problems experienced by these khat users may be due to the use of the drug being removed from its original sociocultural context and transplanted to a foreign (English) setting where previous roles and restraints may be less effective or completely lacking.

Another perspective upon the wider social context of drug taking can be gained by looking at the relationship between drugs and religion. Many religions offer formal guidelines about the use of drugs, and not all of these are prohibitions. Some religions, especially the more ancient ones, have an active involvement with drugs, and many anthropologists who have made a study of religion believe that all knowledge of the supernatural may be derived from the ecstatic experiences of religious visionaries and prophets. Many drugs produce convincing hallucinatory experiences and states of ecstasy, and the use of drugs for religious purposes is extraordinarily widespread. (The word 'ecstasy' is derived from the Greek, *ekstasis*, and it means the flight of the soul from the body.)

There is no general agreement about the role of alcohol in religious experience. In his book, *The Varieties of Religious Experience*, William James wrote that 'the sway of alcohol over mankind is unquestionably due to its power to stimulate the mystical faculties', though he also spoke of drunkenness in its totality as a degrading form of poisoning. Aldous Huxley, on the other hand, was less favourably inclined towards alcohol. He could see nothing elevating in the alcohol-induced state. The only forms of worship based upon ritual drunkenness usually involved an uninhibited and belligerent euphoria. Bacchus or Dionysus was the god of wine, and his worship was characterized by wild dancing, exciting music and general excess. The ancient Roman festival of Saturnalia, too, was a period of licence when customary restraints could be thrown aside. It was a time for feasting, drinking, revelry and the pursuit of all sensual pleasures, and is considered a precursor of the Christmas festivities.

Huxley's view that alcohol is not compatible with more reflective forms of religious experience has been formalized by those for whom it is a proscribed drug, notably the Mormons, the Muslims and certain fundamentalist Protestant sects. The Mormons believe that their sacred text Doctrine and Covenants contains a series of revelations given by God to their founder, Joseph Smith, in 1833. Among these revelations is the prohibition of alcoholic drinks, tobacco and even hot drinks such as tea or coffee; orthodox purists also believe that caffeine-based drinks such as Coca-Cola should be included within this prohibition.

In *The Doors of Perception*, Huxley voiced another opinion which has received rather less sympathetic comment: that 'Christianity and mescaline seem to be much more compatible'. Mescaline and other drugs have played a central part in the religious experience of many cultures. When the Spanish invaded Mexico they found that the Aztecs ate the peyote cactus as a 'divine messenger' to help them communicate directly with the gods. (Mescaline is a derivative of peyote.) Peyote was unquestionably one of the most potent vision-inducing plants to be encountered by the conquerors, and the Conquistadors and the Holy Inquisition immediately began a programme intended to suppress the diabolical practices of the natives. But the sacramental use of peyote survived. During the last hundred years, the use of peyote in religious ceremonies has been adopted by many Native American peoples, including the Comanches, Apaches and Kiowas, and it is currently used by members of the Native American Church as a sacrament in their religious services.

The use of peyote as a divine plant by the Huichol Indians of Mexico is thought to correspond most closely with pre-colonial customs. The Huichol Indians assemble each year in the desert 300 miles from their home in the Sierra Madre mountains where they take part in a peyote hunt led by their shaman. This pilgrimage is preceded by acts of confession and purification through which the participants are initiated into the hunt, and the whole enterprise is surrounded by ritual. The peyote hunt is seen as a return to paradise, the archetypal beginning and end of a mythical past.

Hallucinogenic mushrooms also have a long tradition of use as an aid to religious experience. When the Aryans swept down from the north into the Indus Valley some 3,500 years ago, they brought with them the cult of Soma. These early invaders of India worshipped Soma and drank an extract of it in their most sacred rites. Of more than 1,000 holy hymns in the Rig-Veda, 120 were devoted to this drug, which is now known to be the spectacular red mushroom *Amanita muscaria*, the fly agaric. The sacred psilocybin mushrooms of Mexico are also held in great reverence. The Aztecs called them 'flesh of the gods', and used them only in their most holy ceremonies; to the Indians who still use them they are 'little flowers'. Europeans are more likely to regard these insignificant little toadstools as a symbol of decay and corruption. The Catholic invaders were particularly offended by their use in religious ceremonies; the clerics and their agents were so energetic in suppressing the mushroom cults that they were driven into hiding, and for four centuries nothing was known of them. It was not until the 1930s that they were rediscovered.

> There is a world beyond ours, a world that is far away, nearby, and invisible. And that is where God lives, and where the dead live, the spirits and the saints, a world where everything has already happened and everything is known. That world talks. It has a language of its own. I report what it says. The sacred mushroom takes me by the hand and brings me to the world where everything is known. It is they, the sacred mushrooms, that speak in a way that I can understand. I ask them and they answer me. When I return from the trip that I have taken with them, I tell what they have told me and what they have shown me (a Mazatec shaman, cited in Schultes and Hofmann, 1979).

Other cultures have used other drugs. Kava, which is generally prepared as a drink, is made from the root of a plant. It seems to have sedative properties something like those of alcohol, and has been extensively used by the South Sea Islanders of Samoa, Tonga and Fiji in many of their important social and religious ceremonies. Kava is taken as a way of getting in touch with the supernatural. One of the most recent studies of this drug described how it is used by men on Tanna and the islands of what were the New Hebrides as an aid to meditation and quiet reflection, 'like entering a light, relaxed dream' or 'like looking into a mirror. One's mind goes beyond one's body and looks back.' As elsewhere, the Christian missionaries tried to prevent the use of this heathen drug ('the practice is a serious menace to the work of God') and moves were duly taken to have it forbidden by law. These failed because such laws were impossible to set up and enforce, and kava drinking continues to be a popular custom on the islands.

Cannabis too has been used in religion. A large number of gods in the Hindu pantheon are thought to have a taste for drink and drugs, and bhang (a drink made with cannabis) is a favourite of Shiva. However, cannabis is more often associated with the Ethiopian Zion Coptic Church (EZCC) based in Jamaica. To members of this church, ganja (cannabis) is an indispensable part of their religious worship. It is smoked to help them look deeper into their own consciousness and to help them find a spirit of love, unity and justice within themselves. The Coptics, who have a literal belief in the truth of Leviticus, regard ganja as a symbol of the body and blood of Jesus, and deny that it is a drug: drug taking is forbidden by their religion, as are homosexuality, oral sex, masturbation, adultery, fornication, violence and haircutting. Ganja is seen as the true sacrament. In contrast, wine-alcohol is the false sacrament of Christendom, causing drunkenness and crime. Although the church claims an ancestry dating back 6,000 years to the Ethiopian Coptic Church, the link between the two is revitalistic rather than historical. In its present form, the origins of the EZCC are due much more to the inspiration of Marcus Garvey, whose teachings in the 1920s and 1930s set the scene for the Ethiopian movements in Jamaica (of which the best known is probably that of the Rastafarians).

It is tempting to dismiss these observations as no more than anthropological curiosities, yet the relationship between drugs and religion does extend to Western societies. Increasing numbers of people experimented with LSD (lysergic acid diethylamide) and similar hallucinogenic drugs during the 1960s. On many of them the experience had a powerful impact. It offered a vivid demonstration of what William James had expressed several decades earlier:

> Our normal waking consciousness ... is but one special kind of consciousness, whilst all about it, parted from it, by the filmiest of screens, there lie potential forms of consciousness entirely different. We may go through life without suspecting their existence; but apply the requisite stimulus, and at a touch they are there in all their completeness (James, 1942).

After taking mescaline, Aldous Huxley came to the same conclusion. The brain functions as a reducing-valve. In order to cope with the overwhelming flow of information which bombards the senses, the brain filters it down to a trickle which can be dealt with more efficiently. The hallucinogenic drugs remove these filters.

The hippie subculture of the 1960s took LSD as its sacrament. However, the hippies were never a unified group. They included drug addicts, the emotionally disturbed, social misfits, hangers-on and others who were interested mainly in the extravagant clothes and music of the movement. But, beneath the surface carnival, there was still a core of hippies by whom LSD was used to pursue a new set of religious, spiritual and intellectual values. Their deliberate rejection of the spiritual and religious vacuum of what they contemptuously called 'the plastic society' was summed up in their creed, 'Turn on, tune in, drop out.' This was provided for them by their high priest, Timothy Leary, a psychologist who had worked at Harvard University until his dismissal in 1963. His research and his own experiences with hallucinogenic drugs convinced him of their religious significance. Although Leary felt that these drugs did not provide an automatic ticket to religious illumination, he was convinced that they were powerful aids to such experiences. At least 75 per cent of the subjects in his experiments reported intense mystical–religious experiences, and more than half felt that these drugs provided them with the deepest spiritual experience of their lives. Leary believed that technological society fears and suppresses ecstasy and transcendental experience: religion is reduced to 'a bunch of people getting up on a Sunday morning, going down to a mortgaged building, and staring at the back of someone's neck'. In contrast, psychedelic–hallucinatory drugs could provide a quick and efficient route to religious ecstasy. He prophesied that, in the future, sacramental biochemicals like LSD would be as routinely and tamely used as organ music and incense to assist in the attainment of religious experience. Leary set up two organizations along these lines: IFIF (Institute for the Investigation of Inner Freedom) and LSD (League for Spiritual Discovery). Neither flourished.

The psychedelic experience is often spoken of as if it were a casual diversion. This is misleading, perhaps dangerously so; such drugs are not to be used casually. Gordon Wasson, who made such a thorough study of the religious uses of psilocybin mushrooms, also used them himself:

I am frequently asked why I do not reach for mushrooms every night. But ecstasy is not fun. In our everyday existence we divide experiences into good and bad, 'fun' and pain. There is a third category, ecstasy, that for most of us hovers off stage, a stranger we never meet. The hallucinogenic mushroom introduces ecstasy to us. Your very soul is seized and shaken until it tingles, until you fear you will never recover your equilibrium.

At the heart of many psychedelic experiences was a fundamental sense of the oneness of things, a belief that all contradictions were resolved, all opposites joined. In this, the LSD experience resembles the mystical experience, which is usually defined by its ineffability (it cannot be described or expressed), its noetic quality (to those who experience it, it is a state of knowledge) and its transiency (mystical states cannot usually be sustained for long):

> But these are words ... And you couldn't put it into words. The White Smocks liked to put it into words, like hallucination and dissociative phenomena. They could understand the visual skyrockets ... But the visual stuff was usually just the decor with LSD ... the whole thing was ... the experience ... this certain indescribable feeling (Wolfe, 1969).

It would be a remarkable irony if an ordinary person could, merely by swallowing a pill, attain those exalted states of consciousness which often elude the most committed seekers of mystical enlightenment after a lifetime's spiritual exercises. Not surprisingly, the suggestion has evoked angry dismissals in many quarters. Whatever the true validity of the LSD experience, the hippies shared an immense knowingness, a conviction of their own superiority. Even if they could not reach the profound truth beneath the surface of things, they felt that they had at least travelled beyond the meagre frontiers of normal, rational consciousness.

For the hippies, subjective experience and the present moment were extremely important. Technology and science might be the accepted tools of progress, but they were rejected because they exacted too high a price in terms of the quality of experience. Because of its immediacy, music was an essential part of the hippie life. It did not involve rational understanding or need translation. Leary wrote: 'There are three groups who are bringing about the great evolution of the new age that we are going through now. They are the dope dealers, the rock musicians and the underground artists and writers.' The hippies rejected the pre-packaged commercial products offered to them for a new form of music. This was played by groups like Frank Zappa and the Mothers of Invention, the Jimi Hendrix Experience, Pink Floyd, and the West Coast acid-rock bands, Grateful Dead, Love, Jefferson Airplane, the Doors, and Country Joe and the Fish. The shows put on by these bands were often elaborate, multi-media happenings intended to simulate or enhance the psychedelic experience.

The hippies produced their own underground newspapers and adopted a literature for themselves. Hermann Hesse's short novel *Journey to the East* (first published in 1932) was read and quoted by many hippies, as was another of his works, *Steppenwolf* (1927). The popularity of many such books was related to speculation about the authors' possible involvement with mind-altering drugs. In such a culturally taboo area, these books offered a reminder to the hippies that others had made similar explorations.

William Blake, the 18th-century mystic poet and painter, was also hailed as a fellow-spirit. Blake too hated the narrow scientific, rationalistic vision, and the hippies were enchanted by the dominant themes expressed in his writing, the denial of the reality of matter, revolt against authority, protest against restrictive moral codes and an exaltation of the spirit of love. His aphorisms were adopted as slogans of the hippie revolution, among them 'Prudence is a rich, ugly old maid courted by Incapacity' and 'The road of excess leads to the palace of wisdom'.

In his failure to allow that the hippies' lifestyle could be the reflection of an alternative set of social values, the Swedish psychiatrist Dr Nils Bejerot completely misunderstood what he saw of the hippies. 'Early in 1968,' he wrote in his book *Addiction*, 'I saw a shocking example of how hashish smoking can change young people's attitudes and way of life.' The shock was caused by seeing groups of young Europeans and Americans in New Delhi. 'These hippies were long-haired and bearded. They wore unusual clothes and some had hung bells around their necks. A few of them had the *Tibetan Book of the Dead* in their pocket.'[1] Worse still, they were all totally disillusioned with modern industrial society and many aimed at becoming Buddhist monks. Instead of interpreting their appearance and behaviour as part of an alternative lifestyle, Bejerot reduced their actions to mere symptoms of a drug-induced decay. Indeed, he went even further, in that he diagnosed the lack of industrial progress in many Oriental countries as being due to their widespread use of drugs. It is curious that, at a time when India was discovering Coca-Cola and the delights of the Western consumer society, the hippies turned their backs on the affluent materialism of their parents and turned to the East. At their worst, the hippie tourists gave the impression of scrabbling for mantras as if for the latest clothes in a boutique sale.

One legacy of the hippies' preoccupation with extraordinary states of consciousness is that it gave considerable impetus to an industry in religious and quasi-religious cults that flourished through the 1970s and showed little evidence of decline in the 1990s. Transcendental meditation, the Krishnamurti Foundation, Buddhist groups and Yoga centres are among the less exotic options. Others have looked to witchcraft and flying saucers to satisfy their spiritual longings. In the more sober and prosaic world of Judaeo-Christian orthodoxy, drugs and altered states of consciousness have not generally been received with much sympathy. Nonetheless, a drug (wine) sits at the heart of the Christian mystery of Communion. This is, however, used as a symbol rather than as an intoxicant.

---

1   For many hippies the *Tibetan Book of the Dead* (translated by Timothy Leary) was a popular book of spiritual guidance. Its popularity can be gauged by the fact that a substantial part of it is used on the Beatles' record, *Revolver*: 'Turn off your mind, relax and float downstream. It is not dying. It is not dying.'

It is a curious phenomenon that there are more drinkers among the Jews than in other social and religious groups (87 per cent of Jews use alcohol, compared with 79 per cent of Catholics and 59 per cent of Protestants) and yet they appear to have fewest problems with their drinking. This is true not only of the more minor problems such as public drunkenness but also of the severe disorders such as alcoholic psychoses, liver disease and alcoholism. In one study of admissions to the New York State Hospital system, it was found that the rates of alcoholic psychoses (per 100,000 admissions) were: Irish 25.6; Scandinavian 7.8; Italian 4.8; English 4.3; Jewish 0.5. The same sort of study has been repeated several times and on each occasion the relative position of the Jews remains about the same; they have very few problems with drinking despite their high incidence of alcohol use. Alcoholism is said to be virtually unknown in Israel. This is quite contrary to the conventional wisdom that, as the proportion of drinkers goes up, so the proportion of alcohol casualties (both acute and chronic) must also increase. However, the use of alcohol by the Jews is interesting mainly because it is so atypical. The fact that so many Jews drink, but so few become casualties of alcohol, has sometimes been called the Great Jewish Drink Mystery.

When viewed in its proper social context, this apparent mystery becomes much more intelligible. One of the explanations for this controlled drinking takes account of the complex and socially important network of ritual that surrounds the way in which Jews drink alcohol. The use of wine is surrounded by religious rules which specify when, and where, and how much, wine is to be taken. There are even special occasions on which Jews can break the normal taboo against intoxication. The orthodox Jew regards drunkenness with disgust, as a disgrace. Yet the festival of Purim is a time of licence when it is obligatory to eat, drink and be merry. The habit of moderation in drinking which is practised from childhood as well as the ritual surrounding the use of alcohol help to protect the individual from losing control of their drinking. Other protective factors include a view that having alcohol problems is not consistent with being Jewish, and this is especially strong when combined with a commitment to Orthodox Judaism as a total way of life.

Although it may reduce the likelihood of alcoholism, being an Orthodox Jew provides no guaranteed protection against developing a drinking problem. For those Jews who do become alcoholics, the idea that there are no Jewish alcoholics may deter them from acknowledging their own difficulties because of a sense of shame, and this may delay any move to seek help. Where abstinence is practised, there can be no drug problems. But, where those who are part of an abstinent tradition attempt to use drugs, it may lead to special difficulties since they must reject all conventional restraints upon the use of that particular drug. If a Mormon chooses to drink, he or she is behaving in a deviant manner and their deviance is likely to create an expectation that drinking is primarily a means of becoming intoxicated, since it cannot be part of normal social behaviour. By definition, social drinking is excluded from the acceptable forms of behaviour and, psychologically, it is likely to become dissociated from other inhibitory, controlling parts of the personality of the drinker and from controls in the social system. This is not to imply that when anyone brought up within a tradition of abstinence begins to drink they will necessarily become alcoholic. It does suggest that rates of alcoholism may be comparatively high for such people.

The protective function of these rituals and social sanctions is shown by the way in which the introduction of drugs has affected societies which lack such controlling influences. Native Americans had a long-standing history of controlled use of such psychoactive drugs as peyote, yet they failed to maintain any such control over the white man's drug, alcohol. They rejected or were denied full membership in American society and were correspondingly slow to acquire the white man's cultural controls defining the appropriate uses of alcohol. Native Americans frequently drank to extreme drunkenness rather than to more sociable levels of intoxication, and alcohol problems among them continue to be evident in their higher rates of alcohol-related illnesses and mortality, and in terms of motor vehicle accidents, alcoholic cirrhosis, foetal alcohol syndrome, alcohol dependence and violence. Among the Navajo, for example, the alcohol-related mortality rate is about six times higher than for the rest of the US population. Attempts have been made to restrict access to alcohol through prohibition. The Navajo Reservation is technically 'dry': it is illegal to buy, sell, or possess alcohol on the Navajo Nation's land. However, bootlegging is common, and Thunderbird wine in particular is a fortified wine which is popular with many Navajo drinkers.

The heavy drinking among Native Americans has contributed towards the negative perception of alcohol misuse among Native Americans and gives unfortunate support to the stereotype of the 'drunken Indian'. This stereotype is, at best, only partly correct, and it is incorrect to suggest that there are no social or cultural restraints upon drinking in Native American societies. In Navajo culture, for instance, the traditional norms, values, and expectations of Navajo culture emphasize the importance of living a balanced, harmonious life in a world that is at once natural, social and supernatural. This value system is enmeshed in a system of extended kinship networks and obligations, and its goal is to live to a ripe old age in universal beauty and happiness. Drunkenness and extreme behaviours of all sorts are seen as contrary to Navajo ideals of beauty and well-being, and are strongly disapproved of. Many Navajo choose to reflect their cultural values by not drinking. Not only do a substantial proportion of Navajos abstain from alcohol entirely but many of the heaviest abusers give up alcohol as they get older. The proportion of 'ex-drinkers' living in various different social settings ranged from over one-half (55 per cent) among Navajos living in a rurally isolated area, to a quarter (26 per cent) in an on-reservation community.

The Inuit (Eskimos) had similar difficulties with alcohol when they were first allowed to drink; their lack of previous cultural experience and guidelines for alcohol use led to pronounced abuse, and the Aborigines of Australia also have a long history of problems with alcohol and other drugs. Although it is sometimes suggested that they had no drugs of their own prior to the arrival of the first British settlers in

1788, there is evidence that they used indigenous flora to make fermented beverages and other mind-altering drugs. However, with the introduction of European alcohol the Aborigines learned a cultural norm of excessive drinking from white settlers, often from cattlemen whose infrequent returns from the bush were associated with binges of heavy drinking as well as swearing, fighting and generally uncontrolled riotousness. The use of alcohol by Aborigines often involves excessive binge drinking in public places, and this led to prohibitions directed against Aboriginal drinking from as early as 1838 in New South Wales. The last prohibition laws were not repealed until the mid-1960s.

Aboriginal Australians mainly make use of legal substances. As well as alcohol, these include painkillers, kava and solvents (especially petrol). For Aborigines who do not have ready access to other substances, these drugs are cheap and easily available. Petrol sniffing can be a dangerous form of drug taking. As well as causing a satisfying outrage among one's elders, the short-term effects of inhaling leaded petrol can include loss of appetite, vomiting, tremor, irritability, aggression, confusion and memory impairment. In high doses or in the longer term it can cause fits and degenerative diseases of the brain. As in Western countries, solvent sniffing is mainly (though not exclusively) done by adolescent boys.

About 1982, kava was introduced to Australia and since then it has been mixed and used by north coastal Aborigines in the Northern Territory. Its positive effects are described as relaxing and soporific and it does not lead to the violence that so often follows heavy drinking. On the other hand, the physical health of Aboriginal kava users tends to be poor. They may develop skin problems and many are as much as 20 per cent underweight. Heavy use of kava may also have damaging effects on the liver. Because they lack the cultural norms and controls that surround the use of kava in Fiji and elsewhere, the Aborigines have often used excessive amounts of this drug.

In Western societies, those who use illicit drugs face the same sort of problems. It is not surprising that some of them should become drug casualties. There are no socially accepted rules and rituals governing the use of such drugs, no education in how to take them without damage, and no reinforcement of moderate rather than self-destructive patterns of use. Since mainstream society fails to provide any such restraints, the only rules to help the illicit drug taker control their drug taking are those available within the drug subculture itself. There have been very few studies of drug takers who keep their use of illicit drugs under control. One such investigation looked at a group of more than 100 American controlled users. The most striking feature about them was the way in which their drug taking was influenced by rituals and socially shared expectations. Although some of them used drugs when they were alone, more than 80 per cent of their drug taking took place in a social setting, and most avoided the company of known addicts. Controlled heroin users, for instance, usually restricted their contact with addicts to those occasions on which it was necessary to obtain their drug and declined invitations to inject heroin with their addict suppliers. Several of them drew an analogy with controlled drinking. People who adhere to rules about drinking (such as only drinking at mealtimes, at parties, at weekends, or not drinking during working hours or when alone) are less likely to develop an alcohol problem than those who have no such restraints and who drink whenever they feel like it. One of the drug takers in this study said that he did not feel that he always had to have a good reason for getting high on drugs, but that, if people found they were using drugs regularly without a reason, this should alert them to the dangers of slipping into a dependence on drugs.

On the other hand, not all social customs protect the individual from the hazards of drug taking; some encourage and reinforce the use of drugs. As so often with drug taking, the user is partly in control of, but also influenced by the drugs. The use of drugs within the club scene has become more or less normalized. Some surveys have found rates of drug use as high as 80 per cent. The use of drugs and the club experience have often become assimilated. Drugs such as ecstasy, methamphetamine and poppers are also commonly used in many gay social settings. Where drug use in such social scenes has been associated with unsafe sexual behaviour, this has led to overhasty conclusions that it was the drugs that led to the unsafe sex. Actually, the two things are more often consequences of the prior, and often explicit, intentions of the clubbers who have gone in deliberate search of an uninhibited and wild night out.

Nor are social rituals necessarily protective. Some are seductive. Of his opium smoking, Jean Cocteau wrote (1957): 'It is reassuring. It reassures by its luxury, by its rites, by the antimedical elegance of the lamps, stoves, pipes, by the secular setting of this exquisite elegance.'

More recently, and in the more sordid world of heroin addiction, there are elaborate rituals that surround the act of injection:

> It's not only a question of kicks. The ritual itself, the powder in the spoon, the little ball of cotton, the matches applied, the bubbling liquid drawn up through the cotton filter into the eye-dropper, the tie round the arm to make a vein stand out, the fix often slow because a man will stand there with the needle in the vein and allow the level of the eyedropper to waver up and down, up and down … all this is not for nothing; it is born of a respect for the whole chemistry of alienation (Trocchi, 1960).

The sharing of injecting equipment can also be powerfully influenced by the implicit or symbolic meaning of the act. There are groups of injectors for whom sharing injecting equipment is not merely something forced upon them by the absence of clean equipment but a shared act of defiance and belonging. In the post-AIDS era we may feel alienated from the rituals of 'blood brotherhood' depicted in Hollywood Westerns, but these rituals are not without their modern counterparts. It is to be hoped that today's injectors can be helped to be better informed about infection risks and that they possess sufficient judgement to avoid sharing needles and syringes. But it unlikely that drug use will always be guided primarily by health considerations.

No society is a simple monolithic organization. Within any society is a multitude of groups, each with its own aims, interests and priorities. Most users of alcohol, coffee and tobacco can take their drugs without challenging the 'conventional' social values. It is frequently permissible to use drugs such as Valium, Prozac and analgesics, provided that they can be obtained through under the licence of a medical prescription. The committed hedonistic drug user and the addict, however, are often spoken of as if they existed outside society (whatever that means), and their behaviour is disparagingly described as a bizarre, uncontrolled and meaningless disorder. But most illicit drug users do not live outside society; they live in alternative (though subterranean) societies which are in many respects clearly at odds with conventional, middle-class values. (Whether such alternatives represent any improvement upon other, more conventional, options is another matter. They can be attacked or defended according to the premises that the reader chooses to apply.) The phrase 'alternative society' owes a good deal to the comparatively articulate dissent of the hippies during the 1960s; but even the supposedly amoral world of the street addict has its own set of alternative social rules and values. It is significant that many illicit drug users see drug taking, not as a weakness or a failure, but as a challenge; and far from being an isolated event in their lives, the use of drugs is an integral part of a wider set of social values.

For many addicts, these values are derived from what could be called 'the street culture'. This provides an ill-defined but nonetheless extremely powerful view of the world and how to behave in it. 'The street' is a tough and competitive environment where only the true initiates can survive, and where there is a premium attached to keeping one's own real feelings and thoughts hidden behind a facade. One of the more obvious features of the street is its private language. The tools of the trade are not needles or syringes, they are spikes and guns, not heroin or amphetamine but smack and speed. It is a characteristic of many disadvantaged minority groups that they use a language or dialect to differentiate themselves from the majority. But it is not merely the language of the street that separates it from straight society. It also has its own moral code.

In Trocchi's novel, *Cain's Book*, a friend of his wife gives the narrator some money to buy him some cannabis. Cain leaves with the money and does not return. In the rules of the junkie world, this is a classic burn. If the friend was not knowledgeable enough to avoid this error, he deserved to be ripped off. The friend, however, sees this differently – as stealing – and threatens to call the police. Cain is surprised and appalled by this reaction and argues with his wife that he did not steal the money: 'I beat him. He gave it to me.' 'You stole it, you admit stealing it.' 'Didn't steal anything, I beat that fool, can't you understand that?' Cain goes on to say that, if the friend were to arrive with a gun or a knife, he would give back the money, but to call the police is outside the rules of the street. The overall purpose of these street games is to give meaning to the addict lifestyle. The street addicts, like the rest of us, create a social reality around themselves and their sense of personal identity is closely related to their social world. The tragedy of addiction is that neither the drugs nor the street culture live up to their initial promise.

Chapter 4

Chemical Comforts

The Demand for Health and Happiness

Aldous Huxley's *Brave New World* provided the complete drug. The product of six years' intensive research by 2,000 pharmacologists and biochemists, this drug was a narcotic that also produced euphoria and hallucinations; it had 'all the advantages of Christianity and alcohol; none of their defects'. It fulfilled a variety of social functions. It was drunk from a Communion cup surrounded by quasi-religious ritual; it was routinely issued at the end of each day's work shift – four tablets a day, six on Saturdays. Its main purpose was to make everyone happy in their servitude, a way of eliminating all possibility of unhappiness, the ultimate chemical comfort.

Our own chemical comforts often carry a greater social stigma than in Huxley's fictional society. Most people are confused about their own drug taking. They are told that drugs are dangerous, yet most people are regular drug takers. They try to make sense of this by denying that many of their regular drugs are drugs at all (cigarettes, coffee, alcohol) and they exaggerate the dangers of illegal drugs which in themselves may be comparatively harmless. There are drugs that are used on a massive scale and, in order to legitimize their use, we look to the medical profession for approval.

One of the striking social developments of recent years is the way that health has been elevated to a supreme value. In the name of health and treatment, the medical bureaucracy is increasingly able to violate such important social values as the individual's freedom of choice and rights of privacy. The distinction between good and bad has been largely replaced by that of healthy and unhealthy (or, as it is sometimes expressed, good for you, and bad for you). Whatever is deemed by medical bureaucrats to be healthy is therefore good, correct. It must be encouraged. This could relate to eating a diet low in polyunsaturated fats, drinking water containing fluoride, taking regular exercise or wearing a seat belt when driving. Whatever is deemed unhealthy, such as smoking cigarettes, overeating, drinking too much or working under prolonged stress, is necessarily bad and must be discouraged – or, if necessary, stopped. Medicine has become more and more involved with aspects of social behaviour that are only vaguely and indirectly related to illness and disease. This is a perilous sort of medical imperialism that seeks to control our social affairs on such a narrow principle.

The superficial orthodoxy suggests that drugs should be used as medicine, to cure or alleviate medical problems. Between 1963 and 1978 the number of prescriptions fulfilled in England and Wales each year increased from just over 200 million to more than 300 million. Since this period saw no conspicuous decline in the nation's general health, this trend to more medication should be seen as a reflection of the increased willingness on the part of doctors to prescribe drugs, and on the part of the general population to accept them. Some health surveys have suggested that as many as nine out of ten people who were not seeing a doctor may have been suffering from some problem deemed worthy of treatment. If a complete and unblemished state of health is so unusual, one of the decisive factors that determines whether a person approaches a doctor is their attitude towards their own physical and psychological welfare. As our expectations about health have been raised, so we have become more dissatisfied with any failure to achieve that state. Like chasing a shadow, as medical science has inexorably extended the definition of illness, the idea of health itself has become ever more elusive.

This is especially true of psychological medicine. Many of the 'mental illnesses' which the psychiatrist is expected to treat are not really illnesses at all. They are only illnesses in a metaphorical sense. Most are the product of a complex interaction between the special circumstances of each person's upbringing, their personality and their social environment.

But if few people are completely healthy, it must be a worrying sign that most of the people who go to see a physician in general practice are not ill. The majority of the patients in the general practitioner's clinic are there largely for non-medical reasons. They may be lonely, anxious or unhappy because of the way their lives are going. Their difficulties are more properly regarded as social problems resulting from the circumstances in which they are living. Their expectations of life are not being met. But it is not a medical problem to be unhappy because a member of the family has died, or to be apprehensive about facing some new challenge in one's life. These are precisely the sorts of complaint that many people take to their doctor: and they are precisely the sorts of complaint which commonly lead to a prescription for a psychoactive drug. Behind each of these cases is the specious assumption that problems of living can be solved, or at least 'treated', by medical means. Once this insidious principle has been accepted, there is no end to the number of problems that can be redefined in medical terms.

The public is constantly being told by the scientific optimists that there is no problem so great that it cannot be solved by science and technology. In the medical sciences, there are those who have suggested that one day all diseases may be avoidable. Endless television programmes encourage this view of medicine as a means of eliminating disease by the application of high-powered technological devices. Doctors, politicians and the general public have all acquired this taste for changing hearts, livers and kidneys in preference to changing minds: now we are being promised a pill for every ill.

We are coming to see every ache and pain as a sign that we need medical help. Until recently, we might have used plays, novels or other social and cultural devices to try to understand our pain and distress, to help us to cope with them by giving them meaning. Medical science has rendered them socially meaningless by redefining them as nothing more than mechanical breakdowns in the soft machine. They are to be solved by their removal. But because medicine deprives them of meaning, it alienates us from our own feelings: it makes us less able to understand them and less able to tolerate them. The promise of freedom from pain and suffering, far from producing a happier society, is turning us into anaesthesia consumers.

There appear to be few constraints upon our willingness to believe in a new wonder drug. Our chemical-consuming societies have had several brief flings with antidepressant drugs in recent years. One such substance to be added to the list of failed wonder drugs is Prozac. Released in 1988, this drug quickly established itself as a best-seller. Prozac is similar in some ways to conventional tricyclic antidepressant drugs. It acts by increasing the supply of the mood-altering brain neurotransmitter called serotonin.

The history of Prozac repeats that of many other drugs. At the outset it was hailed as a magical discovery which was capable of producing amazing transformations in people's lives. Not only did it remove depression but it was supposed to produce pleasure and happiness. The media, ever keen to spot (or even to create) a good story, duly fanned the flames of euphoria surrounding the new chemical superstar and contributed towards its promotion. Particularly in the US, the drug assumed a distinctly fashionable status as a sort of psychoactive facelift. It may not be unrelated to its fashionable image that it also led to reduced appetite and could be used as a slimming drug.

Shortly afterwards, the first negative reports started to appear. The more modest adverse effects included headache, nervousness, insomnia, dizziness, sweating, skin rashes and, definitely not fashionably, diarrhoea and loss of sexual capacity. More serious worries were also raised about possible links between Prozac and suicide, and violent and aggressive behaviour. One particularly worrying observation was that it seemed to be linked to increases in suicidal behaviours among children who were given the drug. This finding was subsequently confirmed. Children who received Prozac or similar antidepressants were found to be almost twice as likely to show suicidal thoughts and behaviours as others who received a placebo. The media now responded by exaggeration of the adverse effects and reported over-prescription by doctors and gullibility by users. Gradually, a more balanced view emerged in which Prozac came to be seen as having some merits as an antidepressant, but, as with other such drugs, it can cause side effects and it is by no means a panacea.

One of the future dilemmas that will face us is the extent to which we are willing to use neuroenhancing drugs. The next wave of drugs in the pharmaceutical industry will be capable of enhancing memory, mood and concentration in people who are not impaired. Prozac is an example of a substance that improves mood in people who are not depressed. And it has been widely used for this purpose. The stimulant Ritalin can be used to improve concentration and school performance not just in hyperactive children, but also in normal children. There can be little doubt about our appetite for 'enhancers'. This is already evident in the massive sales of nutrachemicals, functional foods and dietary supplements. There is likely to be an even greater demand for a substance that 'improves memory'. Look out for the neuroenhancers: coming your way soon.

The Prescription

In a somewhat lyrical vein, Professor Trethowan referred to 'the relentless march of the psychotropic drug juggernaut'. Almost half of all the drugs prescribed in England are psychoactive drugs, or drugs which affect the central nervous system. A large proportion of these psychoactive drugs are sleeping tablets, which suggests that a lot of people like to put themselves to sleep at night with knock-out drops. Of the remainder, most are taken for conditions which can only be described as extremely vague. Certainly, it does not look as though they are being prescribed for specific medical conditions, and this is (or should be) worrying. If such huge quantities of drugs are being medically prescribed for what are really personal and social problems, this may establish a vicious circle in which a person who is faced by some upsetting life problem goes to their doctor, the doctor prescribes tranquillizers and, because the patient has received a prescription, they feel that their problem is really a medical one which the doctor understands and is competent to deal with. The pills produce an emotional numbness which makes the patient feel better, but they do not usually solve the problem; so when the pills run out and the original problem makes itself felt again, the patient returns to the doctor for further treatment.

Before prescribing any drug, competent doctors should ask themselves whether it might not be better to prescribe no treatment at all. If they do treat the patient, they should ask themselves what they are trying to achieve, whether the prescribed drug is capable of achieving any such goals, what side effects the drug might have, and whether the possibility of improvement overrides the likelihood of harming the patient. In practice, these five questions often remain unanswered and, in doing all they can, the doctor does too much.

The increased reliance upon prescribing as an adequate treatment response has been evident in many countries but it is especially marked in the US, and it has most often involved the prescription of antidepressant drugs. The over-prescription of drugs is far from being a risk-free option. Thousands of people have been injured by the well-intentioned medicines that they have been given. A survey conducted in one large US hospital found that as many as one patient in every 20 had suffered a major toxic reaction to medicines. All drugs have potentially harmful effects, the more so when they are used unwisely. Any drug which is worth using at all is capable of causing harm. Psychoactive drugs are also increasingly being prescribed to children despite the fact that the research testing of medications is almost always done with adults and most of the commonly prescribed medications are not licensed for use in children. There is often little or no evidence that these medications are either safe or effective for children.

It is tempting but mistaken to put all the blame on either the doctor or their patient for the over-prescription of psychoactive drugs. There is no doubt that the general practitioner feels under intense pressure to respond to the patient's problems by offering a prescription. Many patients actually request a particular drug when they go to see their doctor, and every GP must have had the totally recalcitrant patient who simply refuses to go away until they have been given a prescription. On the other hand, many doctors are all too eager to write out a prescription, especially for those vague psychosomatic disorders that are so difficult to understand. A major problem is that GPs receive insufficient training and therefore have little knowledge of psychology or mental health problems; they are not able or not interested to provide psychological therapies to support drug treatments; and generally, they do not monitor their patients closely enough to detect non-responses or adverse effects.

One survey found that four out of every five doctors agreed that drugs can be very valuable in helping patients to cope with the social demands and stresses of everyday life. As examples of the sort of problem for which drugs might be offered, almost all the doctors who were interviewed agreed that tranquillizers were an appropriate treatment for marital difficulties, and more than half felt that the daily use of these drugs was a legitimate treatment for the anxious college student. In one advertisement, for instance, Librium was proposed as an appropriate treatment for a new student who finds that the changed circumstances of university life 'may force her to re-evaluate herself and her goals' and whose 'newly stimulated intellectual curiosity may make her more sensitive and apprehensive about national and world conditions'. Tranquillizers have also been advertised as an appropriate treatment for the housewife with too little time to pursue a vocation for which she has spent many years in training, and even 'when anxiety and tension create major discord in parent–child relationships'. Whatever the exact circumstances of the consultation, about three-quarters of all visits to the doctor result in the writing of a prescription.

Despite the central position that the prescription occupies in medicine, we still do not properly understand its many different functions. It is, however, increasingly clear that prescribing depends just as much on social and psychological factors as upon medical ones. When a patient takes their complaint to the doctor they expect the doctor to diagnose and treat it. But since many of the complaints that are brought to the modern doctor are not really medical at all, it is unlikely that the doctor will be able to discover any specific cause for the complaint.

It would be mistaken to regard the prescription of psychoactive drugs as the doctor's response to specific medical disorders. Psychoactive drugs are generally given out for vague and undefined problems that cause the patient *dis-ease*. This is clearly recognized by the drug companies who sell their products by emphasizing the 'dual action' or 'broad spectrum activity' of the drugs.

The conventional view of medicine suggests that the doctor diagnoses the problem before prescribing the treatment. In this area the whole procedure is often turned on its head, with the problem being diagnosed according to the drug that is used to treat it: 'This is a case of Valium, there must be some anxiety.' However, if the patient is not given a specific treatment, they may keep returning to the surgery and become a cause of increasing irritation to the doctor. When this happens the most likely outcome is that the doctor will eventually prescribe a psychoactive drug, generally a tranquillizer. Yet many of these 'difficult patients' go to see their doctor not so much for a physical remedy in the shape of pills or medicine as to have someone listen sympathetically to their problems.

Far from being just a medical response to a specific complaint, sociologists have identified as many as 27 different social functions that the prescription can play. These include providing a visible sign of a doctor's power to heal, a recognition that the patient is 'really' ill, an expression of the doctor's concern, and an excuse for the patient's failure to perform their social duties. Last but not least (from the doctor's point of view), the writing of a prescription can provide a satisfactory way of signalling the end of the consultation.

Doctors may now be more aware of the potential hazards of prescribing psychoactive drugs, though this often shows itself in a strange way. Two out of every three doctors feel that *other* physicians prescribe too many tranquillizers. The drug companies have also moderated their claim about the psychoactive drugs. At one time their advertising implied that tranquillizers were non-addictive and could be safely prescribed for all manner of complaints: they are now more circumspect, and rightly so, because these drugs are far from harmless. Adverse reactions to medications are responsible for about 6 per cent of all hospital admissions every year.

Queen Valium

Of all the psychoactive drugs currently being used, among the most widely used are the minor tranquillizers. These drugs (they belong to a family of drugs called the benzodiazepines) include Valium (diazepam), Librium, Ativan and Mogadon, and they are prescribed on a quite prodigious scale for an astonishing variety of complaints and ailments. Although the benzodiazepines are synthesized drugs, several plants, such as potato and wheat, contain trace amounts of naturally occurring diazepam and other benzodiazepines. Librium was the first to be synthesized (in 1955) and it was approved for marketing in the US in 1960; Valium was first marketed in 1963. The popularity of these drugs made them a source of enormous profit and the pharmaceutical companies immediately began a diligent search for more and more of them. In the years since Librium was first introduced, many more drugs of this class have been produced – most of them with virtually identical effects.

The US is the great consumer of drugs. It is top of the international league table, and in 1977 it accounted for one-fifth of the entire world sale of pharmaceuticals, at a cost of 7.8 billion dollars. The prescription of drugs in the US has more than doubled since the 1950s, though this trend is not confined to the US; the same thing is happening throughout the Western world. Among the most prominent class of medications being prescribed are the benzodiazepines. In Germany, in 1980 alone, 28 million packs of benzodiazepines were sold.

Of the prescribed drugs, the most dramatic increases have occurred amongst the psychoactive drugs, and, of these, Diazepam is the most widely prescribed drug in the world. Valium and Librium are said to be first and fourth in the list of drugs prescribed in the US, with as many as one in every 10 Americans taking diazepam because of tension or 'nerves' during any three-month period. US physicians write approximately 50 million prescriptions for diazepam every year, and these drugs are also distributed freely among hospital patients. As early as 1972, a survey of two Boston teaching hospitals found that up to 30 per cent of all medical inpatients were given diazepam and 32 per cent were given a similar drug, Dalmane.

The popularity and prescription of psychoactive drugs, and especially of benzodiazepines, continued to increase for many years and peaked in many Western countries during the mid-to-late 1970s. Diazepam was the top-selling pharmaceutical in the US from 1969 to 1982. Peak sales of 2.3 billion pills were recorded in 1978. In 1975, 47.5 million prescriptions for psychoactive drugs were dispensed at retail chemists in England and Wales. Of these, 43 per cent were for tranquillizers and 35 per cent were for hypnotics (sleeping tablets). Since 1979, there has been a gradual reduction in the prescription of these drugs owing to increased concern about their associated risks and problems. Nonetheless, these drugs are still very widely used. The number of prescriptions for benzodiazepines in England and Wales during 1986 amounted to 15.8 million. By 2004, this had fallen to 12.4 million with about 5 million prescriptions for diazepam. Somewhere between one and 1.5 million people are prescribed benzodiazepines every year, and about 5 per cent of men and 12 per cent of women in the UK consume these drugs on a daily basis for one month or more during the course of a year.

These drugs produce a number of changes in behaviour that can best be described as disinhibition. In animal experiments they reduce the negative effects of stress and frustration, but they also reduce the animal's susceptibility to punishment. They have the same effects on people, which implies that person may be more susceptible to temptation when under the influence of drugs such as diazepam. There are numerous instances of people who have been caught shoplifting while taking these drugs. It is not that the drug itself leads them to commit crimes, but that the fear of punishment, which normally has a deterrent effect, has been chemically suppressed.

Rohypnol is one of the benzodiazepines that has been causing concern in recent years. This drug, which the media love to call the 'date rape drug', is a potent tranquillizer which is intended for the treatment of sleep disorders. It has also been used by young people as cheap way of getting intoxicated when dissolved in either soft drinks or alcohol. It has also been used in the club scene with other drugs such as amphetamines or ecstasy. Because it is easily soluble and leaves no detectable taste, odour or colour, it can be slipped into the drink of an unsuspecting victim who then becomes unaccountably 'drunk', disinhibited or falls asleep. This has happened to a number of women who have then been raped when under the influence of the drug.

It is also worrying that these drugs can increase levels of aggression. Generally, the benzodiazepines lower aggression and hostility, as one would expect of a tranquillizing drug. But under some conditions they can have the opposite effect, producing excitement, outbursts of anger and aggressive, destructive behaviour. In this, they are similar to alcohol, which can make some people 'fighting drunk'. Disinhibition is precisely the sort of psychological state that makes driving under the influence of alcohol such a potentially dangerous combination. Alcohol, barbiturates and the minor tranquillizers all have similar psychological effects, and all are likely to interfere with driving skills. They may do this in one of two ways. All have a depressant effect on the brain. They slow people down. As a result they increase the chances that the intoxicated driver will fail to react quickly enough to any emergency that occurs. At a high enough dose, they may cause the driver to fail to respond altogether. But each of these drugs can also cause the sort of changes in judgement that lead to accidents. The disinhibited driver is more likely to drive too fast, to overtake without checking if it is safe to do so, or to use their car as a weapon.

Drinking drivers have been surveyed and studied in great detail. They have had their body fluids and their breath analysed; they have walked up and down white lines and recited tongue-twisting phrases until it has entered into common knowledge that drinking alcohol increases the risk of having an accident. We are so familiar with Valium, Librium and the other tranquillizers that we often fail to treat them with the respect that is due to any drug. It has been known for years that tranquillizers, far from being completely harmless, can produce a whole range of unpleasant side effects. Drowsiness, tiredness and impaired coordination are fairly common, and other adverse effects that are occasionally reported include confusion, depression, double vision, stammering, headache, incontinence, nausea and dizziness. The makers of Valium recognize these problems and have issued a warning that people using Valium 'should be cautioned against engaging in hazardous occupations requiring complete mental alertness such as operating machinery or driving a motor vehicle'. The risks are undoubtedly increased when such tranquillizers are used in amounts larger than was prescribed or in conjunction with alcohol (as frequently happens), yet at this moment millions of people are driving cars, trains and lorries while under the influence of diazepam and its sister drugs.

Studies carried out in Canada, the US, Italy and Finland have found that drivers who had taken drugs were more likely to be involved in a fatal accident than drivers who were drug-free, and tranquillizers were among the drugs most seriously implicated in such accidents. It is possible that this is partly caused by the sort of problem that led the person to take tranquillizers in the first place – high levels of anxiety, irritability and moodiness; but such factors probably account for only a small part of these drivers' accident-proneness. The rest may be attributed to the drug-induced intoxication. It is a measure of the irrationality that surrounds drug taking that this lethal state of affairs is accepted with such complacency, whereas popular opinion is excited to hysteria by the casual use of illegal drugs.

The dangers of the prescribed drugs are no less than those of many of the illegal drugs. Although diazepam and the other minor tranquillizers are safer than barbiturate drugs in terms of their dangers in an overdose, they are just as likely to produce addiction if they are used continuously. At first the tranquillizers have a dampening effect on emotions, but after a while this fades as the person becomes tolerant to the effects of the drug. Many ordinary people who take these drugs adjust the dose, not according to the doctor's instructions but according to the way they are feeling: when they feel upset or stressed, they increase the dose. This carries many potential dangers and can mark the start of drug dependence. Some of the tranquillizers, such as diazepam and temazepam, seem to have a special sinister attraction as drugs of dependence.

Nor have the attractions of the benzodiazepine tranquillizers escaped the attentions of other drug takers. Heroin injectors began to acquire a taste for intravenous tranquillizers during the 1980s. By the late 1980s these drugs were widely misused, with about one-quarter of the heroin addicts admitted to drug dependence units in London also requiring treatment for their physical addiction to tranquillizers. Once the user is physically addicted, they may suffer from distressing withdrawal symptoms if they are deprived of the drug. These symptoms are very similar to those associated with barbiturate addiction, one of the most serious forms of drug dependence. Withdrawal begins with restlessness, anxiety and tension; sufferers find it very difficult to sleep and, as the withdrawal reaches its peak, they may suffer from stomach cramps and vomiting; sometimes they tremble uncontrollably and have convulsions like an epileptic fit. The fact that a drug is prescribed by a doctor, and is socially acceptable to the millions of people who use it, has little or nothing to do with the damage it can cause. Tranquillizers are far from being safe drugs, and they are massively over-used. This form of drug taking is one of the hidden and more serious forms of drug abuse in our society.

The Hoffmann-La Roche Affair

In 1973, the cost of Librium and Valium to the National Health Service was debated in both the House of Commons and the House of Lords. This marked the culmination of a series of misunderstandings between the UK government and the Swiss pharmaceutical company Hoffmann-La Roche who held the patents for these drugs. The essence of the complaint was that the drug company was taking advantage of the National Health Service (NHS) by selling Librium and Valium at vastly inflated prices. The basic chemical ingredient of these drugs was sold in Italy, for instance, at only £9 and £20 a kilogramme: in the UK the same amount of each drug was costing more than 40 times as much – £370 and £922.

The UK government asked La Roche to justify its profits on the basis of its costs, but when it was asked to present its accounts for examination by government auditors, it flatly refused. Since La Roche does not regard its profits as a matter of public concern, there is no idea as to how much the company really makes on these drugs. However, the Swiss company did offer to return part of its profits to the Treasury 'without prejudice' (this is legal jargon for 'without admitting that we were wrong and without establishing any precedent') and between 1967 and 1970 the company repaid £1,600,000 to the NHS as a rebate against its high prices.

The Monopolies Commission was asked to carry out an investigation into the matter and argued that La Roche was over-pricing these two drugs. La Roche enjoyed a monopoly on the market for the supply of both Librium and Valium, and these two drugs represented more than two-thirds of all the tranquillizers used in the UK. As a result, the company was able to fix arbitrary price levels for these drugs. The Commission recommended that the price of Librium should be reduced by 60 per cent and that of Valium by 70 per cent. In addition, it recommended that La Roche should repay a further amount of the large profit it had made out of the NHS.

La Roche rejected the findings of the Monopolies Commission and clearly felt that it had been victimized and unfairly picked out for special treatment. It argued that, since only a few of the drugs that a drug company produces are ever successful, it is necessary to use the successful drugs to support the entire research programme. In any case, even successful drugs usually return a high profit only for a short time. After that, newer, more advanced rivals appear on the scene to replace them.

In the end, La Roche opened legal proceedings against the UK government and the Monopolies Commission. This set up a curious situation in which a national government was taken to court by a multinational company. As a monopoly supplier of these tranquillizers, La Roche set its own price for the drugs; it also established its own levels of research expenditure and justified one by the other. The Monopolies Commission argued that the company was spending 'excessive' amounts on research and promotion. If a multinational company of this sort is allowed to set its own levels of research expenditure and then as a monopoly supplier to pass on these costs to a nation's health service, this raises interesting questions about who is playing the servant and who the master. Even at a less exalted level, there must be some limit to the price and profit levels that a manufacturer is justified in setting.

In the eventual settlement, La Roche paid a rebate to the NHS of £3.7 million and joined the system of voluntary price control that had been used in the UK since 1957. This system established the price of particular drugs by agreement between the NHS and the drug company.

As a result of the Monopolies Commission report, proceedings were started against Hoffmann-La Roche in several European countries. In view of the allegations of over-pricing that did so much harm to its reputation, it is paradoxical that, in Canada, Hoffmann-La Roche was found guilty by the Ontario Supreme Court of trying to reduce or eliminate competition by selling Valium at unreasonably low prices. Between 1968 and 1974, Valium was given away to hospitals very cheaply (or even at no charge at all) in order to prevent the use of competing versions of the drug. In a four-year period, Hoffmann-La Roche reportedly gave away some 174 million doses of Valium and 26 million doses of Librium.

Self-Medication

Quite apart from the medically prescribed drugs, there are many forms of chemical comfort to which a person can turn in order to soften the stresses and strains of everyday life. The most common, of course, is alcohol. One out of every seven American adults drinks more than usual as a way of coping with a personal crisis, and men are particularly likely to turn to drink under such circumstances. Although heavy drinking is becoming increasingly common in women, they are still more likely to turn to medically prescribed psychoactive drugs as a way of relieving their psychological aches and pains.

The misuse of prescribed drugs, including the diversion of drugs that were prescribed to another person for their psychoactive effects, is increasingly common. National surveys in the US during 2003 estimated that about 15 million Americans were using prescription drugs for purposes other than the intended ones. This places prescription drug use second only to the use of cannabis in the prevalence league. The types of drugs most commonly used were the same as the commonly misused illicit drugs – painkilling drugs, stimulants, tranquillizers and sedatives. By far the most frequently misused of the prescribed medications are the painkillers. The number of people in the US who were estimated to be misusing analgesics increased from about 600,000 in 1990 to 2.4 million in 2001. The second most commonly misused prescription drugs are the tranquillizers. Different types of medications are used for a variety of purposes. Some are taken for their euphoriant or intoxicating effects, some are taken for instrumental purposes (to stay awake, to go to sleep, to gain more energy), and some are taken to reduce negative emotional states.

Few of us enjoy being under stress, and it is natural to look for some way of reducing the pressure. For most of us, the sort of thing that causes us to feel anxious, unhappy or tense is linked to our social life. The most common life events that provoke these feelings are losing one's job, moving house, marital difficulties or the death of a close friend or someone in the family. Sometimes the roots of people's unhappiness are more elusive. They may feel depressed all the time without any obvious reason; they may feel persistently tired or tense or fidgety. By taking a drug, they can easily obtain some relief from their stress. Generally, the drugs fail to resolve the original problem. Students who are worried about failing an examination for which they have not done enough work are no more likely to pass the examination if they are taking tranquillizers; the economic causes of redundancy are not altered by antidepressant drugs, nor are parents and friends brought back to life. Indeed, the drugs may even make the original problems worse. By reducing the student's anxiety, the tranquillizers may reduce their motivation to do some revision. By suppressing feelings of grief and unhappiness, the antidepressants may interfere with a person's ability to come to terms with their bereavement.

Drug taking is generally thought of as something that occurs among young people. What is less often recognized is that drug misuse also occurs among older people. Aging and its losses can be psychologically stressful. Many elderly people outlive their spouses, friends, and even children. They also have to cope with loss of employment, economic problems, failing health, loneliness and social isolation. Many elderly people also have visual and hearing problems, and lose vital communication skills, which serves to aggravate problems of depression, isolation and loneliness. Drugs, alcohol, or both may be used as ways of dealing with or forgetting the problem.

Aging can also be physically stressful. The elderly are more likely to suffer from multiple health problems, and physical ailments leading to disability and pain. Osteoporosis affects millions of elderly women and predisposes to fractures. Arthritis is one of the most common problems of the elderly. Neuropathies, recurrent gout attacks, and cancer may also predispose older people to substance use. Chronic pain is a daily problem for many elderly people.

Between 1 and 3 per cent of hospital inpatients aged 65 and older have been found to have substance abuse disorders. Prescribed drugs, especially when taken in high doses or in inappropriate ways may put the older person at greater risk of falling, with fractures and subsequent institutionalization, and benzodiazepine misuse is one of the most common disorders in this age group.

Elderly people often take over-the-counter medications, or unused medications belonging to family and/or friends. Sedative-hypnotics, anxiolytics and analgesics are among the more commonly misused prescribed or diverted drugs. Many elderly people who take such drugs have been found to do so for more than five years, and they may only recognize their dependence when they stop taking their medication. As a group, the elderly are amongst heaviest consumers of both prescription and over-the-counter medications. 'Classical' patterns of drug misuse such as the use of street heroin or crack cocaine or the use of drugs by injection are believed to be rare among the elderly. However, some survivors from earlier generations of drug addicts are growing old, and some elderly addicts now being treated in methadone treatment programmes.

Drug dependence can also be more problematic among the elderly because tolerance to drugs decreases with age. The use of multiple prescriptions, and combined use of prescription drugs with heavy drinking may also put elderly people at increased risk of accidents and adverse reactions. Benzodiazepines are often prescribed together with antidepressant drugs, and the prescribing of multiple medications is often not appropriate. In a detailed clinical review of prescriptions for elderly patients, one study concluded that almost half of the medications were not justified. Where prescribed drugs are supplemented by other non-sanctioned forms of substance use, elderly drug misusers often try to hide their drug taking. This increases the difficulties of identifying such behaviours, and such problems are very often not recognized by family or carers. Where drug taking is excessive, or where drug interactions (including drug-alcohol interactions) lead to drug-related delirium or dementia, this can be wrongly seen as indicative of Alzheimer's disease and it can easily lead to serious errors in clinical response.

At the same time, it is important not to over-react to the use of drugs. There is an attitude of chemical Calvinism that seems to value suffering and to condemn the easy relief that drugs can bring. There is no great virtue in enduring psychological stress for its own sake, and there are often no easy solutions to the problems that cause so much suffering. It is too readily assumed that psychotherapy (whether of the Freudian variety or in one of its more unorthodox forms) can solve every sort of emotional problem. Those who need a panacea must continue their search. Neither drugs nor psychotherapy can resolve the problem of unhappiness.

In Huxley's *Brave New World*, Soma was used to keep the population compliant and under control. There have been uncomfortable hints that Valium and its sister drugs are being misused in this way. After all, it is much cheaper to tranquillize the distraught housewife who is confined to a remote tower block with nowhere for her children to play than it is to demolish such flats and rebuild a more human environment for her to live in. The government, the drug companies and the doctor all have a vested interest in offering a medical solution to what are really social and political problems.

Illegal psychoactive drugs are often used in the same way and for the same reasons as alcohol and as the drugs prescribed by doctors. In this respect, as in so many others, there are far fewer differences between heroin, Valium and alcohol than we like to pretend. One of the main reasons why people escalate their use of drugs to become dependent upon them (because they are all potentially addictive) is precisely because of the ease with which they can be used to relieve psychological distress.

For the bored teenager, drugs may offer the initial prospect of excitement or social acceptance. Because adolescence is such a difficult period in Western society, the teenager is especially vulnerable to the temptation of using drink or drugs to gain relief from his or her problems. In recent years, it has become increasingly obvious that far more young people get into trouble with drink than with drugs. Alcohol is easily available, socially approved of, and it solves so many of the dilemmas of youth. Shyness, insecurity and feelings of social awkwardness all evaporate after a few drinks. It is easy to relax, talk freely and confidently, and to feel extraverted and sociable after a few drinks. Anyone who has watched a party move from its sober beginnings to its less sober conclusion will appreciate how effectively alcohol works as a social lubricant. But neither heavy drinking nor drug abuse are the exclusive preserve of young people; they merely generate more righteous indignation when teenagers are involved. Anyone in psychological distress is potentially at risk if they persist in using drink or drugs as a prop. Drugs may offer temporary relief if used in this way, but, in the long term, they create far more problems than they can ever solve.

In recent years, researchers have been looking at the ways in which different drugs can be used to relieve different sorts of psychological problems. Alcohol, the barbiturates and Valium, for instance, can all be used as a way of blotting out feelings of anxiety or relieving stress. Just as the harassed executive may reach for a stiff drink to calm themselves down after a difficult day, so the adolescent labouring under feelings of nervousness and awkwardness may feel better after taking barbiturates.

For the person who is insecure or chronically shy, amphetamines supply the confidence and artificial energy that convinces the user that they are brilliant, witty and creative. Objectively, they may be none of these things, but the drug-induced exhilaration is powerful enough to override any more realistic appraisal of their own performance. Many drug addicts find it difficult to express their feelings of anger and aggression in an appropriate way. Heroin helps by suppressing their aggressive feelings directly. Alcohol, Valium and the barbiturates help in a different way, by producing the sort of disinhibited state that allows the person to act out their feelings of hostility and aggression. Drunks and barbiturate addicts are often a particularly irritating problem in hospital casualty departments, where they stumble about, threaten the staff and generally make a nuisance of themselves.

What these drugs have in common is that they can all give a temporary chemical comfort. But in the end, none of them solves the problems of living.

Chapter 5

Alcohol

Alcohol and Its Origins

Alcohol is one of the more potent as well as one of the most widely used of all the psychoactive drugs: paradoxically, it is also the least likely to be recognized as such. Two-thirds of the US population drink alcohol. The average American spends more than 5 per cent of their annual budget on alcohol, consuming 2.6 gallons of spirits, 2.2 gallons of wine and 26.6 gallons of beer every year. The same sort of pattern emerges in most Western countries. Almost half of the UK's population over the age of 16 drink regularly: more than one in 10 drink every day.

Both nationally and internationally, the drinks industry is an extremely powerful political force. This power is obtained through the revenue generated for governments, and through the jobs provided both directly and indirectly by the production, shipping and retail of alcohol. In France, almost a third of the electorate are either wholly or partly dependent upon the drinks industry for their livelihood. World beer sales in 2005 were about 158 billion litres. In the US, the government receives more than $30 billion in taxes from the production and sales of beer alone. The countries of the European Union take 24 billion euros in excise duty from the trade in alcohol. This represents more than the total annual government expenditure of countries such as Finland or Poland.

Alcohol is produced by a small number of extremely powerful multinational companies and by a large number of smaller domestic manufacturers. However, a great deal of alcohol is produced outside the alcohol industry. In low-income countries in particular, the consumption of commercially produced alcohol is often confined to the wealthier groups. The East African countries are amongst the heaviest consumers of non-commercial alcoholic drinks. In Tanzania and Uganda, as much as 90 per cent of the alcohol is produced as (often extremely potent) home-brews.

Nature provides alcohol in liquid form and man has been drinking it for so long that the verb 'to drink' has come to mean to drink alcoholic beverages. There are six basic kinds of alcoholic drink: beers, cider, table wines, fortified wines, liqueurs and distilled drinks. The ways in which these drinks are made, and their relative strengths, are shown in Table 5.1. They differ in their precise chemical composition, and to a certain extent in their physiological effects on the body, but the main component of all of them is ethyl alcohol, or ethanol. (In this book I have used the term 'ethanol' in its strict sense to distinguish the simple solution of ethyl alcohol from the complex mixtures of higher alcohols and other substances that make up the actual drinks that we take: the term 'alcohol' is used more loosely to refer both to the ethanol content of drinks and to alcoholic drinks in general; it seemed unnecessarily pedantic to keep referring to 'alcoholic drinks'.)

Among the other alcohols are methyl, amyl and propyl alcohol. Of these, methyl alcohol is possibly the most important because it is sometimes taken as a substitute for drinks containing ethyl alcohol. Methylated spirit, for instance, contains a mixture of ethanol and methyl alcohol, and methyl alcohol is also used in some paint-strippers and antifreeze mixtures. The intoxicating effect of methyl alcohol is much less than that of ethanol, in that it makes the person less drunk after a given amount, but its side effects are more serious. The most alarming of these are its effects on vision. These can vary from visual disturbances to total blindness. This may be followed by partial or even complete recovery, though there have been many cases in which people have been permanently blinded as a result of drinking methyl alcohol. Aftershave solutions and 'eau de colognes' often contain another of the higher alcohols, isopropyl alcohol, and some people drink these preparations for their alcoholic effect. In Russia, where drinking problems are very prevalent, the consumption of such products has been estimated to cause more than 40,000 deaths each year. However, few of us would willingly resort to such bizarre and dangerous methods of drinking alcohol. Let us return to our more familiar 'poisons'.

All beers are made by the fermentation of brewer's wort. This is made primarily from barley malt, though other cereals may also be used. If an ale, stout or porter beer is wanted, a top-fermenting species of yeast is used, while a bottom-fermenting yeast is used for lager. European beers contain three times as much hops as American beers. The hop is sometimes said to produce a 'heady' sort of intoxication and has been described as 'the English narcotic'.

Historically, wine making is about as old as beer making, with a technology which is probably even more complicated. Variations in the type of grape used, the soil of the vineyard, temperature and weather conditions during the growing period, methods of harvesting, crushing and fermenting the wine, and even the conditions of storage all affect the final quality of the wine. Wines contain literally hundreds of organic compounds. In their physiological effects, however, the differences between wines are less significant. Red wines are richer in pigment-producing compounds than white wines; they also have a higher tannin content. Whereas the still wines are fermented in a single process, the champagnes are produced in two stages of fermentation. During the second stage, the carbon dioxide produced by the fermentation is held in solution under pressure. When a bottle of champagne is chilled, uncorked and served, the carbon dioxide content drops by about half.

Fortified wines such as port, sherry, Marsala and Madeira are ordinary wines to which a form of alcohol has been added to increase their strength. The vermouths are a similar type of drink. These are usually contain 15–20 per cent wine with plant extracts added as flavouring. Their name probably comes from *Wermut*, a German word for wormwood, which has traditionally been thought to possess healing powers and has been added to wines since Greek or Roman times. Among the other flavourings that have been used in vermouth are bitter orange peel, camomile, thistle, cardamom and nutmeg.

Table 5.1 Comparison of alcoholic drinks

Drink	Type	Alcohol content (% by volume)	Produced by
Beers	Lager	3–6	Fermentation of brewer's wort with hops added for flavour
	Extra-strength beer & lager	8–10	
	Ale	3–8	
	Stout & porter	4–8	
Cider		3.5–13.5	Fermentation of apple juice
Table wines	Still wines; red white & rosé;	8–14	Fermentation of grape juice
	champagne	12	Secondary fermentation with carbon dioxide retained under pressure
Fortified wines	Sherry, port, Madeira, vermouth	15–20	Wines with added brandy, neutral spirits or plant-extract flavourings
Distilled spirits	Brandy	40–55	Distillation of grape mash
	Whisky	40–50	Double distillation of fermented barley, rye or corn mash
	Rum	40–75	Distillation of fermented molasses
	Vodka	35–50	Distillation of grain
	Gin	35–50	Tasteless distillate flavoured with juniper berries
Liqueurs	Benedictine, Chartreuse, Kirsch, Kümmel, etc.	25–55	Neutral spirits with various added herbs for flavour

Spirits have been distilled from almost every conceivable source of sugar which could be fermented. Fruits, cereals, potatoes and molasses are among the more common bases. Brandy was probably the first of the spirits to be produced commercially, and is made by the distillation of wine. The spirit is then kept in barrels for at least two years, and sometimes as long as 20 years, before blending and bottling. Calvados, a type of apple brandy, is made from apple cider in the same way that grape brandy is made from wine. In some areas where calvados is widely used, such as Brittany and Normandy, there are especially high levels of alcoholism and liver disease, and there have been suggestions that calvados contains some mysterious and highly toxic ingredient which is responsible for these problems. No such mystery ingredient has been detected.

Whisky is made from various combinations of cereals – malted and unmalted barley, corn and rye. Scotch, for instance, is made from malted barley and corn. Rum is distilled from a solution containing molasses or fresh sugar-cane juice, and the distillate may be flavoured with sherry, Madeira, wine or various fruit extracts. Gin is essentially a tasteless alcohol distillate. It can be made from any fermentable carbohydrate: barley, rye, potatoes, molasses and cane juice have all been used for this purpose. Gin derives its distinctive flavouring from a second distillation with juniper berries and plant extracts. Vodka is a similar drink but without the flavouring.

Liqueurs are among the more exotic alcoholic preparations. Most were originally made as medicines during the Middle Ages, and many of them are associated with religious orders. They were usually made from herbs which had been specially chosen for their medicinal properties, though the ingredients of some have not been revealed (Benedictine and Chartreuse, for instance). In some cases, the herbs are allowed to ferment with water and sugar and the liqueur is then distilled from this mixture. In other cases the alcohol is first distilled and then flavoured. The final preparation is usually a sweet and potent liquid, though there is another group of liqueurs known as 'bitters'; the best known of the bitters is probably angostura bitters which is used to make pink gin.

The Uses of Alcohol

Most people use alcohol fairly intelligently and derive considerable pleasure and benefit from their drinking. But it is still a drug. Indeed, it is one of the more powerful, addictive and destructive drugs that is used on a large scale. Alcohol is used widely throughout the world, but, as with any other drug, the way it is used differs from culture to culture. The Islamic faith, for instance, forbids the use of alcohol, and the majority of Muslims seem to abide by that prohibition. In other societies heavy drinking has been built into religious ceremonies. The Aztecs were required to get drunk at every major religious occasion, otherwise their gods would be displeased. Even within religions there are different attitudes and expectations about alcohol. Certain Protestant denominations of the Christian Church regard alcohol as being so repugnant that it is not allowed in their Communion ceremonies.

The Jews are especially interesting in this respect, since the use of wine plays such a central part in their religious ceremonies. Wine is taken as part of the Kiddush and Habdalah which separate the Sabbath from the secular part of the week; it is taken to honour the annual festivals, and on special occasions such as New Year's Day and Yom Kippur. It is a measure of the importance of wine in Jewish life that the incidence of alcohol use is higher among Jews than among any other religious group. Probably fewer than 10 per cent of adult Jews are abstainers, and in some surveys the percentage of abstainers has been found to be as low as 1 per cent. When set against this high incidence of alcohol use, the low incidence of serious alcohol problems among Jews is quite remarkable; these features together make up what has been called the Great Jewish Drink Mystery (see Chapter 3).

There are also marked differences in national levels of alcohol consumption. Among the more abstemious Western nations is Norway. In certain wine-producing countries, on the other hand, notably in France, the consumption of large amounts of alcohol is part of everyday life. These comparisons between countries, however, are made on the basis of average levels of consumption and because of this they have only a rather general relevance to actual drinking habits within the different countries. It is important to distinguish between average levels of consumption and patterns of drinking. It is possible for an infrequent excessive drinker and a regular light drinker to have exactly the same average level of consumption. However, the two patterns can have very different implications for both the health of the drinker and for the behavioural consequences of drinking, such as drunk driving.

There is evidence that moderate drinking may have health benefits. For example, light to moderate drinking appears to be associated with a reduced risk of coronary heart disease. This effect is found both for men and women, among the elderly, and among smokers and non-smokers. Any protective effects of drinking, however, are found only for light and moderate drinkers. The risk of coronary heart disease increases rapidly among heavy drinkers, and especially among binge drinkers.

Although some health benefits are associated with regular ingestion of low amounts of alcohol, excess alcohol is toxic to the liver. In the UK and other Western countries alcohol abuse continues to be the most common cause of chronic liver disease. Alcohol is quickly absorbed from the stomach through the liver and into the bloodstream. Almost all alcohol is metabolized in the liver. The liver is exposed to the highest concentrations of alcohol and is the bodily organ most prone to alcohol-related problems. However, alcohol also causes toxic effects on other organs in the body including the brain, heart, muscles and pancreas. Heavy drinking can lead to three distinct liver diseases, and at least half of all clinical cases of liver disease in the UK are alcohol-related.

Almost all excessive drinkers will develop the first stage of alcoholic liver disease – fatty liver. If the patient stops drinking at this point, the liver can heal itself. If excessive drinking continues, the next stage of alcoholic liver disease is alcoholic hepatitis, when the liver becomes inflamed. Alcoholic hepatitis can range from a mild condition, with abnormal laboratory tests being the only indication of disease, to severe liver dysfunction and coma. In the final stage, permanent scarring liver damage (cirrhosis) can occur. Liver cirrhosis resulting from alcohol abuse is one of the ten leading causes of death in the US. As a general rule, the more heavily and the more frequently heavy drinking occurs, the more likely it is that the drinker will develop the more advanced forms of liver disease. Women who drink an equal amount of alcohol are at higher risk than men for the development of liver disease.

Alcohol consumption in the UK has been rising steadily since the middle of the 20th century. One unpleasant manifestation of this is the increased prevalence of drinking with the deliberate and explicit purpose of becoming drunk (or even as drunk as possible). Binge drinking is now a common behaviour among young people in many countries, and especially those of Northern Europe. It has become largely socially accepted and normalized among many young drinkers. Binge drinking has certainly established itself as an unpleasant feature of drinking in the UK, and drunken youths can be found shouting, fighting and vomiting in many town centres most Friday and Saturday nights. The UK currently has the worst teenage drinking problem in Europe. The staff of hospital accident and emergency departments have come to dread the influx of violent and abusive drunks every weekend, and deaths due directly to acute alcohol intoxication have doubled in the last 20 years both among men and women. About a thousand under-15s are admitted to hospital every year with alcohol poisoning. For many problem drinkers, their choice of beverage type reflects their drinking intentions. Many problem drinkers and drug takers choose extra-strength lagers, ciders, or fortified wines in order to maximize their 'bang for the buck'.

Alcohol is a food. Unfortunately, it is not a very good food; it contains calories but no minerals or vitamins. Alcohol is also a drug. It acts on the nervous system like an anaesthetic, and in large enough amounts it is a poison which can kill. In sufficiently large doses alcohol is capable of killing any living organism, though the cases in which alcohol poisoning leads to respiratory depression and to death are comparatively rare. A blood-alcohol level of 400mg per 100ml is usually fatal. In smaller amounts alcohol acts as a depressant drug, though it is often mistakenly thought to be a stimulant because some people become talkative, boisterous and excitable after they have been drinking. This is not the result of any stimulant effect, however, but is really the result of alcohol releasing the inhibitions which normally restrain such behaviour, and it is better described as 'disinhibition'.

The depressant effects of alcohol are most clearly found in the central nervous system. The conscious experience of these effects is rewarding to most people, and they are one of the main reasons why people use alcohol as a drug. Unfortunately, there are also less desirable effects and the drinker must try to achieve a balance in their intake of alcohol between drinking enough to maximize the pleasurable effects and avoiding the unpleasant consequences of drinking too much.

In the normal drinker, a small amount of alcohol usually produces a general relaxation and relief of stress. These effects are experienced after drinking quite small amounts. At higher doses the depressant effects on the brain are more marked and the drinker often begins to show obvious signs of disinhibition at this point. They may become euphoric or tearful; they may become aggressive and 'fighting drunk', or over-friendly or amorous. The precise expression of alcohol intoxication will vary widely because it is largely determined by the individual's personality and by social and cultural expectations about the effects of drink. This is true of alcohol as it is of every other psychoactive drug. The effects that anyone experiences after taking it depend at least as much upon psychological and social factors as on any biochemical processes.

Alcohol removes the learned restraints. (Probably the nearest that the psychoanalysts have ever been to cracking a joke was to suggest that the superego – the part of the mind that operates as our conscience – is soluble in alcohol.) But other social, psychological and cultural factors determine how the drinker will then behave. If they continue to drink more alcohol, they will become increasingly clumsy and have difficulty in speaking clearly. Their emotional states will become even more variable, until they become confused, and unable to walk or balance properly. Finally, they will pass out and fall into an alcoholic stupor; if they have taken an extremely high dose, they will die.

Two of the things that are most obviously related to how intoxicated we will become are the strength of the drinks that we have taken and the body's capacity to absorb the alcohol contained in them.

There are several different systems used to grade the potency of alcoholic drinks. The most straightforward indicates the percentage of alcohol by volume (usually abbreviated to per cent v/v). Another system which is widely used, but not very easy to understand, is the 'proof' system. This owes its origin to a practice of some centuries ago. If gunpowder would ignite after being soaked with a particular alcoholic drink, this was 'proof' that the drink contained more than half alcohol. The American proof system can be translated easily into per cent v/v, with every two degrees of proof (American) being equal to 1 per cent v/v. The UK system is more tricky, with 57.15 per cent v/v as the equivalent of 100 degrees proof. With three such different systems, the possibilities of confusion are considerable. All references to alcoholic content in this book are made in percentage by volume.

Alcoholic drinks have a fairly rapid effect, and up to a maximum strength of 40 per cent v/v, the higher the concentration of alcohol, the more quickly it is absorbed into the body. Very strong drinks are absorbed relatively slowly because the high concentration of alcohol slows down the physical processing of the solution through the stomach and the intestines. Absorption is also affected by the other ingredients of a drink. In sweet drinks, the sugars slow down the rate, but the carbon dioxide and bicarbonate of sparkling wines or of a whisky and soda speed up the absorption rate. Food also slows down the absorption of alcohol. Milk is especially effective in this respect, as are carbohydrates such as bread and potatoes; the carbohydrates that are present in beer also interfere with the absorption of the alcohol content.

The rate at which the alcohol is absorbed has a direct influence on the intoxicating effects of the drink. The body can metabolize alcohol at a rate equivalent to about three-quarters of an ounce to an ounce of whisky every hour. Provided that it were taken gradually and in small amounts, it should be possible to drink as much as 20 ounces of whisky (almost a whole bottle) over a 24-hour period without feeling any effect from the alcohol or, indeed, even showing any sign of alcohol in the body if physiological tests were used. The body would have metabolized the alcohol as fast as it was drunk. Should anyone be so unwise as to drink the same amount of whisky over a much shorter period of time – say one or two hours – they would be considerably indisposed by it.

The rate at which alcohol is absorbed in the body, therefore, depends on several factors, including the total amount of alcohol, the alcoholic strength of the drink itself, the time taken to drink the total amount, the presence or absence of food, and whether the food was eaten before, after, or at the same time as the drink. The absorption of alcohol is also affected by the sex of the drinker. Women show higher blood-alcohol levels than men after drinking equivalent amounts of alcohol; they absorb the alcohol faster and reach a peak level of intoxication sooner. In tests of their memory and speed of reactions women also perform worse than men after drinking. Because female hormones affect the metabolism of certain drugs, their response to alcohol is altered by their menstrual cycle and women who use oral contraceptives tend to remain intoxicated for longer than those not taking the pill.

About 90 per cent of the absorbed alcohol is metabolized by the body, and the rest is excreted in the breath, the urine and the sweat. The alcohol is metabolized by the liver, first into acetaldehyde (AcH) which in turn is broken down into acetate, carbon dioxide and water. Some drugs used in the treatment of alcoholism prevent the completion of this process so that the AcH cannot be converted and the accumulation of this substance in the blood makes the person feel sick. This experience is so unpleasant that the drinker generally has little wish to repeat it, and the drug is used to help them avoid further drinking.

Drink and Occupation

There is a rich folklore which associates certain occupations with heavy drinking and with various alcohol problems. Sailors, for instance, are notorious for their heavy drinking. It does not require any great effort of imagination to see why this should be the case. The sailor spends long periods of time in an isolated, exclusively male, work-centred environment with little opportunity to spend his wages. These work periods alternate with the free time that is spent in a port, and the contrast between work and leisure conditions encourages the sort of celebration traditionally associated with sailors. In the armed forces, drink is quite freely available and is usually subsidized, which makes it easier to develop the habit of drinking regularly and in large amounts.

For others, alcoholic drinks are even more immediately available. Barmen, waiters and publicans are constantly exposed both to alcoholic drinks and to an environment which is calculated to promote drinking. As a result, the incidence both of alcohol-related diseases such as cirrhosis of the liver, and of alcoholism, is higher among these groups.

Other groups who are known to be at risk in this way are journalists and businessmen who regularly entertain customers or colleagues to expense account meals. An additional complication for such people as journalists is the stress inherent in their work. They often have to work through periods of comparative inertia when drink provides a pleasant means of passing the time; at other times they are required to work under conditions of intense physical and intellectual stress. In these conditions, alcohol can serve as a tranquillizer. Coupled with all of this, they usually have to cope with the more chronic strain of having to work to a deadline. One consequence of these conditions is the comparatively high rate of alcoholism in the profession.

Of course journalists have no monopoly on occupational stress. The practice of medicine puts many different sorts of stress on the doctor and, as a profession, physicians are not noted for their aversion to alcohol. This can certainly be seen in those cradles of medicine, the medical schools. Unfortunately, doctors are not trained to understand the non-medical uses of drugs, and their understanding of the problems that can be associated with alcohol is often equally poor. Little wonder, then, that many doctors who start to drink too much do not properly understand what they are doing. Doctors are affected by the same problems and illnesses as their patients, though often at different rates. Drinking problems are generally more common among doctors than among the general population. It has, only half jokingly, been suggested that an alcoholic is someone who drinks more than their doctor.

Problem drinkers are not just the alcoholic down-and-outs who stumble around our cities. Drinking problems usually develop slowly and insidiously. It is easy gradually to increase the frequency and amount of alcohol consumption. It is easy to pour a larger measure into the whisky glass. The majority of people with a drink problem continue to work. Often their colleagues are aware of their drinking, but for various reasons they turn a blind eye to it. Sometimes, inappropriate beliefs about what an alcoholic is 'really' like (that is, the skid row alcoholic) prevents them from realizing that alcoholism can take many forms, some of them apparently quite ordinary. The standard of work that the person is capable of producing often suffers; occasionally, a crisis develops and it becomes impossible to carry on as if the problem did not exist. Sadly, this often leads to mutual misunderstanding, rejection and recrimination which could probably have been avoided by a more open recognition of the problem at an earlier stage. However, it is easier to suggest this than actually to do it. There is an understandable tendency for any group to avoid making any unnecessary trouble for itself – such as by identifying one of its members as a problem drinker. In any case, there are no definite criteria which can be used to decide when a particular level of drinking becomes 'problem drinking'.

Drink and Driving

Most people in the US, the UK and Europe drive a car. Most of them drink alcohol. At some time or other, most of them do both. In 1904, the *Quarterly Journal of Inebriety* carried an editorial condemning the use of alcohol by drivers of automobile wagons: 'The general policy and diminished power of control of both the reason and senses are certain to invite disaster in every attempt to guide such wagons.' Since that time, the internal combustion engine has transformed our lives. None of us can escape the ubiquitous motor car and, because of this, the question of drink and driving has become more and more important to each one of us.

The costs of drunken driving are enormous both in personal and in economic terms. In the US, roughly half of all road traffic deaths involve heavy use of alcohol on the part of the drivers or pedestrians involved, and during the late 1960s more people were killed on the roads of America by alcohol than were killed in the Vietnam War. Road traffic deaths on American roads since the 1980s have averaged at about 40,000–45,000 every year. The Blennerhassett Committee report on drunken driving to the UK government estimated the annual costs of road traffic accidents due to drinking at about £1,100 million.

The first scientific investigations of how alcohol affected driving ability were conducted in America during the 1930s. Measures of blood-alcohol concentration showed that drivers who were involved in fatal crashes often had high levels of alcohol in their systems. About half of the drivers who were involved in fatal crashes had been drinking large amounts of alcohol. Of the other drivers who were stopped at the same times and places as the accident, only a few (between 1 and 4 per cent) had drunk enough alcohol to give them blood alcohol levels above 10mg per 100ml (10mg per cent).

The same sort of result has been obtained in more recent research studies. In the UK, about one-third of the drivers killed in fatal accidents in 1976 had blood-alcohol levels above the legal limit; on Saturday nights, the proportion of fatal accidents involving drivers with blood-alcohol levels above the legal limit rose to an appalling 71 per cent. During 1976, 63,000 people were convicted of drunken driving offences. The highest risk group for drink driving is young men (aged 20–24); the highest risk times for drink driving fatalities are after 10pm; and the highest risk days are Fridays and Saturdays.

At a blood alcohol level of 80mg per 100ml (or 80mg per cent, the legal limit in the UK), the risk of having an accident increases rapidly. This limit was set in 1967, and at this level, the risk of an accident is about twice as high as for the sober driver. At 150mg per cent the risk has increased to 10 times the normal level, and by 200mg per cent it is 20 times as high as for the non-drinking driver. After larger amounts of alcohol, the driver cannot counteract the effects of drink merely by making a special effort. Worse still, once the driver begins to feel the intoxicating effects of alcohol, they are inclined to become over-confident and to take unnecessary risks, and drink probably leads to as many accidents because of errors of judgement as because of its physically debilitating effects.

The decision to set the legal limit at 80mg per cent is somewhat arbitrary. It is also higher than in almost all other European countries. In Sweden it is 20mg per cent. And even in the wine producing countries of France, Italy, Spain and Germany, the limit is 50mg per cent. Only Cyprus has a higher limit (90mg per cent). There is considerable evidence that driving is impaired at levels below the UK legal limit. The Department of Transport has estimated that around 80 deaths a year can be attributed to drivers with blood-alcohol levels just below the limit (between 50 and 80mg per cent). Before its election, and again in 1998, the Blair government announced that it intended to reduce the legal limit (to 50mg per cent) to be more consistent with other European countries. By 2000, and probably due to its susceptibility to pressure from the alcohol industry, the government changed its mind.

Any road traffic accident is the result of a whole series of events, all of which combine to produce the final crash. It is a mistake to look for a single cause in such a complicated situation. The driver's personality, their level of driving skill when sober, and the road traffic conditions at the time all play a vital part. But having taken account of these factors, there can be little doubt that alcohol in large, or even in fairly moderate, amounts increases the chances of the driver being involved in an accident. In the sort of 'near misses' that happen so often during ordinary driving, the alcohol may make just enough difference to the driver's reaction times, to their skill, or to their judgement, to produce a serious accident.

In 1967, UK drivers were introduced to the use of the breathalyser as a result of the Road Safety Act. This was preceded by an intensive publicity campaign, and the introduction of the breathalyser had an immediate and dramatic effect. Road casualties fell by 11 per cent, and deaths on the road by 15 per cent. Within a few years, however, its deterrent effect had disappeared. This was probably due, as much as anything, to the realization by drivers that their chances of being caught were comparatively low. In order to counteract the rising figures of drunken driving, the government looked again at the possibility of random breath tests. In 1968, a poll conducted by the Automobile Association on the acceptability of random breathalyser tests showed that only 25 per cent were in favour, whereas 68 per cent were against random tests. By 1975, another poll showed that opinion had moved in the opposite direction: 48 per cent were in favour of random tests, and 37 per cent were opposed to them. It is not clear why such a marked change in public attitudes should have occurred during this period.

In most EU countries the police can carry out random breath testing, though the current laws do not permit random testing in the UK. A police officer can require a breath test only if they have reasonable cause to suspect that the driver has been drinking, has committed a traffic offence, or has been involved in an accident. However, since a police officer can stop a vehicle at random and then ask for a breath test if they suspect the driver of drinking, this produces a similar end result in practice.

Increased awareness of the dangers of drinking and driving, increased social disapproval of the practice, the introduction of low-alcohol drinks, the use of breathalysers, and the use of high-visibility publicity campaigns about breath testing all appear to have contributed towards a decrease in the numbers of people who drink and drive. In 1979, more than half (51 per cent) of UK drivers were willing to admit to drinking and driving during the previous week. By 1997, this had dropped to less than a quarter (23 per cent). In Australia, the percentage of traffic deaths due to alcohol fell from 50 per cent in 1978 to 40 per cent in 1985 and to 31 per cent in 1988. In the UK, there has also been a substantial decline in drink driving and in the number of alcohol-related deaths since the early 1980s. However, the number of casualties has been rising again since 2000 and, as always, about half of the casualties are people other than the alcohol-using driver.

The Hangover

One of the most common and more immediate forms of retribution that is experienced as the result of heavy drinking is the hangover.

> Who hath woe? who hath sorrow? who hath contentions? who hath babbling? who hath wounds without a cause? who hath redness of eyes? They that tarry long at the wine; they that go to seek mixed wine … At the last it biteth like a serpent and stingeth like an adder (Proverbs 23:29–30, 32).

As well as woe, sorrow and so forth, this unpleasant state is characterized by headache, dizziness, fatigue, nausea and digestive disturbances, and it is almost always the consequence of too much alcohol. Among the few real exceptions to this are people whose state of physical health does not permit alcoholic drinks, even in moderation. People with liver disorders, for instance, may suffer from headaches and indigestion after only a few drinks and the effects of alcohol on stomach ulcers can be extremely painful. It is doubtful, however, whether these adverse effects of alcohol should really be considered in the same category as the hangover which follows excessive drinking.

Alcoholic drinks consist mainly of ethyl alcohol and water, but they also contain small amounts of other substances called congeners. These congeners include other forms of alcohol, ethyl acetate, various sugars, salt, acids, minerals and B-group vitamins, and the concentration of these components varies in different drinks. Although most people are unaware of their existence, the congeners are important to the drinker because they give the characteristic flavour and colouring to the different drinks. They also contribute towards the hangover. When the higher alcohols have been distilled off from brandy, people who were given this congener concentrate to drink developed headaches and drowsiness which persisted for up to 18 hours. No such symptoms were recorded in another group who drank a solution containing a comparable amount of ethanol.

The congener content of various drinks seems to affect not only the likelihood of waking up with a hangover after a given amount of alcohol, but also the severity of the hangover symptoms themselves. This has usually been tested experimentally, having volunteer subjects drink either a high-congener or a low-congener drink. Vodka and bourbon are the two drinks that have generally been used in experiments because they are so different in their congener content. Vodka, for instance, is very nearly a neutral spirit and may contain as little as 33 grams per 100 litres. Bourbon, on the other hand, contains a massive 286 grams. At a given dose of ethanol both drinks can produce hangovers, but people who have drunk too much bourbon are likely to feel much worse than the vodka drinkers.

One of the congeners which has been associated with such hangover symptoms as headaches, sweating and feeling of sickness is acetaldehyde (AcH). Interestingly, AcH occurs in higher quantities in white than in red wines, which is contrary to certain folklore about red wines causing worse after-effects. On the other hand, calvados, which has the reputation of being a particularly fierce form of brandy, contains extremely high levels of certain congeners (notably the esters).

One of the reasons that people regularly give for drinking beers and lagers – and one that features in several advertisements – is to quench a raging thirst. Paradoxically, alcohol has the opposite effect. It produces dehydration, and after excessive drinking this is felt as one of the symptoms of the hangover. It has been suggested that, after drinking too much, it is possible to reduce the severity of the hangover by drinking large amounts of water to counter the after-effects caused by the drying action of the alcohol.

Alcoholism

When a persistent heavy drinker begins to treat their hangover with further alcohol, they are running a serious risk of becoming a dependent drinker. This 'hair of the dog' treatment may lessen the immediate physical and mental distress, but it helps to establish a pernicious habit. As with the person who has learnt to use drugs as a psychological prop to deal with real or imaginary difficulties, this sort of 'morning after' drinking is often a further step to long-term dependent alcohol use. Indeed, morning drinking is often used as an indicator of alcohol dependence. The estimation of the number of alcoholics (or drug addicts) is notoriously unreliable, not least because of the difficulties of defining precisely who is and who is not 'addicted'. Some of the more carefully crafted estimates of the prevalence of alcohol problems in the US have suggested that about 7 per cent of the adult population (almost 14 million people) meet the diagnostic criteria for alcohol abuse or alcohol dependence (alcoholism).

As with other forms of drug dependence, there is some confusion about what we mean by the term 'alcoholism'. During the past century there has been a shift of perspective. Alcoholism was once regarded primarily as a sin and a vice; it is now more frequently seen as a disease. In fact, this polarization of attitudes towards alcoholism is quite unhelpful. The person who has become dependent on alcohol (or on other drugs for that matter) should not be seen as morally weak or necessarily as being sick. By focusing attention on alcoholism merely as a bad habit, the moral viewpoint underestimates the extent to which alcohol can become a central feature of the alcoholic's life and, because of this, it also underestimates the difficulties inherent in the individual's attempt to stop drinking. The disease conception of alcoholism falls into the opposite error; it encourages a view of alcoholism as a specific illness over which the alcoholic has no control. Alcoholism is not a specific disorder; in almost every case, it is a complex mixture of social, psychological and physical problems. Although several eminent specialists in this field have expressed the belief that it is still more humane to regard the alcoholic as 'sick' rather than as morally weak, the disease concept of alcoholism can be equally misleading since it can encourage both the doctor and the alcoholic patient to ignore the active role that the individual plays in determining their own drinking behaviour.

Alcoholism, like drug addiction, can be more easily understood if it is seen not as something that the user either has or does not have. Dependence upon any sort of drug is something that the user can have in varying amounts. It is more useful to know someone's actual height than merely to know that they are tall or short. Dependence on drugs can also be seen in this way. But unlike height, dependence is changeable. It can increase or decrease and it is influenced by many different circumstances.

It is often more useful to remove any medical mystique from the problem by not using a term such as 'alcoholism' but to talk more simply and more directly of drinking problems. These can vary from drunkenness and the familiar hangover, through problems with social relationships and various psychological difficulties, to full medical disorders such as liver damage. The more of these complications from alcohol use that the individual experiences, the more concerned they ought to be to change their drinking habits. Certain problems are especially significant. Regularly drinking more than was intended, being intoxicated at inappropriate times, the conviction that alcohol is a necessary aid to functioning properly or the feeling that one's drinking is not really under voluntary control – any of these things should be treated as danger signs. The drinker who recognizes their own attitudes and behaviour among these problems would be well advised to consider changing their drinking patterns.

Of course, the notion of 'drinking problems' is itself not without a certain vagueness. In the first place, it does not specify whose problems are involved. If a person is drinking so much that they are damaging their health, and are unable to give up their heavy drinking, there is little difficulty in deciding whose problem is involved. But in many other cases the drinker would be quite happy to go on drinking if only others would let them. Whose problem is it then? Drunkenness, for instance, is just such a public nuisance.

During the 20 years between 1957 and 1977 there was a steady rise in the incidence of drunkenness offences in England and Wales. This was most marked for males (rising from about 370 to 540 per 100,000 of the population). The most marked increase during this period was for young men aged between 18 and 21, which more than doubled, rising from just over 600 per 100,000 to almost 1,500. For various reasons, drunkenness offences among women are far less common than they are among men, but the rise in convictions among women aged 18 to 21 was even more dramatic in this period, increasing from about 35 per 100,000 to almost 100. These trends have continued to the present.

Drunkenness is one of the more visible drinking problems, but it is rather different from the chronic forms of alcohol intoxication. These are not really about getting drunk at all. Someone who is chronically intoxicated on alcohol may not show any of the acute effects that are usually seen in the drunk. The most common features of alcoholism are usually described as: (a) an increased physiological tolerance to alcohol, (b) withdrawal symptoms and craving when alcohol is not available, and (c) inability to drink moderately: most alcoholics have serious difficulty in controlling their drinking after having even a single drink and go on to drink to excess.

The acute withdrawal syndrome that is provoked in alcoholics when they are deprived of their drug has been a known part of the human condition for thousands of years. It is also one of the most severe drug withdrawal states, far more serious, for instance, than that provoked by heroin withdrawal. Symptoms can include insomnia, tremor ('the shakes'), a general state of confusion, and auditory, tactile or visual hallucinations. Withdrawal from alcohol can also provoke seizures in which the unfortunate alcoholic suddenly falls into an epileptic fit with convulsions. These fits almost always occur during the first 48 hours after drinking has stopped.

Delirium tremens (DTs) has been the topic of many jokes over the years (usually featuring pink elephants), but for the person involved they are a terrifying (and dangerous) experience. DTs represent the most severe form of alcohol withdrawal. The onset of DTs is often abrupt and is often at night, and it may be preceded by increasing restlessness and feelings of apprehension, and nightmares. Once the condition is established, it tends to be associated with restlessness and agitation, fear increasing to panic, confusion, disorientation and hallucinations. Delirium tremens usually subsides in 2–3 days but it is a medically serious condition, and sometimes leads to fatalities.

The experience of losing control over one's ability to assess when and how much to drink, and, especially, when to stop drinking, has been the subject of considerable controversy. It appears to fit quite well with the 'disease' model of alcoholism, in so far as it suggests that the individual is powerless to control their own drinking; and it is also consistent with the belief that the only realistic goal for an alcoholic is total abstinence. Many of the people who believe that they have lost control over their drinking try to cope with this by 'going on the wagon' for days, weeks, or even longer between their binges.

It is better and more appropriate to refer to impaired control than to loss of control, since very few drinkers or drug takers completely lose control of their consumption patterns. The true significance of this impairment of control is interesting. The drinker tends to experience this impairment as a craving or compulsion for alcohol. The discomfort of this craving is relieved by drinking and the repeated experience and reinforcement of this pattern – craving and discomfort leading to drink and relief – establishes and confirms the user's own beliefs about impaired control. The user's beliefs about their impaired capacity to control their drinking is a central feature of what we mean by addiction or dependence.

Early beliefs about alcoholism often included the notion that lifelong abstinence was the only realistic goal for recovery. In recent years there has been much debate about whether people with alcohol problems are able to return to normal drinking. One of the first papers to report this was published by Dr D.L. Davies of the Maudsley Hospital and it provoked an outburst of hostile criticism. Since then, other researchers have found that many people who have had drinking problems can learn to control their intake of alcohol and develop normal or at least controlled drinking habits. However, controlled drinking appears to be more appropriate for younger and less severely dependent drinkers. For the most severely dependent drinkers abstinence may still be the best goal, and many people who have been dependent upon alcohol find that their chances of recovery are greater and that it is more satisfactory to get off alcohol and to stick to an abstinent lifestyle than to struggle to maintain a moderate intake of alcohol.

These three features – increased tolerance, craving and withdrawal symptoms when alcohol is not available, and loss of control – seem to be more common in North America and in Anglo-Saxon countries. In France, on the other hand, the predominant pattern of alcoholism reflects the first two features, but instead of feeling that they have lost control of their drinking after the first drink, the French alcoholic drinks steadily but cannot do without their drink. Instead of binges alternating with periods of abstinence, the pattern is one of constant heavy drinking without marked intoxication. A survey carried out in France asked what amount of wine a workman could consume every day 'without inconvenience'. The response was a staggering 1.8 litres (almost 2½ bottles of wine, or 6 ounces of ethanol). A quarter of the people in the survey described wine as 'indispensable' to their lives.

One of the most interesting comparisons to be made between European countries is that between the rates of alcoholism in France and Italy. Although both countries produce and consume large amounts of wine, the incidence of alcoholism in France is five or six times as high as that in Italy. This is not simply related to the prevalence of drinking, because wine is used by a larger proportion of the population in Italy than in France. Sociologists have noted several differences that could have an influence. Among these are the French belief that drinking large amounts of wine is somehow associated with virility; the Italians do not share this belief. The French are also more tolerant of drunkenness, seeing it as amusing or at least as tolerable, whereas the Italians regard it as a personal and family disgrace. There are also differences in national attitudes towards drinking among children. The Italians are inclined to regard the matter unemotionally and as a normal and unexceptional part of the child's social development; French parental attitudes, on the other hand, tend to be more rigid and are usually either strongly in favour or strongly opposed to drink.

National differences are, however, becoming less evident with the increasing globalization of tastes and behaviours. The 'Mediterranean' style of moderate, social drinking is gradually being challenged and replaced by binge drinking and other, less moderate patterns. Until recently, drinking in Spain tended to involve drinking wine or beer in restaurants and bars, and public drunkenness was regarded as a social disgrace. Lately, there has developed a form of drinking among teenagers which involves sitting in public places drinking whisky and coke from plastic bottles. This is known as *el botellon*, the big bottle. The number of 15–19-year-old boys in Spain who regularly get drunk doubled from 22 per cent to 44 per cent between 2002 and 2004. The rate among teenage girls more than doubled from 10 per cent to 24 per cent. Similar trends have also been noted in other Mediterranean countries such as Italy and Portugal. The American affectation of drinking beer straight from the bottle (why?) has become a worldwide style among young drinkers. Like fast food, drinking patterns have also spread from America to the rest of the world.

For many years, the former communist countries of Eastern Europe played down their problems with alcohol. However, alcohol consumption in the Eastern bloc is amongst the highest in the world. Vodka is consumed in large amounts in Northern and Eastern Europe, and various public campaigns have been mounted against the problem of drunkenness. In Poland, the nation's three million hard-core drinkers account for something like half of the total amount of alcohol that is drunk by a population of 34 million. The Baltic port of Szczecin had such a bad reputation as a Polish version of Sodom and Gomorrah that a form of total prohibition was introduced in the area for a time. The results were much the same as in the US between 1920 and 1933. From 1 January 1980 another system designed to restrict the availability of alcohol was tried in Warsaw, with a ban on the sale of drinks containing more than 45 per cent alcohol during weekends, holidays and pay-days. Before it was torn apart by civil war, the former Yugoslavia also introduced restrictive measures by placing a ban on all forms of advertising designed to promote the use of alcohol (and tobacco).

Heavy use of alcohol over a prolonged period of time certainly increases the risk of developing various physical illnesses, but there are no convenient signposts to show at what point someone moves from moderate and acceptable levels of drinking to a pattern of heavy drinking which may cause damage to health. It seems as though this threshold may be a great deal lower than it was once thought to be. Converted to standard units of alcohol, one unit is equivalent (approximately) to half a pint of beer, one glass of wine or a single measure of spirits (or, more precisely, to 8 grams of ethanol). Such guidelines are only approximate since some drinks contain surprisingly large amounts of alcohol. A 500ml can of extra-strength lager contains four and a half units, and drinks poured at home are almost inevitably more generous than acknowledged by these rough guidelines.

The UK Department of Health guidelines for 'sensible drinking' issued in 1995 set the limits for safe drinking at 21 units per week for men and 14 per week for women. If that looks too severe, an even more conservative estimate has been suggested by the American Liver Foundation, with moderate drinking for men defined as an average of 2 drinks or less per day, and for women, an average of 1 drink or less per day. Do not blame me: I did not set these limits and it is not my fault that drinking is bad for your liver.

Regular heavy alcohol use puts the drinker at risk of establishing a pattern of addictive drinking, and of a variety of diseases, including inflammation of the stomach and diseases of the pancreas, as well as damage to the heart, liver and nervous system. For cirrhosis of the liver, if different countries are arranged in order of their consumption of alcohol per person, this also puts them in roughly the same order of their death rate from cirrhosis. France, Portugal and Italy are high on the liver disease table. At the bottom of the table are the UK, Eire and the Netherlands. It is rather surprising to find the UK at the bottom of the table since its per capita consumption is comparatively high – higher, for instance, than that of the US which has a higher incidence of cirrhosis. In New York State, cirrhosis is the third most frequent cause of death for adults in their productive years; in California it is the fourth most frequent cause. In Ontario, Canada, it is the most rapidly increasing cause of death among people over the age of 25.

For the average drinker, of course, this catalogue of alcoholic disasters seems remote, and they find it difficult to reconcile their own enjoyment of wine or beer with the havoc that alcohol can wreak. Nonetheless, it is the same drug, alcohol, that is involved. But it is a mistake to focus only upon the substance. It is not just the alcohol that causes drunkenness and alcoholism; it is the thoughtless or unintelligent ways in which the individual uses alcohol and the insidious development of the drinking habit that are responsible.

Chapter 6

Tobacco

In 1604, King James I published his *Counterblaste to Tobacco*, one of the first and most strident condemnations of 'This Filthy Custom':

> 'A custom loathsome to the eye, hateful to the nose, harmful to the brain, dangerous to the lungs, and in the black stinking fumes thereof nearest resembling the horrible Stygian smoke of the pit that is bottomless.'

Like one of his successors, King James was very clearly not amused. Tobacco can be taken as snuff or it can be chewed; it can be smoked in pipes, as cigars or as cigarettes. Each of these forms has been popular at one time or another, but during the 20th century one increasingly established its supremacy over the others: cigarette smoking. For the Western world, the discovery of tobacco can be directly traced to Christopher Columbus' voyage to the New World in 1492. Columbus himself was far too preoccupied by his lust for gold to take much notice of the curious customs of the natives, and it was not until later voyages that the smoking of tobacco was given any real consideration. At first, the Spanish sailors found it an unpleasant experience, but they soon became enthusiastic smokers themselves.

The dubious honour of being the first man to smoke tobacco in Europe belongs to Rodrigo de Jerez, a companion of Christopher Columbus. On his return to Spain, he so alarmed his countrymen by breathing smoke that they concluded the Devil had entered him, and hurried off to the priest who in turn referred the matter to the Holy Inquisition. As a result, de Jerez spent some years in prison. When he was let out, he may have been considerably piqued to find that smoking had established itself as a popular pastime.

The current preoccupation with the adverse effects of smoking is not new. In 1526, Oviedo the Spanish historian described it as 'a bad and pernicious custom' and King James' *Counterblaste* is hardly a recommendation of the habit. James I combined his distaste for tobacco with his financial acumen and imposed a tax on it. Others adopted more drastic measures. In Russia, Turkey, Persia and parts of Germany smoking was punished by death. In Transylvania the smoker was dealt with more leniently: all their money and possessions were confiscated by the state. Torture and mutilation have also been used to persuade smokers not to harm themselves by smoking. Since its discovery many physicians have been convinced that smoking was harmful, though the nature of the supposed damage has changed. It was once thought to 'blacken the brain'. Indeed, this was said to have been demonstrated beyond all doubt by autopsies carried out on the bodies of smokers.

The tobacco trade has always been a lucrative enterprise and during the 20th century vast industrial and political influence came to be linked with this drug. About 16 million people in China are employed in tobacco cultivation. Even in Europe, a continent not normally associated with the cultivation of tobacco, the total production (for 1990) was a massive 419,000 metric tons. In Greece and Italy, 35 per cent and 17 per cent, respectively, of all the people working in agriculture are involved in growing tobacco. Tobacco is particularly important in China, Zimbabwe, Malawi and Greece, where it accounts for between 10 per cent and 25 per cent of the total national agricultural income.

There are many reasons for the economic importance of tobacco. One is that it is an extremely profitable crop. The gross returns per hectare on tobacco in Zimbabwe are about twice those of coffee, the next most profitable crop, and about 10 times greater than those of food crops.

If you pop into your local tobacconist's shop, you will be confronted by an impressive array of brightly packaged cigarettes, cigars and tobaccos. Everything seems to point to an enormous variety of choice for the consumer. The facts of the matter are rather different. Seven large multinational tobacco corporations control almost all aspects of cigarette production in the Western world. Their control extends from growing the leaf to selling the packets of cigarettes. Between 85 and 90 per cent of the leaf tobacco in international trade is already directly or indirectly controlled by only six multinationals. The efforts of these companies to control the consumption of cigarettes are mainly concentrated in advertising. In their attempt to conceal the full extent of their advertising costs, the multinational tobacco companies have all acted in unison to keep details of this expenditure from an investigation by the Federal Trades Commission. One estimate is that, each year, these firms spend about 18 billion dollars on advertising.

It is difficult to see how the public could benefit from this massive expenditure. Rather than providing information, cigarette advertising mainly produces confusion and vagueness. The advertisements themselves are little more than emotionally loaded image-boosters, and one could be forgiven for believing that the main effect of such advertising is to debase and corrupt society's understanding of this form of drug taking. However, it is notable that advertising is often deliberately aimed. A 1995 advert for Embassy cigarettes suggested, 'Hold your friend's cigarette while *she* powders *her* nose' (italics added).

One of the purposes of such advertisements seems to be to protect the market position of the established multinational tobacco companies by erecting massive barriers to the entry of any rival. But apart from excluding potential rivals, advertising seems to be concerned with exploiting already existing tastes and directing them towards specific brands. One of the classic studies of the effects of advertising suggested that

... if underlying conditions are favourable to an increase in demand for a product ... the use of advertising tends to enhance and accelerate the rising trend of demand. In the case of declining trend in demand ... advertising is powerless to halt or reverse the trend. It can do no more than temporarily delay it.

It is very difficult to carry out controlled research studies to determine what are the effects of advertising. It seems likely that these effects will vary according to the types of substance being advertised, existing levels of demand, personal attitudes and predispositions, and social attitudes towards the use of that particular product. Recent studies of advertising and cigarette smoking suggest that advertising bans can reduce consumption, though their effect is not especially strong and changes in other factors (such as price and income) can have a more powerful influence.

After Canada's Tobacco Products Control Act banned tobacco advertising in 1988, sales fell by 15 per cent in the next two years. In New Zealand, the Smoke-free Environments Act banned advertising in 1990 and sales fell by 8 per cent. The ban in Finland in 1978 produced a drop in consumption of 7 per cent and advertising bans in the Nordic countries have held consumption on a downward path despite rising income levels and a fall in the inflation-adjusted price of cigarettes.

UK governments (both Conservative and Labour) have resisted pressure from the anti-smoking lobbies to introduce smoking restrictions and advertising bans. This failure to act is almost certainly due to a fair and impartial appraisal of the evidence and to a real concern about the health of the nation; it would be absurd to suggest that it might be due lobbying from the tobacco industry or to economic self-interest. For example, the reluctance to act among the previous Conservative government can surely have nothing to do with the fact that during the closely fought election of 1992 the tobacco industry provided 2,000 poster sites to be used for the support of the Conservative Party.

The multinational tobacco companies are also said to have more questionable techniques of protecting their profits. A United Nations report has described how another component of the marketing of tobacco involves 'global corporate bribery'. The same report suggests that pay-offs (some involving millions of dollars) have been issued to politicians and political parties both in the US and elsewhere in the world by several of the largest multinational tobacco companies.

There is a common feeling that drug taking can be controlled by taxation. This idea seems appealing, but like other systems of drug control that attempt to impose themselves upon the consumer, it may raise as many problems as it solves. Since 1960, tobacco taxes have steadily increased. In 1975, the total tax revenue from tobacco in the US was almost twice that from alcohol. The UK government earned £8,093 million in revenue from tobacco duty in 2004. As a result, the tobacco lobby can apply immense political pressure for its own ends.

For developing countries with limited opportunities for raising tax revenues, tobacco taxes can be extremely important. In Haiti, for instance, the amount of money raised through tobacco taxes in 1983 represented 41 per cent of all central government tax revenue. Even in developed countries the proportion of taxes raised in this way can be very considerable. In the UK it is about 6 per cent.

One of the other interesting developments that has followed the rise in tobacco taxation is the development of the black market. About a third of all cigarettes on international sale (355 billion per year) come from the black market. In Italy, bootleg cigarettes make up 35 to 40 per cent of all sales. In 2004, 71 billion cigarettes were consumed in the UK. Of these, 10.5 billion were smuggled, accounting for about 15 per cent of the total cigarette market. This reduces the price, increases demand, and undermines national tobacco tax policies.

In the US, the tax on a packet of cigarettes varies from state to state. The combined state and city taxes in New York City make it the most expensive place in the country to buy cigarettes. North Carolina, on the other hand, is one of the cheapest places. A single truckload of cigarettes bought in North Carolina and brought to New York could easily produce a profit of more than $60,000. As a result of this bootleg trade in cigarettes, more than half of the traditional wholesalers have been put out of business during the past decade, and criminal conspiracy charges have been brought against nine members of the Wholesale Tobacco Distributors in New York. All five of New York's Mafia families are said to have moved into cigarette marketing operations. Their annual profits may be as much as $100 million. It is thought that the Mafia involvement in this lucrative trade will continue to increase.

A less dramatic form of tax avoidance is currently taking place in the UK, where the taxes on cigarettes are higher than for the mainland European countries. At least one entrepreneurial company has now started to send cigarettes by post from Luxembourg to UK smokers, thereby evading excise duty. Not surprisingly, the UK government, which receives so much money from tobacco, takes a dim view of this, and has declared such activities to be illegal. In March 1999, the UK government faced an annual shortfall of more than £1 billion in tax revenue. About one in every eight cigarettes smoked in the UK was estimated to have been smuggled into the country and organized crime syndicates were said to be becoming increasingly involved. A similar differential between Canada (with its high tariffs) and the US caused so much smuggling and cross-border shopping that several Canadian provinces were forced to lower their rates of tax.

Americans smoke 620 billion cigarettes every year, one-sixth of the entire world output. In 1978, they paid some 158 billion dollars for this doubtful privilege. The trend in the UK, the US and in the industrialized countries, however, is towards a gradual reduction in the consumption of cigarettes. In the UK, the percentage of men smoking manufactured cigarettes fell from 65 per cent in 1978 to 35 per cent in 1985, and by 1992 it had fallen to about 28 per cent, with approximately equal numbers of men and women smoking. At the time of writing this edition, about 12 million adults in the UK smoke cigarettes, 28 per cent of men and 24 per cent of women. The exceptions to this generally falling trend are interesting. The decline in smoking has occurred mostly among older age groups. Almost as many young people are taking up smoking but more established smokers are quitting. More than 80 per cent of smokers take up the habit as teenagers, and smoking rates are highest among young adults. Among 20–24 year olds, 38 per cent of men and 34 per cent of women are smokers. Among people aged 60 and over, only 15 per cent are smokers. This is due to many former smokers giving up smoking in middle age (and also to about a quarter of the smokers having already died before reaching this age).

The overall decline in smoking prevalence has not been evident among adolescents, and higher rates of cigarette smoking have become particularly marked among girls. Among the UK's schoolchildren, more girls than boys are regular smokers, and about a quarter of 11-year-olds have tried smoking, despite the fact that it is illegal to sell cigarettes to children aged under 16. The decline in smoking has also varied according to social class. In 1958, the percentage of smokers was similar in all social classes. By 1985, the percentage of smokers in social class I (professional and managerial) had declined to 20 per cent but only to 40 per cent in social class V (the lowest socioeconomic group). One of the lowest rates of smoking is in Australia where 24 per cent of the population smoked in 1993, falling to less than 20 per cent in 2001.

In the Third World, there is a rapid increase in consumption; this is a great potential market for the tobacco companies. Now that there is an increasing awareness of the potential hazards of smoking, the advertising and marketing practices of the tobacco companies have come under special scrutiny in the West. In the Third World, where there is less awareness of the risks and fewer regulations, the opportunities are much greater, and it seems unlikely that there will be any alteration in the present increase in smoking in these countries.

One current multinational absurdity is the contribution of the European Union to the subsidy for the tobacco-growing industry, which is based mainly in Italy and Greece. Almost every one of the countries which belong to the EU has a policy of reducing tobacco consumption within its own borders. Despite this, tobacco is the most heavily subsidized EU crop, and the EU spends almost €1 billion a year subsidizing tobacco farming.

What is Tobacco Smoke?

A burning cigarette is a miniature chemical factory. From the 15 or so major constituents of tobacco, some 4,720 separate compounds have been identified in the smoke. These vary with the type of tobacco plant from which the leaf was gathered and the way in which it was cured. Among its many appetizing ingredients, tobacco smoke also contains hydrogen cyanide, carbon monoxide, ammonia and formaldehyde. Some of these ingredients are put there deliberately. The addition of an alkali such as ammonia increases the availability of free nicotine and therefore increases the nicotine 'hit'.

The components of tobacco smoke that are of most medical interest are nicotine, carbon monoxide and tobacco tar. But the mixture that eventually reaches the smoker's body depends upon more than just the chemistry of tobacco. It depends upon the way in which the smoker smokes it. The more vigorously they puff on the tobacco, the higher the temperature at which it burns: this affects the chemical products of combustion. The smoker who keeps a cigarette between their lips when smoking will inhale more of the 'sidestream' smoke than someone who holds the cigarette away from their mouth: sidestream smoke that curls away from the end of a burning cigarette is more concentrated than the mainstream smoke inhaled through the cigarette itself. Cigarette smoke also becomes more concentrated as the cigarette burns down.

The ingredients of tobacco smoke can act in the mouth, in the air passages or in the lungs. Cigarette smoke is acidic and the nicotine in cigarette smoke can be best absorbed through the lungs. The smoke from cigars and pipes is alkaline and can also be absorbed through the membrane lining the mouth. Cigarette smoke is also less irritating to the lungs than cigar and pipe smoke, and because of this it is the most likely to be inhaled.

There has never been any doubt about the remarkable and insidious attractions that tobacco has for some people. In 1527, a Spanish bishop described how the native habit of smoking was taken up by Europeans: 'When reproached for such a disgusting habit, [they] replied that they found it impossible to give it up. I cannot understand what enjoyment or advantage they derive from it.' To the non-smoker, it seems inconceivable that countless millions of people should persistently inhale the smoke of dried leaves. It produces no obvious intoxication, and the initial experience of inhaling cigarette smoke is almost always unpleasant. Many people are actually sick the first time they smoke. Despite this, it is amazing to find that for every 100 teenagers who smoke more than a single cigarette, 85 will continue to smoke and only 15 will not. Cigarette smoking is one of the most addictive of all drug habits. It appears to be more likely to produce dependence than using either tranquillizers or alcohol: the nearest drug habit, in terms of the risk of becoming dependent, is injecting heroin. Its high addictive potential is further increased by the fact that, unlike many other types of drug taking, smoking is believed by smokers to improve their performance in normal social and work settings. Nonetheless, neither cigarette smoking nor any other habit is so addictive that there is no escape. In the US there may be as many as 43 million ex-smokers, the vast majority of whom gave up without any form of treatment.

Nicotine is a powerful drug with a variety of effects, many of which are unpredictable. Generally speaking, it is a stimulant drug and it has some amphetamine-like properties. Among its other effects, it stimulates the secretion of adrenaline and noradrenaline, which produces an increase in heart rate and blood pressure. Yet when smokers are asked why they smoke they usually say something like, 'It relaxes me', or 'It helps to calm me down.' In other words, they are suggesting that smoking has primarily tranquillizing or sedating effects. In large doses nicotine can produce vomiting, tremor and convulsions. Nicotine is also one of the most powerful poisons and is used in a number of agricultural pesticides. The fatal dose for a man may be as low as 60 milligrams, though it seems to be less dangerous when swallowed in the form of tobacco. A strong cigarette may contain 20 milligrams of nicotine, though only a small amount of this reaches the brain when it is smoked (perhaps 2 milligrams). Death from nicotine poisoning, as with cyanide poisoning, occurs within minutes (both cyanide and ammonia are also present in tobacco smoke, though, mercifully, only in very small quantities).

Nicotine reaches the brain within a few seconds of each puff and the average smoker may deliver something like 70,000 separate doses of the drug to their brain every year. Several experiments have shown that, when smokers are given cigarettes containing very little nicotine, they tend to smoke more, and when they are given cigarettes with very high nicotine levels they smoke less. All of this might be thought to point directly to nicotine as the crucial addictive agent in smoking. However, the effect that nicotine has had on smoking in these experiments has often been extremely crude and variable. In one study, the strong cigarettes contained more than four times as much nicotine as the weak ones, yet the smokers who were given the low-nicotine cigarettes smoked only about a quarter as many more than the high-nicotine group. There are other problems involved in this sort of experiment. It is difficult to vary the nicotine content of cigarettes without altering other constituents. Nicotine and tar are closely related, and since tar is largely responsible for the flavour of the cigarette this could produce a bias in the results which was not directly related to nicotine at all. Some studies have even used cigarettes made of dried lettuce leaves with nicotine added to them. These tasted so unpleasant that the subjects in the experiment probably smoked fewer of them because of their vile flavour rather than because of their drug content. Another way of investigating the role played by nicotine involves giving measured doses of nicotine to smokers and then seeing how this affects their smoking.

An important early experiment on the effect of nicotine upon smoking was carried out at the Institute of Psychiatry in London. A group of volunteer smokers was divided into three groups who received different doses of nicotine: one group received a high dose, the second a low dose, and the third only a nicotine-free placebo. In the first part of the study, the three groups were asked to inhale from cigarettes containing different amounts of nicotine (or no nicotine at all). In the second part of the study a few weeks later, instead of receiving their nicotine by smoking, they were given the different doses of drug directly by injection. The experimenters took various physiological measures to check that the drug had an active effect. Throughout both parts of the study, all the subjects were allowed to smoke whenever they wanted to. The results clearly show that inhaled doses of smoke postponed and reduced further smoking and that this was related to the content of the smoke. When the results of the second part of the experiment were analysed, they showed, contrary to all expectations, that the intravenous doses of nicotine had no effect on the person's subsequent smoking. This result indicates that smoking cannot be explained simply in terms of the smoker's need for nicotine. Nonetheless, nicotine clearly has a powerful effect upon smoking and the effects of nicotine on the brain act as major reinforcers for smoking. This has implications for people who are trying to give up smoking, and nicotine replacement methods have been developed to support such efforts. The best known method involves replacement therapies, usually with nicotine patches or nicotine chewing gum (but also with nasal sprays, inhalers, tablets and lozenges). The rationale for these treatments is that, since the smoking habit involves physiological dependence on nicotine, alternative methods of delivering nicotine which do not involve tobacco and which reduce the health risks should be useful.

Nicotine replacement therapy is now being used in at least 35 countries and clinical trials have been carried out in 20 countries. It has been estimated that about 3 million Americans used the nicotine patch to try to give up smoking in the first seven months after it was approved for use in the US. Nicotine gum is often administered for between one and three months and the number of pieces chewed per day varies between five and 10 (each containing between 2 milligrams and 4 milligrams of nicotine). The result of these trials has led to considerable enthusiasm. A prescription for nicotine gum combined with a brief explanation of why and how it should be used appears to double quitting rates among patients approaching their family doctors for help. Nicotine patches deliver the nicotine into the bloodstream through the skin and provide an effective substitute for smoking which can reduce nicotine withdrawal symptoms and help smokers trying to quit.

An overview of the effectiveness of nicotine replacement treatments suggested that smokers who use these may be twice as likely to give up successfully as those given a placebo treatment. When nicotine chewing gum has been used in smoking clinics it has increased the proportion of people who successfully quit smoking from 13 per cent who received a placebo to 23 per cent. However, nicotine gum appeared to have little or no impact on success rates when used in a general practice or other medical setting. Nicotine patches may have certain advantages over nicotine gum, not the least of which is that patches are easier to use with minimal explanation. The evidence for the effectiveness of patches is more convincing and in at least eight controlled research studies nicotine patches doubled the numbers of smokers who were able to stop smoking and remain abstinent. An even more recent nicotine replacement therapy involves nicotine nasal spray in an aerosol form.

However, nicotine is only one of the factors which makes cigarette smoking such a difficult habit to break. This is partly reflected by the relatively low success rates of nicotine replacement therapies. There are other aspects of smoking that also provide powerful rewards for the smoker. For instance, the smoker's craving for cigarettes can be satisfied by the irritation that smoke causes to the throat and upper respiratory tract as well as by the direct pharmacological effect of pure nicotine. Taste, smell, sociability and the manual manipulation of the cigarette all appear to play an important role. The psychological effects and social significance that the habit has for the smoker are among the most important but least well understood aspects of smoking.

Smoking and Illness

The idea that smoking is a direct cause of various diseases is not new. In one form or another it has been with us for centuries. King James asserted that smoking caused damage to the lungs and to the brain, and physicians claimed to have demonstrated how it 'blackened the brain'. The US anti-cigarette lobby that demanded prohibition was convinced that smoking was a certain cause of moral degradation. Smoking is clearly as much a moral and political issue as a scientific and medical one and, as in so many other cases where the two have become entangled, rational argument is often the first victim. The great smoking debate is characterized, as it always has been, by dogmatism, impatience and self-righteousness as much as by impartial investigation of the issues. The facts themselves, however, are quite clear. Smokers are at much greater risk of contracting lung cancer. They run a much greater risk of developing chronic bronchitis and emphysema. Smokers are more than 10 times more likely to develop circulatory disease which leads to the amputation of one or both legs. Smokers are twice as likely to die of coronary heart disease as non-smokers. No one disputes these observations; there has, however, been some argument about how to explain them.

One of the weaknesses of the evidence linking smoking with lung cancer and with heart disease is that it is generally based on correlational statistics – these simply show that the two often go together. They do not show how they are caused. As an example, correlational statistics show that people who take tranquillizers are more anxious than people who do not. This does not prove that tranquillizers cause anxiety. The same is true of smoking and illnesses; both may be due to other factors. The same sort of statistics show that smoking is positively correlated with suicide: this does not prove that smoking causes suicide. Smoking is negatively correlated with Parkinson's disease and diabetes: this does not show that smoking prevents these diseases.

Nonetheless, correlational studies can help to draw attention to possible causal links even if they do not confirm them, and there is little doubt that the weight and consistency of evidence demonstrating the widespread and seriously damaging effects of smoking is now compelling.

Certainly, there is little doubt about the official medical view of the matter. The Royal College of Physicians has stated this as clearly as anyone could hope: 'Cigarette smoking is now as important a cause of death as were the great epidemic diseases such as typhoid, cholera and tuberculosis' (*Smoking and Health Now*) and the College has also reached a clear verdict that there is a direct causal link between smoking and various fatal and disabling diseases. A World Health Organization estimate suggested that there may be as many as 10 million deaths a year that are attributable to smoking. The British Medical Association has suggested that as many as 15–20 per cent of all deaths in the UK throughout all age groups may be related to smoking. These estimates point to 63,000 deaths each year from lung cancer and 32,000 deaths from coronary heart disease, with smoking implicated in about 84 per cent of lung cancer deaths and 17 per cent of all heart disease deaths. Such figures dwarf the number of deaths resulting from any other single hazard. To put it another way, smoking in the UK kills more than 300 people every day – the equivalent of a passenger jet crashing every day and killing all of its passengers.

For most of the 20th century there was a steady increase in the number of smokers and in the incidence of lung cancer. This is usually put forward as support for the causal view (that is, smoking causes lung cancer). However, there are problems involved in this interpretation. Medical diagnoses are far from being completely reliable; in fact, for some diseases they are extremely unreliable. During the past century there have been many changes in diagnostic practice in relation to such diseases as lung cancer. A medical article written in 1904 found that, out of 178 cases of lung cancer detected by autopsy, only six were diagnosed while the patient was alive. Without an autopsy they would have remained undetected. With modern techniques, many more of these cases would have been recognized. So a good deal of the apparent increase in lung cancer may actually be due to improved diagnostic techniques (radiology, broncoscopy, sputum examination and surgery). This leads on to another problem: although lung cancer is less likely to be missed by modern medicine, it can still be falsely diagnosed. Pathologists are often in disagreement with doctors in clinical practice on the question of this particular diagnosis, and it has been suggested that the interest in lung cancer stimulated by the new techniques may have led doctors to diagnose lung cancer too often. There are fads and fashions in diagnosis as in other non-medical areas of life.

A study of the accuracy of medical diagnoses (Cameron and McGoogan, 1981) confirms that there are still many inaccuracies in the identification of illnesses. In about 40 per cent of all cases, the diagnosed cause of death was found to be incorrect when an autopsy was carried out and, despite the vastly improved modern techniques of screening for lung cancer, this is one of the most frequently misdiagnosed forms of cancer; generally, these are errors of under-diagnosis. In the Cameron studies the disease was confirmed at autopsy in 59 per cent of cases. Under-diagnosis was about three times as common as over-diagnosis (31 per cent and 10 per cent, respectively). Coronary heart disease is also subject to many diagnostic errors, and it is probably used as a convenient label whenever the cause of an unexpected death is not known. Heart attacks (acute myocardial infarctions) were misdiagnosed in 36 per cent of cases: it was offered incorrectly (over-diagnosed) in 19 per cent of cases, and missed (under-diagnosed) in 17 per cent.

These results raise doubts about the extent to which death certification can be used as a precise measure for estimating public health trends. For instance, if there were a systematic bias such that lung cancer or coronary heart disease were over-diagnosed among smokers but under-diagnosed among non-smokers, this would lead to a systematic bias. On the other hand, it does not seem likely that any such bias towards misdiagnosis could account for the massive increase during the 20th century in deaths from lung cancer.

Assuming that no such bias does operate, errors in the diagnosis of lung cancer should be no different for men than for women. The period 1890–1920 saw a massive increase in the numbers of men who smoked. It was not until 1920–40 that women began to smoke in any numbers, during which time there was no marked increase in smoking among men. It is usually assumed that there is a delay of something like 30 years before the effects of smoking begin to show themselves as lung cancer. If smoking does indeed cause cancer, we would expect the incidence of the disease among men to show a rapid increase long before it appears for women. Between 1911 and 1915, men were twice as likely to die of lung cancer as women. This risk gradually increased. By the 1950s, men were 10 times more likely to die of this disease. By this time, however, the sex ratio had begun to decrease. All of these changes are consistent with the patterns of smoking by men and women earlier in the century; they are also consistent with the suggestion that smoking causes lung cancer.

Cigarette smoke is known to contain chemicals which can cause cancers when they are applied in sufficient concentrations to some wretched laboratory animal; it also contains other chemicals which can encourage the development of cancer. The precise constituents of tobacco smoke that cause cancer have not been identified with any certainty, though it is suspected that they are likely to be found in the small droplets that condense out as tar. One of the research groups that is most strongly convinced that cigarettes are a direct cause of lung cancer is that at Oxford University, which conducted the investigations of the smoking habits of UK doctors. In a paper published by the Royal Statistical Society of London, Richard Doll argued that we are all exposed from birth to agents that are capable of causing the disease, and that these agents interact to multiply the degree of risk (Doll, 1971). Industrial studies have shown that, among workers who are exposed to asbestos or irradiation, smokers are at even greater risk than usual of contracting lung cancer. Of these various agents, Doll and his colleagues are convinced that cigarette smoke is most clearly implicated as a cause of this disease.

If smoking does cause lung cancer we might expect heavy smokers to contract the disease earlier than light smokers. But although heavy smokers are more likely to develop lung cancer than light smokers, the amount smoked seems to make little difference to the age at which a person contracts lung cancer. Light smokers are afflicted with the disease at about the same age as heavy smokers. On the other hand, there does seem to be a clear mathematical relationship between the incidence of lung cancer and both the number of years during which a person has smoked cigarettes and the average number of cigarettes smoked per day.

The experimental work that has been done with animals strongly supports this view that duration of exposure to cigarette smoke is a crucial factor in causing cancer; and in human studies, among people of a given age, those who started to smoke earliest are most likely to develop lung cancer. A 60-year-old who has smoked more than 20 cigarettes a day since their early teens runs a 33 times greater risk of contracting the disease than a non-smoker; if they started smoking in their early twenties they are at 15 times the risk of a non-smoker, and if they started smoking after they were 25 years old, they run an eight times greater risk. When information from different countries is compared, with this time-lag taken into account, there is a close relationship between the number of manufactured cigarettes sold (per adult) in 1950 and the incidence of lung cancer in 1975.

It is sometimes said that the way in which cigarette tobacco is cured has an influence upon the health of the smoker. The most common brands of cigarettes sold in the UK and the US contain Virginia tobacco. This is a tobacco that has been flue-cured by heating for five to seven days and it is chemically different from that used in some European cigarettes (for example, Turkish tobacco) which has been air-dried. Flue-cured tobacco has a sugar content which may be 20 or 30 times as high as that of air-cured tobacco, and its smoke is acidic and easier to inhale than that of the alkaline air-dried tobacco. It is not inconceivable that these different tobacco-curing processes might relate to the smoker's chances of contracting lung cancer.

Countries such as France and the UK differ in terms of the type of cigarette tobacco that is generally smoked. Interestingly, France has a lower incidence of lung cancer. At one time this could have been explained in terms of the fact that the French tended to consume fewer cigarettes than the UK's citizens, and the incidence of lung cancer in France was just as one would have expected from the number of smokers in the country. However, the prevalence of smoking and the daily number of cigarettes consumed by smokers in the UK and France have become much more similar. As the smoking habits of the British and French have become more similar, so have the rates of respiratory disease. Nonetheless it is still rather odd that so little is known about this question of curing processes. For the moment, it is not clear whether or not flue-cured Virginia tobacco is intrinsically more harmful than air-dried tobacco, or whether it could be harmful in a less direct way because its acidic smoke is easier to inhale.

Lung cancer is the most notorious smoking-related disease. It is, however, far less common than coronary heart disease, which is now the leading cause of death in many developed countries. Although we know that smokers are more likely to die of this disease than non-smokers, there has been some argument about the nature of this relationship. It has been suggested that the observed association between the two is not due to cause and effect but may also reflect the presence in the population of people who have inherited a predisposition to both smoking and specific diseases.

One of the most interesting experimental techniques in psychology and medicine involves the study of twins, particularly identical twins. Identical twins are nature's gift to experimentation since they share the same genetic endowment. If we can find a large enough number of identical twins where one twin is a smoker and the other is not, then this provides an extremely valuable test of whether genetic factors, smoking, or both, contribute towards the various diseases to which smokers are so prone. If genetic factors are partly responsible for the common basis of smoking and disease, the twin who does not smoke will still be at risk of becoming ill, even though they do not smoke. In a Swedish study of more than 23,000 twin pairs, it was quite clear that identical twins are more likely either to be both smokers or both non-smokers than is the case for two people with different genetic endowments: they are also more alike in such other aspects of their drug taking as their use of tranquillizers, sleeping tablets and alcohol. They even show a greater similarity in terms of the number of cups of coffee that they drink during the day, and in such other aspects of their behaviour as sleeping difficulties and feelings of stress. The Swedish study showed that smokers are genetically different from non-smokers. The differences between them cover a wide range of personality characteristics and behaviours, many of which are known to be implicated in the smoking-related diseases. For instance, susceptibility to stress is partly determined by genetic factors and this is known to be related to coronary heart disease.

However, despite the fact that smokers state that smoking helps to reduce stress, there is little evidence that it actually does so. Smokers score higher than non-smokers on psychological measures of stress and smokers who give up show reduced stress scores after quitting unless they relapse, when their stress levels go up again. Far from being stress-relieving, smoking may be stress-inducing.

There is considerable evidence that implicates smoking as one of the contributory factors in coronary heart disease, though the relative risk of the smoker developing this disease is less than for lung cancer or chronic bronchitis. A report in the *New England Journal of Medicine* (vol. 304, 1981) compared the effects of smoking on heart disease when such differences as age, sex (coronary heart disease is more common among men), alcohol consumption, prior symptoms of heart disease and obesity were taken into account. Persistent smokers were found to be more than twice as liable to contract heart disease as people who had once smoked but who had since given it up. In the age range 45–55, smokers are more than four times as prone to this disease than non-smokers. Most studies have also shown that this liability is dose-related: the more cigarettes the person smokes, the greater the risk of heart disease.

But whatever doubt there is about the causal relationship between smoking and heart disease (and many smoking researchers would argue that there is no longer any doubt at all), for respiratory problems the evidence is indisputable. Cigarette smoking is the most important cause of chronic bronchitis; and again, the degree of risk is related to the number of cigarettes smoked. Among men who smoke more than 25 cigarettes a day, the death rate from bronchitis and emphysema is more than 20 times higher than for non-smokers. The highest death rate in the world for bronchitis and emphysema is in England and Wales, where it is estimated that about 25,000 people die each year from these diseases because of their smoking. On this question, the results of the Swedish twin study are quite clear. When one identical twin is a smoker and the other is not, the smoker is more likely to develop such symptoms as persistent cough, shortness of breath and severe chest pains. This difference between smokers and non-smokers is just as evident in ordinary twins as it is in identical twins, so the effect seems to be independent of genetics and can be attributed to the smoking. It is probably due to those substances in tobacco smoke which irritate the respiratory system by creating mucus and by clogging up the self-cleaning processes of the lungs and bronchial tubes. The strongest evidence about the health damage caused by smoking is undoubtedly that linking it with various respiratory disorders, some of which may have serious, disabling and often fatal consequences.

There are also hazards associated with the high concentrations of carbon monoxide contained in cigarette smoke. When the smoke is inhaled, the carbon monoxide is diluted to about 3–6 per cent, which exposes the smoker to levels of carbon monoxide about twice as high as those encountered in the most polluted city traffic conditions, and eight times those permitted in industry. One of the main dangers associated with carbon monoxide is the way that it replaces oxygen in the blood; and the heart, which has a great demand for oxygen, is among the first parts of the body to suffer. Under most normal circumstances, this may have no obvious effect on a young and healthy person. However, it can limit the athletic performance of smokers; it can interfere with the growth of the unborn child among pregnant mothers; and among patients with arterial disease or those recovering from a heart attack it may impose a fatal stress on the weakened heart.

In short, smoking is almost certainly the most physically destructive of all of the forms of drug taking discussed in this book. In terms of its physical damage it is more dangerous than heroin addiction. There may still be some uncertainty about the precise mechanisms which are involved in smoking-related illnesses, but as a serious health hazard there can no longer be any doubt.

Health Warnings and Smoking Bans

Whether or not the risks to the health of the smoker prevent people either from starting to smoke or from continuing the habit is another matter. Most smokers acknowledge the health risks associated with smoking, and some even accept the most pessimistic interpretation of the evidence, yet they go on smoking. When drugs offer sufficiently powerful psychological rewards, these can override health considerations. But the drug user cannot even begin to make a rational assessment of the potential problems that they face unless they are accurately informed of the risks.

There have been enormous changes in the nature of the health warnings that have appeared on tobacco products since the first edition of *Living with Drugs*. These have been mandatory in the UK since 1971. Until 1991, the warnings were determined by a voluntary agreement between the tobacco industry and government, and, not surprisingly, the tobacco industry sought to negotiate the weakest messages. However, despite the resistance of the tobacco companies, the health warnings were significantly strengthened over the years.

The first warning in 1971 tentatively suggested that 'Smoking can damage your health'. In 1983 this became 'Smoking can seriously damage your health'. In 1986 six new warnings were introduced that listed specific diseases caused by smoking. These informed the smoker that smoking can cause heart disease, lung cancer, bronchitis and other chest diseases, that smoking can cause premature death, and that smoking when pregnant can injure your baby. The physical size of the warning has also increased. The space devoted the warning on posters increased from 9 per cent of the whole area in 1971 to 15 per cent, and on cigarette ads, it increased from 15 per cent to 17.5 per cent.

It is only since 1991 that health warnings on tobacco products have been regulated by law when an EU directive required that the completely uncompromising message 'Smoking kills' should cover one side of the cigarette pack, with an additional warning to be included on the reverse side. More warnings were now included, touching upon issues such as passive smoking – 'Smoking damages the health of those around you, and 'Protect children: don't make them breathe your smoke'.

When health warnings first appeared, they tended to be printed with the same typeface as their pack designs, rendering them virtually invisible. Under the new directive, warnings were printed in a black typeface on a white background, and surrounded by an ominous black border to help them to stand out. The warnings also now increased in size to cover at least 30 per cent of the front surface of the cigarette pack and 40 per cent of the rear surface. Because of concerns that the text warnings have lost their visual impact, consideration is also being given to having graphic images of diseases on cigarette packs.

A further indication of how much things have changed since *Living with Drugs* first appeared has been the introduction of smoking bans in workplaces and in public places including restaurants, pubs and bars. In the UK, there has been a gradual but increasingly obvious trend towards restrictions on smoking. This has been reflected in providing smoke-free offices, shops, cinemas and public transport. Some of the earliest policy changes included an increase in no-smoking spaces on public transport. In London, for example, smoking was banned on single-decker buses in 1971, and the proportion of smoke-free carriages on underground trains increased from 50 per cent to 75 per cent. However, it took another 16 years for smoking to be banned completely on the London Underground, and it might have taken longer had it not been for the King's Cross fire which claimed 31 lives.

The trend towards anti-smoking bans in public places has moved more swiftly in other countries. Bans on smoking in bars and restaurants were in place by 2006 in Ireland, Norway, Italy, Malta, Sweden and Scotland (Scots will be delighted to point out that the English will be following in their footsteps shortly). Many other European countries (including Spain, Finland, Iceland, the Netherlands and Belgium) have introduced similar, but less comprehensive smoking bans in public places and in the workplace. The principal aim of these laws has been to protect third parties, particularly workers, from the harmful effects of exposure to second-hand tobacco smoke. Interestingly, there has been good public support for the introduction of these laws. Compliance with the law has generally been high from the outset, and support from both smokers and non-smokers has increased since these were implemented.

Alcohol, too, is known to carry considerable risks to health, and at a meeting of the American Medical Association it was once proposed that alcohol should carry a similar warning to that on cigarette packets:

Direction for use: use moderately and not on successive days. Eat well while drinking and, if necessary, supplement food with vitamin tablets while drinking. WARNING: May be habit forming; not for use by children. If this beverage is indulged in immoderately it may cause intoxication (drunkenness), later neuralgia and paralysis (neuritis), and serious mental derangement, such as delirium tremens and other curable and incurable mental diseases, as well as kidney and liver damage.

Strong stuff! But in the end, health warnings may not have a particularly strong deterrent effect upon the use of drugs. People do not use drugs because they believe them to be safe, nor do they necessarily stop using them because they think they are dangerous.

An alternative tactic against smoking, and arguably a more effective one, may be to focus upon reducing the social nuisance and possible health risks that smokers inflict upon others. Smoking clearly involves some risk to health, and most authorities are agreed that the risk is considerable. Whatever the degree of risk, it is important that the individual should be provided with a clear, factual account of the effects of smoking.   However, unlike most other forms of drug taking, the smoker also inflicts their habit on others in a very direct way. Non-smokers who sit in a room polluted by tobacco smoke are forced to become smokers merely by breathing. Over a prolonged period of time such as an eight-hour working day, and in a small, enclosed space such as a small office or a car in which there are several heavy smokers, the non-smoker may inhale the equivalent of several cigarettes, and those with asthma, allergies or chest complaints may have to endure acute discomfort under such circumstances.

In a 1981 study of more than 91,000 Japanese wives, a paper in the *British Medical Journal* reported that women who were married to cigarette smokers were more likely to develop lung cancer than those married to non-smokers, and that the risk of developing lung cancer increased with the number of cigarettes smoked by the husband (Hirayama, 1981). At first, there was some dispute about the validity of these results, but subsequent studies have continued to find that passive smokers are exposed to health risks as a result of breathing other people's smoke. In a later paper in the *British Medical Journal*, Professor Nicholas Wald estimated that passive smokers face a 35 per cent higher risk of getting lung cancer, and a US report concluded that children are at 20–30 per cent greater risk of respiratory problems requiring medical attention if they are raised by smoking rather than non-smoking parents.

In June 1986, *The Times* of London ran a story under the banner headline 'Passive Smoking: No Significant Danger' and the Tobacco Advisory Council immediately circulated this to all Members of Parliament. A few days later the Tobacco Institute of Australia published an advertisement referring to the *Times* study. The Australian Federation of Consumer Unions took the Tobacco Institute to court and the outcome was one which the tobacco industry must bitterly regret. After hearing all the evidence, the judge ruled that 'there is compelling scientific evidence that cigarette smoke causes lung cancer in non-smokers' and also that there was 'overwhelming evidence' to show a causal relationship between passive smoking and respiratory disease in children and between passive smoking and asthma. The judge commented also upon the evasiveness of the industry's witnesses and upon their demands for near unobtainable levels of scientific proof.

The California ballot for the 1980 presidential election contained an anti-smoking referendum. Specifically at issue was Proposition 10. If accepted, this would have made it an offence to smoke in any enclosed public space, and offenders would have been issued with the equivalent of a parking ticket and fined $15. Several other states in America had already passed similar laws. The issue had been put before Californian voters two years previously, when it was rejected by 54 per cent to 46 per cent. On both occasions, the tobacco companies ploughed millions of dollars into a campaign to sway public opinion against such measures. In 1978, the companies are reputed to have spent more than $6 million, and about $2 million in 1980. As in 1978, the investment was repaid and Proposition 10 failed. The reason for this investment is that the stakes are high. Despite the fact that California is way down the league of cigarette smoking states in terms of the percentage of the population who are smokers, Californians still spend more than $1.5 billion on cigarettes each year.

But whether or not the argument for limiting smoking in public is linked to evidence about the proven medical hazards of exposure to cigarette smoke, it is, in any case, unpleasant for someone who chooses not to smoke to have to tolerate such air pollution. We are more familiar with other measures to limit air pollution. England has had laws against air pollution since the 13th century. By the 19th century, the Industrial Revolution had produced conditions worse than ever before. These persisted well into the 20th century and some are with us today. One, thankfully now extinct, was the dense yellow fog known as a 'London particular'. This was certainly unpleasant and it is difficult to imagine how it could have been anything but harmful to health. The 1952 London fog produced such a disastrous crop of deaths that it provided a powerful stimulus for the passage of the Clean Air Act. Some prominent physicians have drawn parallels between the evidence relating to air pollution and to smoking. Even now we remain as unsure about the precise ways in which air pollution can damage health as we are about smoking.

The Search for a Safer Cigarette

The search for a safer cigarette dates back to the mid-1950s when the notion that cigarette smoking might have physically damaging effects began to gain ground. By the 1960s, it had become the established view. As people became more and more nervous about the effect that smoking might have on their health, so the filter-tip revolution occurred. The filter-tip cigarette was originally devised as a means of capturing a larger share of the consumer market. Its success was due to the way in which it also came to symbolize the possibility of a less harmful cigarette. In the early 1950s, tipped cigarettes accounted for less than 1 per cent of the market. By the mid-1970s, they made up 95 per cent.

For the tobacco companies, this was a challenge to their ingenuity. For instance, as the fashion in smoking moved to filter-tip cigarettes, there was a corresponding preference for cigarettes with a narrower column (that is, the manufacturer needed to put less tobacco in each cigarette). And although cigarettes have become longer, so have the filter-tips. The other advantages of using filter-tips are that the tobacco can be more loosely packed, and it is easier to use the sort of waste material that would once have been discarded. As a result of all these changes, cigarettes now contain only about half as much tobacco as they did in the 1930s.

Cigarettes are also weaker than they were. In the 1950s, the average cigarette delivered more than twice as much tar and nicotine as in the mid-1970s. This has happened in the US, the UK and most European countries. Since this change coincided with the switch to filter-tip cigarettes, these two developments mean that the smoker today is inhaling considerably less tar and nicotine than their counterpart 30 years ago. The search for a safer cigarette has also been closely linked to the production of lower-tar cigarettes. The move towards low-tar, low-nicotine cigarettes is, however, limited by the taste of the smoker. It is possible to extract virtually all of the nicotine from a cigarette. Tar is rather different. Whatever material is burned in a cigarette will produce tar. In principle, this could be filtered out, but since the tar carries the flavour, the resulting no-tar cigarette would have no appeal to the smoker. It would deliver nothing but a flavourless and chemically inert warm gas. But this very fact creates a problem. It is impossible to remove the harmful ingredients that are created by the burning of dried organic material. Carcinogens are found in almost every class of the chemical compounds in tobacco smoke. A safe cigarette that is smoked is impossible.

There is some evidence that filter-tip cigarettes may be less harmful than the non-tipped variety, probably because of the way in which they reduce the tar content of the inhaled smoke. The latest technology has produced 'trionic' filters with 3 layers, each designed to remove a different set of toxic compounds while allowing the nicotine to pass through. But filters can also have a paradoxical effect, in that many brands of filter-tip cigarettes deliver more carbon monoxide than plain cigarettes. By reducing the amount of one of the harmful agents in cigarette smoke, filter-tip cigarettes, instead of producing a 'safer' cigarette, may have merely altered the balance of the harmful constituents. Some filter-tip cigarettes (those with unventilated filters) may be more dangerous than non-tipped cigarettes in terms of the carbon monoxide that the smoker inhales. A study in the *American Journal of Public Health* found that if smokers block the holes of low-tar cigarettes, this could increase the toxic by-products of smoke by up to 300 per cent. People smoke mainly for nicotine but die to a large extent from tar and carbon monoxide, and paradoxically, the search for a less harmful cigarette might be better directed towards one that delivers low tar and low carbon monoxide but a medium dose of nicotine.

Low-tar cigarettes probably do not deliver significant health benefits despite the much lower official tar yields. The measures that are made of tar and nicotine yields are made by smoking machine. These do not duplicate the behaviour of real smokers.

Smoking behaviour is determined largely by the smoker's need to consume nicotine and maintain a satisfactory blood/nicotine level. With low-tar cigarettes, smokers adjust their smoking behaviour to take in the required levels of nicotine, even if the cigarette is supposed to be low in tar and nicotine when smoked by a machine. Since tar intake is closely linked to nicotine intake, the tar exposure also increases. This effect is known as 'compensation'. Because of compensation, smoking low-tar cigarettes may even increase, not decrease, the risks of smoking.

Smokers of low-tar cigarettes inhale more deeply, take puffs more often, and even cover up the tiny holes near the filter that were put there to reduce the amount of smoke, and subsequently the amount of tar, that a smoker inhales.

Some of the reasons why low-tar cigarettes have a low-tar yield are quite surprising. The expectation fostered by the multinational tobacco companies is that these cigarettes contain some new and specially developed low-tar tobacco. This is partly true. The nicotine and tar content of tobacco can be reduced in several ways, one of which is through the selective breeding of the plants, and by special methods of cultivation. A less well-publicized reason why these cigarettes produce low levels of tar is that they contain smaller amounts of tobacco.

One American consumer magazine made a direct comparison between low-tar and ordinary cigarettes by buying packets from local stores and unwrapping the contents; these were left to stabilize under room conditions for two days. After this time, the contents were weighed. The low-tar cigarettes contained less than two-thirds as much tobacco as the ordinary brand. In addition, low-tar cigarettes contain a high level of reconstituted 'tobacco sheet'. This is made by salvaging the sweepings and stems, in other words the remnants that have been discarded during the manufacture of other cigarettes. One can only gasp in amazement at the genius that could persuade people to choose a low-tar, low-nicotine cigarette that is also a low-tobacco, low-quality cigarette. The manufacturers must still be laughing.

Among the other developments in this field is the search for an effective tobacco substitute. A new smoking material (NSM) cigarette was tried in the UK in the 1960s. This owed a great deal to the desire of ICI to find new uses for cellulose and the hopes of Imperial Tobacco that they could find some way to protect themselves from fluctuations in the supply of the natural product. Most substitutes are nicotine-free and contain less tar than tobacco smoke; they also produce smoke which is less complicated in its chemical components than tobacco smoke. In the long term, they may offer a less harmful alternative to cigarettes containing tobacco. For the moment, however, no satisfactory or commercially successful tobacco substitute has been found. Men have tried smoking cabbage leaves, tomato leaves, spinach, wild hydrangea, cocoa beans and lettuce leaves – with varying degrees of pleasure. Few of these seem likely to replace tobacco. Nonetheless, the search for a tobacco substitute continues. British American Tobacco has announced that it will launch a new safe cigarette product in 2006.

Chapter 7

Cannabis

Marihuana, hashish, pot, weed, bush, tea, Mary Jane, grass, shit, dope, bhang and ganja are a few of the different names for preparations of the plant, *Cannabis sativa L*, otherwise called Indian hemp. The drug can be eaten, drunk or, as is more common in Europe and America, smoked. Cannabis is the general term for the different preparations of this herbaceous annual plant, of which there are different varieties, with somewhat different physical, as well as chemical, characteristics. Most botanists agree that these should be regarded as belonging to a single species, though others suggest that there are really three species.

Cannabis is closely related to the hop, and grows vigorously both in its wild state and under cultivation. Indeed, it is so vigorous that it still grows wild in countries where systematic efforts to eradicate it have been going on for centuries. It was one of the first plants to be cultivated by man for its non-food properties, and is thought to have originated in Asia. The earliest Indian Vedas which were composed before 1400 BCE refer to the chemical virtues of cannabis, and those who worship the Hindu deity Shiva have used bhang in their religious practices.

The cultivation of cannabis seems to have been introduced into North America in 1606 by Louis Hébert, an apothecary. Apart from yielding a drug, the plant also produced the fibre which was used at that time to provide sails and rigging for ships of the Royal Navy. King James I commanded his American colonies to cultivate the plant, and in 1630 cannabis was a staple crop of the East Coast. The government of Virginia awarded bounties to those producing cannabis and imposed penalties on those who produced other crops. On the whole, the early colonists seem either not to have known, or to have had no interest in, its intoxicating effects.

The drug probably first reached Europe more than a thousand years ago following the Muslim invasion of Spain. François Rabelais, the eminent French physician and satirist of the 16th century, wrote of it in his book, *Gargantua and Pantagruel*, but it was not until quite recently that it inspired any serious interest. This probably dates back to the invasion of Egypt by Napoleon's expeditionary force in 1798. On their return to France, many of the troops brought cannabis with them, and by the middle of the 19th century the medical profession had begun to show an interest in the drug. It had also intrigued a small group of writers, artists and intellectuals, and in 1844 Paris saw the founding of the Club des Hachischins. Théophile Gautier and Charles Baudelaire both wrote of their fantastic hallucinatory experiences after eating large amounts of the drug. This they took in the form of 'a green sweetmeat, the size of a nut and singularly odious' (Baudelaire). Gautier also writes of 'a piece of greenish paste or jam, about the size of one's thumb'. However, it was not until very much more recently that the drug became used by more than a small minority of the intelligentsia in Europe. This seems to have occurred with the developments of the mid-1960s, and it was probably as much the result of American cultural influences as of any other single factor.

There are an estimated 200 million to 250 million people throughout the world who use cannabis. Most of them live in Asia and Africa, but over the past 40 years or so the West has seen a remarkable surge of interest in the drug. By the 1970s, it was suggested that as many as 24 million Americans had tried the drug and about eight million had continued to use it on a regular or occasional basis. In 1977, more than half of the US population between the ages of 18 and 25 had used illegal cannabis. In the UK too, the drug is very widely used. The British Crime Survey for 2002/3 found that cannabis was the most widely used of the illegal drugs, with about 3 million people having used it in the previous year and about 2 million having used it in the previous month. Rates of use were highest among younger adults, with more than a quarter of 20–24-year-olds having used it.

Cannabis is a unique drug. It defies attempts at precise pharmacological classification since its effects are so various. Under different conditions it can act as a stimulant, as a sedative, as an analgesic or as a mildly hallucinogenic drug. It has superficial similarities to many other drugs but, on the whole, the differences between cannabis and other drugs are more striking than the similarities. In its chemical composition, cannabis is an exceedingly complex substance. The main active ingredients of the drug are the cannabinoids, a group of compounds which, for the sake of simplicity, are generally referred to as THC. This is an abbreviation for tetrahydrocannabinol, which seems to be the most important psychoactive constituent. The potency of the drug varies according to the plant from which it was taken, and genetic factors play an important role here. Stronger cannabis is generally grown from the seeds of plants which were themselves high in THC. The plant can be grown from suitable seed in most temperate conditions and cannabis of reasonable potency has been grown in the UK and Canada.

So many people have insisted that hashish, the resinous form of cannabis, is stronger than marihuana (grass), the herbal form, that this has become a generally accepted truth. Some people have gone further and argued that hashish and marihuana have different effects. Neither of these ideas is correct. The active drug is the same in both forms of cannabis, and there is no necessary reason for hashish to be more potent than grass, though it often is the stronger of the two. However, the active THC content of hash seems to be less stable, and over a period of months its potency declines more rapidly than that of marihuana.

It is always a somewhat hazardous procedure to describe the subjective effects of a drug, and this is especially true of a drug such as cannabis where the effects are even more variable than those of most other psychoactive drugs:

What does one experience? What does one see? Wonderful things, eh? Amazing sights? … This is an ill-informed notion, a complete misunderstanding … The brain and organism on which hashish operates will produce only the normal phenomena peculiar to that individual – increased, admittedly, in number and force, but always faithful to their origin. A man will never escape from his destined physical and moral temperament: hashish will be a mirror of his impressions and private thoughts – a magnifying mirror, it is true, but only a mirror (Charles Baudelaire).

Bearing this in mind, there is a surprising consensus among cannabis users about the effects that they do experience. The most common of these seem to be a general sense of relaxation and peacefulness coupled with heightened sensory awareness. All the senses seem to be more acute, but most cannabis smokers report that the experience of listening to music is particularly intense and pleasurable under the influence of the drug. Many users become euphoric and find that the most mundane events and objects are sources of considerable amusement. Other common effects include a changed sense of the passage of time; time usually is described as appearing to be stretched out and to be passing more slowly. Users also describe an increased sense of sexual pleasure, and the drug has often been used as an aid to imagination and fantasy.

Erich Goode, the American sociologist, has suggested that almost all the reported effects of cannabis are *whimsical* in nature: 'happy, silly, euphoric, relaxed, hedonistic, sensual, foolish and decidedly unserious'. The drug is often used in connection with activities which are themselves highly pleasurable: eating, listening to music, watching a film, having sex, meeting friends and so on. Cannabis is used as a means of intensifying the level of enjoyment. To this extent it is accurately described as a recreational drug. Cannabis is seldom used (or it is used far less) during serious work-related activities, because most users recognize that it interferes with these.

Users overwhelmingly describe their experience in pleasurable terms. This is not to say that the drug does not also produce some effects which are actually or potentially unpleasant. Confusion, irrational thoughts, increased tension, impaired memory, sadness, rapid heart rate, dizziness and nausea have all been reported as occasional effects. Nonetheless, it remains true that most users, most of the time, enjoy their cannabis experiences.

Those who wish to prevent people from being able to use cannabis generally use one or both of the following arguments: that cannabis may be pleasurable but is physically or psychologically dangerous; that cannabis itself may be comparatively harmless, but leads to other more dangerous forms of drug taking.

Physical Hazards of Cannabis Use

The medical and scientific journals have published a number of papers which set out to prove that the use of cannabis is not completely safe. Of course it is not completely safe. No drug is completely safe. In sufficient quantities, common salt can be lethal. It is possible to find isolated cases of people who have suffered damage as a result of ingesting almost any substance, including food and water.

The short-term physiological effects of cannabis are fairly unremarkable. One of the most common effects is a reddening of the eyes. This seems to have no real clinical significance, and contrary to popular belief cannabis does not produce dilation of the pupils. The drug also causes dryness of the mouth, an increase in pulse rate and, at high doses, a slight increase in blood pressure. These effects disappear within a few hours unless the dose is repeated. Cannabis does not produce any significant changes in hormonal activity or in blood biochemistry. Nor does it seem to have any effect on the liver or kidneys. Its effects upon the electrical activity of the brain are equally unremarkable, and in some studies of brainwave activity it has proved very difficult to detect any changes at all. The changes that do occur in the brain seem to be predominantly changes in brain chemistry, but the significance of these has yet to be established.

In terms of its lethal dose, cannabis is an exceptionally safe drug. The safety of a drug, in this respect, is calculated as the difference between the effective dose and the lethal dose. In the case of the barbiturate drugs, for instance, this difference is comparatively small. With cannabis it would be virtually impossible to ingest enough of the drug for it to have a lethal effect. It has been estimated that the lethal dose could be as high as 40,000 times that of the effective dose. Cannabis is one of the least toxic drugs known to man, and there is no evidence that anyone has ever died as a direct result of taking an overdose of it.

In terms of its chronic effects, there is surprisingly little reliable information. It seems probable that cannabis smoking might lead to bronchial and respiratory disorders in long-term heavy users. Chronic cannabis smoking is likely to have some of the same health risks as those that are now linked with tobacco, notably lung cancer. The tar yield from marihuana, for instance, is similar to that of tobacco. But as yet no firm evidence has appeared to link cannabis with lung cancer. There is also puzzling evidence from a study of chronic cannabis smokers in Costa Rica which suggested that cannabis smokers who also smoke cigarettes appear to have healthier small airways in their lungs than people who *only* smoke cigarettes (this is consistent with the claim sometimes made by cannabis users who suffer from asthma that cannabis alleviates their asthma attacks). This result is surprising and needs to be approached with some caution. In general, the available evidence suggests that regular users of cannabis are at increased risk of bronchitis and this problem will be greater still among cannabis smokers who also smoke tobacco. There is also some evidence that regular cannabis smoking over a period of decades may increase the risk of cancers of the upper respiratory system.

On the question of lung damage, it is unfortunately necessary to add that several governments, notably the Mexican government, have been spraying cannabis crops with highly toxic weed killers such as paraquat. Paraquat has no odour and no known taste, and it is invisible to the eye. As a result, several people have suffered irreversible lung damage through consuming cannabis which has been poisoned as a result of these legally sanctioned anti-cannabis campaigns. Yet in an outline of its plans for the 1980s, an American Drug Enforcement Administration official complained that, if it were not for the existence of certain unnecessary restrictions, it would be prepared to use even more powerful poisons.

As with every other illegal drug, there have been several sensational reports linking cannabis with brain damage, genetic damage and deformed babies. There is no convincing evidence associating cannabis with any of these effects, though, on the last point, pregnant women might be well advised to avoid any unnecessary drugs during their term of pregnancy. This is certainly true of the first few months, during which time the foetus is especially vulnerable. Since cigarette smoking is known to have some adverse effects on the baby, cannabis smoking might have similar effects.

To understand why the idea developed that cannabis causes brain damage, we must look at the way science *actually* works. Whereas science may be a rational procedure, scientists remain as human, fallible and irrational as anyone else. When the needs and emotions of the scientist are sufficiently strong they can influence his or her work to produce the conclusions that they want to reach. Scientists and doctors who work in less media-attractive areas find that if they want to get onto the TV or into the newspapers, their opinions on drugs give them easy access. And the stories that the media wants to hear are always the more dramatic stories. Look out for more tales of brain damage, killer drugs and discoveries of miracle cures. And look for who is telling these tales.

In Nazi Germany, there was a rush to provide 'scientific evidence' about the genetic inferiority of the Jews. In Stalinist Russia, there was the remarkable case of T.D. Lysenko, whose completely spurious theory of heredity dominated Russian science for decades. Lysenko refused to acknowledge the existence of genes and proposed that heredity was a general property of living organisms. The theory held out the promise of being able to produce hereditary changes in a particular direction by environmental means: and because this was such an appealing idea it enabled Lysenko and his followers to reject the actual results of scientific experiments in favour of what they already 'knew' to be correct. This bias, though on a lesser scale, is constantly present in science, and in recent years psychologists have begun to investigate how this 'experimenter effect' operates. There are a number of scientists who have a deep-rooted need to show that cannabis is an evil and dangerous drug. To prove that would be to justify their dislike of the drug and their need to keep it illegal.

One example of the sort of research that is supposed to have 'shown' that cannabis causes brain damage appeared in that most prestigious medical journal, *The Lancet*,[1]

1   Campbell, Evans, Thomson and Williams (1971), 'Cerebral atrophy in young cannabis smokers', *The Lancet*, 4 December, 1219–24.

but when examined in detail the investigation shows nothing of the sort. Among its scientific weaknesses are the following:

- All the patients in the study were known to use drugs other than cannabis. Every one of them had an extensive history of drug use. All had used LSD: one is even described as having taken an overdose of LSD. No detailed information is given about their use of alcohol, which is already known to cause the sort of changes in the brain that were found (though two out of 10 were described as heavy drinkers). Therefore any abnormalities in these patients could have been due to drugs other than cannabis.
- The patients were drawn from an abnormal sample who were not representative of long-term cannabis users. One had had a schizophrenic illness, another had a possible psychotic illness and three had a history of head injury. All of them were people who had sought medical or psychiatric help because of various troubling symptoms. Four already had neurological problems; two were attending a drug addiction centre; one had a history of drug abuse and had recently taken an overdose of drugs other than cannabis, and the other three were receiving psychiatric treatment. Any abnormality is probably completely independent of the cannabis use, and even the authors of this paper admit that their sample could have been abnormal before they started to use cannabis.
- The technique used to measure brain damage (air encephalography) is imperfect, often imprecise, and neurologists acknowledge that it is impossible to define exactly the difference between normal and abnormal levels.

In fact, the article is entirely inconclusive. But because it reached the conclusions that many people wanted to hear, they disregarded all of these faults. Typical of the responses that the paper generated is a letter (also published in *The Lancet*) arguing that this 'evidence' should be used to justify 'the continuation and strengthening of every possible measure to suppress cannabis'.

Psychological Hazards

Most psychoactive drugs produce adverse reactions amongst some individuals. In a study of more than 5,000 patients, as many as one in every 10 showed an adverse reaction to the psychoactive drugs that were being medically prescribed for them. When we are dealing with the non-medical use of drugs, the problem is further complicated by the fact that the beliefs and expectations of the individual play an even more crucial part in determining how they will experience the drug effects. What is seen as a highly pleasurable hallucinatory experience by one person may be seen as a terrifying symptom of impending madness by another.

Although adverse reactions to cannabis are fortunately quite rare, about three-quarters of them take the form of a panic attack in which the user experiences intense anxiety. Often this is caused by the user coming to believe that they are going mad, or dying. Such panic attacks are often found among novice or inexperienced users who have taken a relatively large amount of the drug and are startled by their internal psychological reactions, or who are exposed to sudden unpleasant forms of stress while intoxicated. It is likely that many of the studies of cannabis psychosis are complicated by misdiagnosis of these sorts of reactions.

At low doses, the subjective effects of cannabis are similar in some ways to those of alcohol, but, at higher doses, the effects are quite different, and for the inexperienced user they may be quite unexpected. The experienced smoker recognizes these as effects of the drug. But if the novice mistakenly interprets them as signs of madness, this can provoke a panic attack. Such reactions are generally self-limiting, and last for a matter of minutes or for a few hours. The best treatment is to reassure the user that what they are experiencing is the effect of the drug and nothing more sinister. If the user is taken to a mental hospital and treated as if they were suffering from some psychiatric illness, this is likely to intensify and to prolong the reaction.

The possibility that cannabis might provoke a serious, long-term psychotic illness like schizophrenia has also been suggested. This view has a history dating back over centuries, but in recent years this debate has been reopened with some psychiatrists arguing strongly that cannabis can cause schizophrenia.

Much of the early evidence about 'cannabis psychosis' was essentially anecdotal. The first full-scale enquiry into the effects of cannabis was the Indian Hemp Commission of 1893–94. Even at that time, to many people it seemed unnecessary to reopen this question of whether cannabis caused insanity: some even suggested that the Commission deliberately chose to ignore what had already been proved. Certainly, the statistics sent in from mental hospitals all over India cited cannabis drugs as one of the chief causes of mental illness. In an article in the *Indian Medical Gazette*, one of the foremost experts at the time, Surgeon Lt. Col. Crombie, had described cannabis as 'the actual and immediate cause of … insanity'. However, when the Commission re-examined the evidence that had been used to justify this conclusion, it was found to be extremely weak. The statistics were not based on any medical diagnosis, but were simply comments entered by the admissions clerk, and were usually taken from the policemen or whoever brought the patient to the asylum. The examining magistrate required some specific cause of illness to be shown and it was standard procedure to enter 'hemp drugs' as the cause whenever the patient had been known to use them. When the commission made a detailed examination of specific cases, even Lt. Col. Crombie was forced to admit that the cannabis could not have caused the illness. The Commission concluded that 'it may well seem extraordinary that statistics based on such absolutely untrustworthy material should be submitted year after year in the asylum report'.

Almost a century later, the quality of the evidence from Eastern countries was not much better. In 1972, the Canadian Le Dain Commission concluded that 'thorough controlled studies in these countries, which isolate the long-term effects of cannabis from the powerful and pervasive sociocultural, economic, nutritional and hygienic conditions described, have yet to be reported'.

A major problem for those who argue that cannabis causes schizophrenia is how to explain the decline (or at least the stable trend) in cases of early onset schizophrenia during the 1970s and 1980s when the number of cannabis users was increasing greatly. Since California probably contains as many cannabis users as most other parts of the Western world, it is interesting to look at the incidence of cannabis psychosis there. A study of students at the Berkeley University campus in 1968 found no cases of this supposed disorder despite the fact that at least a quarter of the 40,000 students there had tried the drug. Another survey of more than 700,000 medical admissions in California found that only nine were related to cannabis, and none required treatment for more than eight days. The question here is not whether cannabis smokers can develop a psychosis. Undoubtedly they can. The incidence of psychotic illness in the general population is about 1 per cent, so it would be no surprise if 1 per cent of cannabis smokers developed such a disorder. Also, for people who have a schizophrenic illness (as for the general population) cannabis is the most commonly used illegal drug. The important question is whether the use of cannabis increases the risk of developing a psychotic disorder. It is, therefore puzzling that the treated incidence of schizophrenia declined (or remained stable) during the 1970s and 1980s despite very substantial increases in cannabis use among young adults both in the US and in many other countries.

The recent proponents of the view that cannabis causes schizophrenia have referred to the results of several large-scale surveys. For example, one 15-year survey looked at cannabis use and schizophrenia among Swedish army conscripts. Those who used cannabis were reported to be more likely to develop schizophrenia, and the heavier users were more likely to develop the illness than lower-dose users. Similar results have also been reported in surveys from Denmark, Holland and New Zealand. However, in all of these studies, the relationship between cannabis use and the timing of the onset of psychotic symptoms was uncertain.

Also, the authors of some of these studies have been more modest than the extravagant claims made by their more excitable readers. In the Danish study, the authors state that it is not possible to say whether the results point to a causal link between cannabis use and the development of schizophrenia, and draw attention to the important observation that 'cannabis-induced psychotic disorders … are rare'. For instance, it has been estimated that the rate of cannabis psychosis among English cannabis users is about one in 10,000. It seems likely that these more recent findings point to cannabis as a potential contributory cause of psychosis in people who are vulnerable to such illnesses. In many respects, the 'new' findings are consistent with what has long been known. There is undoubtedly evidence that the symptoms of schizophrenia can be exacerbated by cannabis, and people with schizophrenia should certainly be advised to avoid or to reduce their intake of the drug.

One opinion that is frequently aired is that modern users of cannabis are at greater risk of psychotic illness because the potency of today's cannabis is so much greater than it was. Reports in the media have asserted that modern cannabis can be 10 or even 20 times stronger than its earlier forms. Like much of the drugs debate, these assertions are largely evidence-free. In the US, which is probably the only country that has analysed the THC content of cannabis products over the past three decades, the results show that the THC content more than doubled between the 1970s and the 1990s. In Europe, the average potency of imported forms of both resin and herbal cannabis has remained largely unchanged during the past decade. It is true that some of the domestically produced 'sinsemilla' or 'skunk' can be about twice as strong as other forms, but there has always been considerable variation in the strength of different batches of cannabis with some imported cannabis being stronger than some of the sinsemilla. The Netherlands is an exceptional case where sinsemilla dominates the domestic market and there are also some extra-strong forms available. But even in the Netherlands there is no evidence that this has led to increased problems.

In any case, the argument about potency is rather specious. Whisky is stronger than wine. Wine is stronger than beer. And the effect on the user? Whisky is sipped from smaller glasses in smaller amounts rather than swigged from pint pots. Most cannabis smokers know the effect that they are seeking and adjust the dose of stronger or weaker batches of cannabis accordingly. And if they wanted a rough guide to potency this is already available by courtesy of the illicit market. More potent forms carry higher prices. But in any case, what is more important than the potency of the product is the total amount consumed.

There has also been a long-running argument surrounding the suggestion that cannabis leads to a general withdrawal from 'straight' society (otherwise dignified by the scientific-sounding term 'amotivational syndrome'). The psychological studies that have been carried out have produced conflicting results. Some found no differences between users and non-users; others found that cannabis smokers were sometimes less successful in situations requiring high levels of drive and ambition, or in performing routine and repetitive tasks. An article in the *Journal of the American Medical Association* (1971) expressed doubt that there was any relationship at all between cannabis use and educational performance. Cannabis users did no better than non-users; nor did they do any worse. This was true, regardless of the amount of the drug involved. Interestingly, 18 per cent of the chronic users planned to work for their doctorate (against only 11 per cent of the non-users). However, where differences of this sort do emerge, they are best seen in terms of the psychological characteristics of the individuals taking part in the study rather than as the direct result of any drug effect. It is comparatively easy to remember this when the results suggest that drug takers do better than non-users. It is soon forgotten when the results point to some psychological deficit among users. In the case of the 'amotivational syndrome' there are many reasons why the individual who does not want to involve himself with routine or competitive tasks should choose to take cannabis rather than alcohol.

There has been a reappraisal of the question of cannabis dependence in the years since 1980. For many years, this question was largely neglected. Recent studies have suggested that some cannabis users who want to stop or to cut down their use of cannabis find it very difficult to do so and they continue to use the drug despite the adverse effects that it may be having on their lives. The essence of a drug dependence problem consists of feelings of compulsion to use a drug, impaired capacity to control its use, discomfort or distress when not using it, and persisting with drug taking despite evidence that it is leading to problems. On this basis, there unquestionably are people who become dependent upon cannabis. Several attempts have been made to estimate the numbers of people who become dependent users. Such estimates vary widely and are of questionable validity. One suggestion is that maybe something in the order of one in 10 cannabis users may become dependent upon the drug. Several efforts have been made to establish treatment services for people with cannabis problems. These services appear to have met a real demand, since there has been no reluctance on the part of cannabis users to seek help with their drug problems.

The Escalation Theory

In the absence of any convincing evidence that cannabis is an especially dangerous drug, another justification for preventing people from using it is that, although it may not be dangerous in itself, it can lead on to other more dangerous forms of drug taking. In its usual form, the escalation theory states that smoking cannabis leads to heroin addiction.

The reason why so many people have been convinced that cannabis use leads to heroin addiction is that many (though not all) heroin addicts begin their drug career by smoking cannabis. Sometimes there is a similar link between other drugs and cannabis in that cannabis is often one of the first illegal drugs that people take. If, for the moment, we ignore the question of legality, most heroin addicts and other heavy drug users began by taking alcohol or tobacco (or even tea or coffee). Few people would care to argue the case that smoking cigarettes or drinking alcohol causes heroin addiction.

The escalation theory is riddled with errors – both of logic and of fact. In its report to the UK government, the Wootton Committee (1968) stated that there was no reason to believe that the use of cannabis led to other more harmful forms of drug taking. The Home Secretary of the day, James Callaghan, disagreed. So did some members of the medical profession. Dr Tylden, a London psychiatrist, called the report 'a junkie's charter' and stated that cannabis was the main cause of heroin addiction among young people in the UK. Many people continue to believe the escalation theory because they would like it to be true.

There is one slight vestige of truth in the escalation idea, but this has much more to do with the reasons why people want to take drugs and the social circumstances in which they take them than with any property of cannabis itself. Many people who use cannabis have a general interest in the use of drugs to change their states of consciousness. Because they must obtain cannabis illegally, they are likely to come into contact with members of the drug subculture who have access to other drugs. It is not entirely surprising, therefore, that some cannabis users should experiment with these drugs, perhaps on the grounds that if cannabis is illegal and it has not harmed them, maybe the other drugs will be equally pleasant and forgiving in their effects. A few may go on to become dependent upon these, but, under the circumstances, it is remarkable that so few cannabis users progress to other drugs.

In view of the different types and degrees of risk attached to cannabis use and heroin use, society should seek to protect cannabis smokers from any unnecessary escalation of risk. There are millions of people who have tried cannabis but a very much smaller population of heroin users. It is an act of grave social irresponsibility to continue to force cannabis users to buy their drugs from people who are also able to supply heroin or other injectable drugs.

Medical Uses of Cannabis

Although this book is primarily concerned with the non-medical use of drugs, it is interesting to note a recent and increasingly strong revival of interest in the medical potential of cannabis. During the 19th century cannabis preparations had been used to treat a wide variety of disorders. *The American Dispensatory* of 1851 recommended extracts of hemp as a treatment for gout, rheumatism, tetanus, convulsions, depression and delirium tremens. In England, Dr J.R. Reynolds, who was Queen Victoria's physician, described cannabis as 'one of the most valuable medicines we possess', and a 19th-century chemist's brochure recommending 'Indian Cigarettes' as a treatment for asthma described how

> … a refreshing sleep soon removes all the alarming symptoms. … To facilitate the use of Indian Cigarettes and enable the patient to benefit by them under all circumstances, whether travelling or walking, they are sold in elegant little cigar cases which can be carried in a breast-pocket with the least inconvenience.

With the rapid developments that occurred in drug research during the 20th century, interest in many natural medicines declined, and during the past 60 or 70 years it has been generally assumed that cannabis is primarily a recreational drug with no specific medical application. Recent research, however, has suggested that cannabis may have several potentially valuable applications.

Glaucoma is a disease of the eye caused by increased levels of pressure inside the eye, which can lead to progressive blindness. In the US, a series of trials were carried out in which glaucoma patients were treated with THC-based drugs. As a result, fluid pressure in the eye dropped by more than a third.

Cannabis-based drugs have also been found to be useful in the treatment of cancer. One of the most distressing side effects of the drugs used in the treatment of cancer is that they often cause nausea and vomiting. This is a major problem both for the patient and for the doctor. In some cases the side effects can be so severe that the patient suffers from vomiting or retching every few minutes for 12 to 24 hours a day. Occasionally the patient finds this so intolerable that they would rather have no treatment at all than face the persistent feeling of sickness. Although many different medications are available for prescription which are meant to prevent feelings of sickness, very few of these drugs have proved successful in suppressing the nausea caused by the anti-cancer medications.

In recent years, there has been an increasing interest in the medical applications of cannabis and this is reflected in the growing number of research articles in medical journals which suggest that cannabis can be an effective treatment for these side effects. For some years, doctors in the US have known of cancer patients who were also regular cannabis smokers and who reported that cannabis seemed to reduce the nausea and vomiting associated with the cancer treatment. Recent medical research confirms that cigarettes or capsules containing THC produced a remarkable reduction in the side effects from the primary treatment. In one study, THC reduced the incidence of nausea and vomiting from 72 per cent to a mere 6 per cent. In another investigation, more than two-thirds of a group of patients who had not benefited from conventional anti-emetic drugs improved when given THC. A recent book on the therapeutic applications of cannabis which was issued by the British Medical Association (1997) notes that 'cannabinoids are undoubtedly effective as anti-emetic agents in vomiting induced by anti-cancer drugs'.

In addition, there are possible applications for using cannabis to treat or manage such conditions as muscle spasticity associated with multiple sclerosis and spinal cord injury, and as a bronchodilator for patients with asthma. In 2002, the results of clinical trials were pointing to the positive results of a cannabis nasal spray as a treatment for some of the symptoms of multiple sclerosis such as pain and spasticity. Cannabis has also been used to increase appetite among patients receiving anti-cancer or other treatments which reduce appetite and lead to weight loss. This can be useful, for example, in the treatment of AIDS-related illnesses.

April 1999 saw the death of Brownie Mary, an elderly lady who, for many years, took it upon herself to bake 'special' chocolate brownies for the AIDS patients of San Francisco General Hospital. Despite being arrested from time to time, she became a figurehead of the movement to promote the medical uses of cannabis.

If cannabis does live up to expectations as a treatment for multiple sclerosis, glaucoma, as an aid to the treatment of cancer, or for other medical purposes, this will add a further complication to the discussion about the drug. For a long time it has been convenient for those authorities who wished to prohibit any use of the drug to deny that it has any beneficial effects at all. Despite the positive uses of the drug that have been reported in respectable medical journals, as recently as 1979 the American Food and Drug Administration and the Department of Health, Education and Welfare were still denying that cannabis was of any medical value. It is encouraging, however, to note that, at the time of writing this book, many of the states have permitted the medical use of cannabis and its active ingredient THC. Synthetic preparations of cannabis which can be used for therapeutic purposes are now available in several countries, including the UK (nabilone) and the US (dronabinol). However, there remains considerable resistance to the granting of a licence to permit its use in clinical practice.

The illegal use of cannabis for medical purposes is now widespread. In those countries where cannabis is classified as an illegal drug, this turns sick people and sometimes their carers into criminals. This is not sensible, and it is certainly not compassionate. It makes little sense as a medical response and it is ineffective as a preventive measure. A 1998 Select Committee report to the House of Lords recommended that the law regarding the medical use of cannabis should be changed, and that – even though to change the law in this way would mean that the UK might have to move 'out of step with many other countries – we consider that the Government should not be afraid to give a lead in this matter'.

The Evidence

I am well aware that some readers will take exception to things that I have written in this book. Nowhere is this more likely to be more obvious than in the present chapter on cannabis. So for those who are interested, I include a brief research commentary.

First of all, let me say that questions about the effects of a particular drug cannot be answered satisfactorily on the basis of any single experiment. In order to understand such questions we need to look at a whole series of experiments. There are hundreds of psychological factors that can interfere with an experiment to produce an unreliable result. If the same experiment were repeated by another researcher, a quite different result could easily be obtained. The chances of error decrease when the researcher has greater control over the conditions of their experiment. In drug research, the experimenter often has comparatively little control, but it is unfortunately true that a good deal of drug research has been made even weaker by the use of badly designed experiments.

Because of this, there will be many occasions when different experiments produce what seem to be directly conflicting results. The newspapers, which are always eager for some new sensation, seize upon any scientific report that has shock value, and as a result the general public is told only of the more lurid research findings; yet these are often the least reliable of all. Another factor that complicates matters is that the medical and scientific journals will usually only publish positive results: that is, results which show that drug X causes certain effects. For various reasons the journals are uninterested in research which fails to demonstrate any effect. This means that, if a hundred apparently identical experiments are carried out but only one of them suggests that cannabis may cause brain damage, that paper will almost certainly get published and receive wide coverage in the media; the other 99 will probably be rejected and forgotten.

The article published in *The Lancet* by Campbell and his associates (1971) is a case in point. The experiment is full of design faults and its conclusions are extremely suspect. Further research has not confirmed its results. Yet its shock value was enough to fire it into the headlines. Even today, people are still referring to it as proof that cannabis causes brain damage.

Since there are literally thousands upon thousands of scientific and medical reports dealing with cannabis, it would be both tedious and confusing for the reader to attempt to evaluate and summarize even the most important research studies. As a compromise, it is informative to look at the conclusions of the various expert committees that have wrestled with this problem.

Before the 1960s there was virtually no controlled experimental research on cannabis. The available evidence was based mainly upon rather haphazard observational methods. One of the best early summaries of this evidence is the seven-volume report that the Indian Hemp Drugs Commission submitted to the UK government in 1894. More than 1,000 witnesses were called before the Commission and, as today, all manner of conflicting opinions emerged. With respect to the possible physical harm caused by cannabis, the Commission concluded:

> The most striking feature of the medical evidence is perhaps the large number of practitioners of long experience who have seen no evidence of any connection between hemp drugs and disease, and when witnesses who speak to these ill effects from its moderate use are cross-examined, it is found that (a) their opinions are based on popular ideas on the subject; (b) they have not discriminated between the effects of moderate and excessive use of the drugs; (c) they have accepted the diseases as being induced by hemp drugs because the patients confessed to the habit; and (d) the fact has been overlooked that the smoking of hemp drugs is recognized as a remedial agent in asthma and bronchitis ... the evidence shows the moderate use of ganja or charas not to be appreciably harmful, while in the case of moderate bhang drinking the evidence shows the habit to be quite harmless.

The Commission did, however, suggest that long-term or excessive cannabis smoking may well be associated with disorders such as bronchial irritation, to which cigarette smokers are prone.

During the late 1930s, the US was in the grip of anti-cannabis fever. The American newspapers competed with each other in the race to publish more and more lurid headlines. As with public officials at other times and in other places, most politicians passively accepted the cannabis myths and used them for their own ends. One of the few people to hesitate before this wave of hysteria was Fiorello LaGuardia, the mayor of New York City, who asked the New York Academy of Medicine to prepare a scientific report on the issue. The LaGuardia Committee, consisting of 31 eminent doctors, psychologists, chemists, pharmacologists and sociologists, published its findings in 1944. Like the report of the Indian Hemp Drugs Commission, it was limited by the weaknesses inherent in much of the evidence available at that time. Nonetheless, the report represents a reasonable attempt to evaluate the evidence for and against the drug. It concluded that cannabis is not addictive in the medical sense of the term and that it did not lead to the use of drugs such as morphine or cocaine; it had no effect on the user's underlying personality and was not a cause of crime or juvenile delinquency. Finally, it commented that the current publicity about its catastrophic effects was completely without foundation.

In 1966, the Wootton Committee was set up to advise the UK government about cannabis. Its report, submitted in 1968, found no evidence that it led to crime or aggressive behaviour, or that it produced psychotic states in otherwise normal users:

> Having reviewed all the material available to us we find ourselves in agreement with the conclusions reached by the Indian Hemp Drugs Commission ... and the [LaGuardia Report], that the long-term consumption of cannabis in moderate doses has no harmful effects.

The next major investigation was authorized in America by Richard Nixon, and the Shafer Report, entitled *Marihuana, A Signal of Misunderstanding*, was submitted to Congress in 1972. It stated that there is no reliable evidence that cannabis causes genetic defects in man; from a public health viewpoint, the effects of cannabis in the body are of little significance and have little or no permanent effect; no objective evidence of brain damage has been shown (in direct contrast to alcohol). Cannabis causes no psychological deterioration, either intellectual or in terms of motivation; it does not produce physical dependence and 'the overwhelming majority' of cannabis users do not progress to other drugs. The report notes that 'marihuana's relative potential for harm to the vast majority of individual users and its actual impact on society does not justify a social policy designed to seek out and firmly punish those who use it'. This was especially true in view of the manifest failure of the law to prevent an estimated 24 million Americans trying the drug and eight million of them continuing to use it.

At about the same time, the Le Dain Commission reported its findings to the Canadian government. The Le Dain Report is a model of balanced and reasonable thinking and is well worth reading in full. Its conclusions are, as before, that cannabis is non-addictive, its short-term effects on the body are of little clinical significance and it carries no real dangers even in an overdose. The Commission took very seriously the suggestion that cannabis might cause lung damage, but found no evidence to support this view. As a postscript to the usual attempts to frighten young people away from drugs, the Commission advised:

> It is a grave error to indulge in deliberate distortion or exaggeration concerning the alleged dangers of a particular drug, or to base a programme of drug education upon a strategy of fear. It is no use playing 'chicken' with young people; in nine cases out of ten they will accept the challenge.

The abrupt and hostile dismissal that the Wootton Report received from the UK government is similar to the official response that has greeted the publication of each of these reports. Their conclusions and recommendations have generally either been ignored, because they failed to confirm the comfortable prejudices of the politicians, or else used as a way of catching votes. Prior to the 1979 Canadian federal election, all three major parties agreed that cannabis penalties should be reduced and that criminal records for cannabis offences should be eliminated. After the election, however, there was no sign of action from the new government, and it looks as though the issue is to be put back on the shelf.

In 1978, the Royal Commission into the Non-Medical Use of Drugs (South Australia) reached a sad and disillusioned conclusion about how these issues were being handled:

> The regulation of the non-medical use of cannabis has been the subject of many official inquiries. These inquiries have reached strikingly uniform conclusions on the effects of cannabis use, both on the user and the community as a whole. The failure of legislators … to accept these conclusions suggests that legislative responses are affected more by the perceived social status of users and the values and perhaps prejudices of powerful groups in the community, than by a careful evaluation of the pharmacological, medical and sociological evidence.

Since that time, South Australia was one of the first states to take action. The South Australian approach to the management of cannabis use offers an important, pragmatic and effective way of handling this issue. It deserves to be better known. Within South Australia a penalty system is now applied by the police to people in possession of cannabis. Although possession of cannabis has not been legalized, it has, in effect, been decriminalized, and is treated in much the same way as a parking offence. Those who are caught by the police for 'simple cannabis offences' are issued with an 'expiation notice', and provided that they pay this fine within 60 days, they are able to avoid prosecution. Payment of the fine avoids any further legal action, and they collect no criminal record as a result. Current fines are $A50 for possession of less than 25 grams (about one ounce) and $A150 for possession of 25–100 grams. Cultivation of 10 plants or fewer carries a fine of $A150. The average fine imposed in the years between 1991 and 1996 was $A74. More serious offences involving the cultivation or trafficking in large amounts of cannabis are still dealt with by the criminal law. One important function of the South Australian approach is that it acknowledges the different degrees of harm associated with the use of cannabis or with other illicit drugs, and provides a greater degree of separation between offences involving cannabis and those involving other drugs.

A somewhat similar approach was adopted in the Netherlands, where possession of cannabis was also treated as a misdemeanour leading to a fine and not as a criminal offence which may lead to imprisonment. In some parts of Holland, cannabis is on sale in youth centres and coffee bars. The Dutch view, as put forward by Eddy Engelsman, Head of Drugs Policy at the Ministry of Welfare in the Netherlands, was that:

> If criminal proceedings against cannabis users do not eliminate the problem but aggravate it, the law steps aside … The aim is to achieve a strict separation of the markets in which

hard drugs and soft drugs circulate … This … should not be misinterpreted as a tolerant or lenient policy. It is, on the contrary, a well-considered and very practical concept.

It is also one that has been found to work very well. The prevalence of cannabis use in the Netherlands has not rocketed out of control as a result of these changes in the law. Cross-national comparisons of rates of drug use are always tricky, but levels of cannabis use in the Netherlands are probably about the same as those in the US. More to the point, cannabis use in the Netherlands was probably declining slightly prior to the 1976 changes in Dutch drug policy, and the changes appear to have had little if any impact upon levels of use during the years immediately following the change.

Chapter 8

The Hallucinogens

Everything connected with the hallucinogenic drugs has aroused intense controversy. Nowhere are the problems of classifying drugs more obvious than in this chapter. Most drugs meet the defining requirements for membership of more than one class of drugs, and some fail to fit comfortably into any major class. There is not even agreement about what these drugs should be called. At different times they have been classified as psychedelics, psychotomimetics, psychodysleptics and hallucinogens.

'Psychedelic' is derived from the Greek words for mind (*psyche*) and visible (*delos*), and it was coined by the psychiatrist Humphrey Osmond in a correspondence with Aldous Huxley in 1956. Certainly, it captured much of Huxley's enthusiasm for his mescaline experiences, and it was later taken up in the 1960s by Timothy Leary and the psychedelic movement of the American hippies who regarded it as synonymous with 'mind-expanding'.

'Psychotomimetic' and 'psychodysleptic' carry entirely the opposite connotations. 'Psychotomimetic' means that the drug has effects which resemble those of the psychotic illnesses such as schizophrenia – and by implication, therefore, that they are undesirable. Whether or not LSD-induced states of mind do resemble the psychoses is discussed later in the chapter. The term itself is rejected not only because of its negative connotations, but also because it is such an ugly word. 'Psychodysleptic' is equally negative and equally ugly: this means 'mind-disrupting'.

There are other unfamiliar names for this category of drugs. The term coined by Louis Lewin, 'phantastica', has a pleasant ring to it and conveys a good deal of the quality of the drug effects. Another was suggested by Moreau – 'oneirogenic' (causing dreams). Again this is reasonably accurate, but both these terms must be rejected because of their unfamiliarity.

The final term, 'hallucinogenic', is misleading. These drugs do not generally cause true hallucinations in which the person becomes immersed in a world of unreality. The effects are more accurately described as perceptual distortions than as hallucinations, though the effects of these drugs also extend beyond perception. Changes in thought, mood and personality integration are all important effects, which are not really included in the term 'hallucinogenic'. What is worse, some of the drugs in this category – such as MDA and MMDA (see below) – tend to produce changes in self-awareness, and in mood and intellectual functioning, without any sensory distortions at all. However, despite its inaccuracies, 'hallucinogenic' is the term most commonly used, and even Dr Osmond who coined the term 'psychedelic' eventually adopted it. There is also some historical justification for using this word rather than its alternatives, since the mental voyages of sorcerers have been described as hallucinogenic.

Before the advent of the 20th-century synthetic alkaloids, most of the hallucinogenic drugs were derived from plants. Many of these plants have been used for magical and religious purposes (see Chapter 3). Some of these naturally occurring drugs are still used occasionally (for example, psilocybin); others are often mentioned but not often taken (for example, mescaline). Finally, some of the hallucinogenic drugs are seldom if ever used nowadays (belladonna, henbane, fly agaric). This chapter is concerned mainly with the drugs that are used (or discussed) most frequently.

Mescaline

Mescaline is one of the alkaloids of the peyote cactus which grows in Mexico. Peyote has played an important part in the religious traditions of Mexico for centuries. Mescaline first became known to science as a result of the interest of a young German pharmacologist, Louis Lewin. During the time he spent in America in 1886, he obtained some specimens of the cactus from which mescaline was subsequently extracted. 'No other plant brings about such marvellous functional modifications of the brain,' he wrote. Those who took the drug experienced

> … pleasures of a special kind. Even if these sensations merely take the form of sensorial phantasms, or of an extreme concentration of the inner life, they are of such a special nature and so superior to reality, so unimaginable … it is easy to understand why the Indians of old time venerated this plant as a god.

Oddly enough, Lewin himself experienced no such visions after taking the drug. It merely made him feel sick. Other famous men of the day were more fortunate in their experiences. Havelock Ellis, who took mescaline after reading reports of it in the *British Medical Journal*, found the visions that it produced entrancing. Colours seemed indescribably vivid and delightful. At the same time, it made him feel both physically healthy and intellectually acute. Much later, Aldous Huxley found the drug equally attractive.

In terms of its current availability and usage, mescaline is a rare drug. Although reports of the drug are fairly common among illicit drug users, what is called mescaline almost always turns out to be LSD – possibly adulterated with amphetamines. Among the hallucinogens seized and analysed by the London police, very few have contained any mescaline.

Psilocybin/Magic Mushrooms

Psilocybin is another hallucinogenic alkaloid which is derived from a plant, though in this case from a mushroom instead of a cactus. To the Aztecs, the mushroom was sacred: they called it *teonanacatl* which translates as 'flesh of the gods'. There are several different varieties of the psilocybin mushroom. Most are insignificant tawny-brown toadstools which seldom grow to a height of more than one or two inches. One of the common varieties is otherwise called the 'Liberty Cap' because the shape of the head of the mushroom resembles that of the hats worn during the French Revolution. These are a widespread species throughout Europe and America and grow on grasslands and pastures during the autumn months. An average hallucinogenic dose of psilocybin would appear to be in the region of 20–60 milligrams, though in its pure form the drug is seldom found on the black market. Samples of drugs called psilocybin, like mescaline, usually turn out to be adulterated forms of LSD.

MDA and MMDA

These semi-synthetic drugs are produced by a modification of the psychoactive ingredients in nutmeg and mace. Nutmeg and mace come from the same tree, *Myristica fragrans*. This is native to the East Indies, and produces a fruit about two inches in diameter. The seed is a dark brown or purple colour. This is the nutmeg, the outer covering of which is the mace. Both have been known as psychoactive drugs for thousands of years, though nowadays they are seldom used as a drug of choice. MDA and MMDA resemble the hallucinogens in many respects, though in others they are closer to central nervous system stimulants such as cocaine and the amphetamines.

DMT

DMT has a similar background. It is the active agent in many Central and South American snuffs such as those that Columbus described being used by the natives of Hispaniola. It is a major constituent of the virola tree bark. In its effects, it is like LSD. But whereas the LSD experience has been described as a long, strange journey, that of DMT has been compared to the experience of being shot out of a cannon. Its hallucinatory effects are intense, but short-lived, reaching a peak in five to 20 minutes, and ending after about half an hour. Because of this it has been called 'the businessman's trip'.

LSD

The most widely used and the best-known hallucinogenic drug is LSD (lysergic acid diethylamide). This is one of the most potent drugs known to man. Whereas other drugs are measured in milligrams (thousandths of a gram), doses of LSD are measured in micrograms – millionths of a gram. Doses as small as 20 micrograms produce effects similar to cannabis intoxication, but when it is taken for its full hallucinatory effects, doses of between 50 and 250 micrograms are more usual.

Weight for weight, LSD is about 5,000 times more powerful than mescaline and 200 times more potent than psilocybin. As a further measure of its potency, only about 1 per cent of the tiny amount originally taken reaches the brain. It is difficult to know how much LSD would constitute a lethal overdose. One estimate puts it at about 2 milligrams per kilo, or about 150,000 micrograms for the average man.

The drug was discovered in 1943 by Dr Albert Hofmann at Sandoz Laboratories in Switzerland. (Hofmann also synthesized psilocybin from the Liberty Cap mushroom.) One afternoon, while working on derivatives of ergot, he felt rather strange and, believing himself to be ill, went home. He lay down, and as he closed his eyes, he saw fantastic visions and vividly coloured kaleidoscopic patterns. After about two hours these symptoms disappeared. Some days later, Dr Hofmann took what he considered to be a small dose of one of the drugs that he had been working on, to see if it was responsible for the symptoms of the previous week. The small dose was one quarter of one milligram. With almost any other drug this would be unlikely to produce any effect at all. By the standards of LSD, however, 250 micrograms is a substantial dose, and Dr Hofmann was about to embark on a long and strange trip:

> My field of vision wavered and was distorted like the image in a curved mirror ... like the reflection in an agitated sheet of water ... with my eyes closed, colourful and changing fantastic images invaded my mind continuously. It was especially remarkable how all sounds ... were transposed into visual sensations, so that with each tone and noise a corresponding coloured image, changing in form and colour like a kaleidoscope was produced.

Synaesthesia is one of the more curious perceptual effects that LSD users sometimes report. It is an unusual but fascinating effect in which the senses seem to get mixed up. As a result the person has the experience of 'seeing' music or of 'hearing' colours.

The next day, Dr Hofmann felt tired but otherwise completely well. Indeed, he felt so well that he describes feeling as if the world were 'newly created'. Hofmann's description of his experiences is a model of careful objective reporting. It is all the more fascinating in that it represents the first-ever account of the LSD experience. We now know that any drug experience is powerfully influenced by the taker's expectations about how the drug might affect him. In Hofmann's case, the experience was untainted by any such ideas. His description picks out the three characteristic effects of the drug: the psychological changes in mood and thought processes, the physical changes and, most especially, the perceptual changes.

Visual perception is strikingly altered by the drug. One of the first signs of the drug taking effect is that the grey field that is seen with the eyes closed starts to become lighter. Later, this field becomes patterned with coloured lights. The patterns are usually described as kaleidoscopic, geometric or 'like a Persian carpet'. With increasing intoxication, the patterns become progressively less symmetrical and more complex. When the eyes are opened, ordinary objects seem to glow as if they were illuminated from within. Colours seem to be deeper and more intense, and not infrequently quite mundane objects seem to assume tremendous symbolic significance. At the peak of the drug experience, pseudo-hallucinations occur in which the person's visual perceptions are comparatively independent of the outside world. True hallucinations, however, are rare, though they do sometimes occur. Generally, they are linked to high doses of the drug, though some individuals may be more sensitive to LSD than others. Unlike the visual pseudo-hallucinations, in which the person is aware that their experiences are drug-induced, true hallucinations usually carry no such insight. The person mistakes their hallucinations for reality itself.

Thought processes are also altered by the drug. Thinking becomes non-logical, and often it has a strong magical quality to it. The person may believe that they can read the thoughts of other people or that they are able to transmit their own thoughts. Several people have been convinced that they could fly, and one or two unfortunate cases have occurred in which they actually tried to put their beliefs into practice. This delusional idea has even led to deaths.

These incidents were well publicized at the time, and the idea that LSD caused people to jump from windows under the impression that they could fly became a part of the assorted myths and misconceptions of drug taking. I have only seen one such case. This woman was referred to a drug unit by a consultant psychiatrist who had identified a case of 'LSD psychosis' on the basis of the flying incident. However, the role played by LSD in the incident is uncertain. It is quite likely that the attempt to fly owed more to the woman's unusual personality than to any drug effect. For instance, she continued to believe that she could fly long after the effects of the drug had worn off. But she also claimed to see the Virgin Mary outside her window, heard voices, regularly took all her clothes off 'so that I could be like the angels', and was seriously negligent about her personal hygiene. In the end, it was decided that she was suffering from a schizophrenic disorder which had developed independently of her use of drugs.

However, as with true hallucinations, serious delusional ideas of this sort are rare. What is more typical is that the user may have pseudo-delusional thoughts – incorrect or irrational ideas, but with some insight into their strangeness. Although the user may believe that they are having profound or brilliant ideas, any attempt to express them usually reveals only banal or fragmented thoughts.

LSD has some of its most striking effects on the personality of the user. During the peak of the LSD experience, the individual begins to lose their sense of personal identity. They seem to lose that pervasive sense of being oneself that characterizes our everyday experience. During the earlier stages of LSD intoxication the user is usually capable of erecting various psychological defences to guard against this, but as the effects increase in strength they tend to overwhelm the defences. As a result, the person moves from a sense of independent personal identity to feeling at one with the universe. Different people react to this in different ways. Some become euphoric or joyful, and regard the experience as a sort of mystical or religious revelation. Others are terrified by the apparent loss of their comfortable feelings of secure selfhood.

These major alterations in personality integration resemble either the transcendental or the psychotic experience. They are the heaven and hell of which Huxley wrote.

Although no one had experienced the effects of LSD before Hofmann, there had been numerous historical instances of people developing bizarre mental disturbances after eating flour contaminated by ergot. This purple fungus is a veritable chemical factory, and for centuries, during wet summers, this parasitic growth spoiled the rye crops from Spain through to Russia. Whether because of greed, ignorance or hunger, the spoiled flour was often eaten, with spectacular and distressing results. 'St Anthony's Fire' was characterized by visual disturbances in which the sufferer seemed to see a shimmering light surrounding things, making them look as though they were on fire. Consequently, it seemed as though people were being consumed by the fire. This impression was confirmed by the blackened fingers and toes that were another result of the poisoning (in fact, this was gangrene). Ergotism also led to mental disturbances, hallucinations and madness, and there are several well-documented descriptions of such epidemics during the Middle Ages. The derivatives of ergot now play a more domesticated role in the treatment of migraine headaches and in assisting delivery in childbirth.

Ever since its discovery, LSD has polarized attitudes and generated hysteria. Every conceivable claim has been made about it: that it causes insanity and irreversible brain damage, that it leads to profound spiritual enlightenment, that it causes genetic damage and that it is a powerful aid to artistic creativity. In fact, LSD seems to produce very few physiological changes other than dilated pupils, increased muscle tension and a slight incoordination. Despite the powerful effects that LSD has upon consciousness, it has been found to have surprisingly little effect upon the electrical activity of the brain. Several studies have been unable to detect any changes in subjects even after they had taken substantial doses of hallucinogenic drugs (up to 400 micrograms of LSD and 1,000 milligrams of mescaline). The only changes that have been detected seem to indicate that these drugs produce a slight desynchronization of brain rhythms similar to that produced by stimulant drugs. This desynchronization has no particular relevance to psychiatric disturbances and is probably of no clinical significance. Considering the impressive range of psychological effects that the drug produces, its physiological correlates are fairly unremarkable.

LSD and the Search for Mind Control

For many of our political leaders, the most seductive dream of all remains that of controlling the mind itself. For centuries there have been crude but comparatively efficient methods by which this dream might be pursued. The Holy Inquisition made a long and loving study of the theory and practice of such techniques. The discovery of LSD reawakened the ancient dream – and, with it, the fear that others might achieve the means of chemical conversion and use them against us.

Albert Hofmann described how the US Army repeatedly approached him with the request that he take a more active part in their research programmes. Much of this early 'research' was organized by the CIA during the 1950s and 1960s. The specialists (if the word encompasses such incompetence) concerned with LSD at that time worked in one of the many subdivisions of the agency. The euphemistically named Technical Services Staff (TSS) were interested in the application of biological and chemical material to spying, and within the TSS was the little-known Chemical Division, which specialized in the use of chemicals against specific individuals. Using chemicals rather than magic, the Chemical Division was concerned with such problems as whether LSD could be used to turn Russians into loyal Americans. Or (appalling thought) would the beliefs of the loyal American collapse before the chemical might of Soviet LSD? Rumours filtered through military intelligence that the Russians had made a deal with the Swiss pharmaceutical firm, Sandoz Laboratories, to obtain enough LSD for 50 million doses. Then another intelligence report suggested that Sandoz were trying to sell 10 kilos of LSD (enough for about 100 million doses) on the open market. Both reports were false, but they were sufficient to provoke the CIA to approach Sandoz with a deal of their own. Despite the fact that Sandoz had only manufactured 40 grams (about one and a half ounces) of the drug during the previous 10 years, they agreed to sell 100 grams of LSD to the US government every week for an indefinite period. Back home in the US, CIA men took LSD. It was given to army recruits and to mental hospital inmates. And it was given to people who had no idea that they had taken any drug, sometimes with tragic consequences. With the publication in 1975 of the report of the Rockefeller Commission, the public learned that the CIA's inept tinkering with LSD had led to the deaths of two men after they had been given the drug without their awareness.

There were other unforeseen consequences of the CIA's incompetence. So much LSD had been distributed throughout the US that the youth of America had become aware of the non-military uses of the new drug. The LSD research project at Timothy Leary's university had been funded by the CIA. By a supreme twist of irony, the CIA's search for a mind-control drug had led it into the role of pusher. By the mid-1960s, a whole counterculture had evolved, centred upon the West Coast of America. LSD had ceased to be simply a drug. It had become symbolic of a way of life, and Richard Nixon's hatred and contempt for 'college punks' and hippies led to talk of introducing the death penalty for possession offences.

Of Chromosomes and Hallucinogens

Few scientific questions have been so obscured by the emotional over-involvement of scientists as this issue of whether or not certain drugs can cause genetic damage in those who use them. The same question has been raised about every one of the illicit drugs, but most especially about LSD. As in other areas of science, when emotions run high the standards of scientific enquiry are allowed to fall. The investigator knows in advance what they want to find. Consequently, the quality of experimental research in this area has often been abysmal. It has left a blot upon the entire study of cellular and chromosomal function.

   The spectre of genetic damage first attached itself to LSD in 1967 after an article appeared in the journal *Science*. This reported that, when human blood cells were exposed to LSD, the cells showed some chromosome breakage. Within a matter of days, this disturbing but otherwise rather vague and ambiguous finding had been translated by newspapers and television into an incontrovertible 'fact'. Parallels were drawn with the thalidomide disaster, and unpleasantly sensational reports appeared linking articles about LSD with pictures of deformed children. The impact of these pitiful photographs was sufficiently powerful to override any reasoned objections at the time.

   Yet, in scientific terms, the original article was so weak that none of this panic could possibly have been justified. The only explanation as to why it provoked an anti-drug crusade of such intensity is that the public, and more especially the media, needed this sort of campaign. The *Science* article relied heavily upon observations made on a 51-year-old schizophrenic patient who had been given LSD on 15 occasions while in hospital. But he had also regularly been given two tranquillizing drugs, Librium and chlorpromazine. These are among the most commonly used drugs in psychiatry, and both are now known to cause chromosomal breakage.

   If any weight can be attached to single case studies of the sort that originally set off the chromosome panic (and this is in itself rather doubtful), it is worth mentioning the analysis that was made using Timothy Leary as the subject. Despite the fact that Leary had taken LSD in spectacular amounts and on repeated occasions, no evidence was found to suggest abnormally high levels of chromosomal breakage.

   But before going any further into this particular issue, it is necessary to remind oneself that even the experts are in considerable doubt about such basic issues as what actually counts as chromosomal breakage, and how we should interpret the significance of any breakages that are identified on the microscope slide. To the layman, chromosomal breakage certainly sounds more sinister than it really is. Chromosomal breaks have been observed in the cells of many perfectly normal individuals. The argument turns on the question of whether such breaks occur more often in LSD users. None of the sensational reports have even bothered to tell their readers that many other quite mundane substances have also been linked with chromosomal breakage. These include caffeine, aspirin, antibiotics and even water unless it has been twice distilled. It is notable that the incidence of chromosomal breaks among people who have used adulterated black-market drugs is more than three times as high as among those who have taken pharmacologically pure LSD.

   Now that more research (and better research) has been done on this question, it is beginning to seem increasingly unlikely that LSD causes chromosomal aberrations. The few reports that suggest the drug does cause damage of this sort have exposed cells to massive concentrations of LSD and for unrealistically long periods of time. Even so, they have failed to prove that the resulting damage is any greater than that produced by many commonly used substances. One study found that aspirin and

LSD led to comparable levels of chromosomal breakage; in another study, one of the largest experimental investigations of chromosomal damage in LSD users, the authors found no evidence that LSD caused any change in the level of chromosomal abnormalities. During the course of this investigation, five out of the 50 subjects gave birth to seven normal, healthy infants (four boys and three girls).

Hallucinogenic Drugs and Psychological Medicine

Many people know that LSD (and some of the other hallucinogenic drugs) have been used in psychiatry. Few realize quite how extensively they have been used. Between 1950 and the mid-1960s, more than 1,000 articles were published dealing with more than 40,000 patients. Historically, medical interest in the psychiatric application of such drugs probably dates back to Moreau's work with cannabis. In his treatise, *Hashish and Mental Illness* (1845), Moreau asserted that 'There is not a single elementary manifestation of mental illness that cannot be found in the mental changes caused by hashish', from simple manic excitement to frenzied delirium.

In the late 19th and early 20th centuries, mescaline was regarded as a chemical model of the psychotic disorders and was occasionally prescribed for the treatment of certain psychosomatic complaints. But it was not until the discovery of LSD that a real interest developed in the therapeutic application of such drugs. One of the initial hopes of LSD (as of cannabis and mescaline) was that it might provide a chemical model of unusual states of consciousness. For the physician, the most immediate interest was in the relevance of such drugs to schizophrenia. If we could discover how LSD affected the brain, the hope was that we would then be able to apply that knowledge to the treatment of the psychotic disorders.

Today, this hope has almost completely vanished. Despite the many similarities between the experiences of the LSD-intoxicated individual and the schizophrenic, there are also many significant differences. Unlike the schizophrenic, whose hallucinations are usually auditory, the person on LSD tends to have perceptual distortions or visual hallucinations, and LSD-induced mood states tend towards the emotional extremes rather than the more usual schizophrenic apathy. These and other differences led many researchers to question the value of LSD intoxication as a model of schizophrenia, though the main reason why research into this topic fell out of favour may have more to do with the fact that such research was largely unproductive. Certainly, no naturally occurring chemical has been discovered that might explain the development of the psychoses, as was originally hoped.

LSD made more impact upon psychiatry as an aid to therapy. Many people who have taken LSD have reported that their lives have been changed for the better as a result. In one study, normal subjects were given a single high dose of LSD and mescaline. Several months later, more than three-quarters of them stated that they were happier, less anxious, more able to love other people and more able to understand themselves. As many as 78 per cent described it as the greatest thing that had ever happened to them. It was hoped that LSD might have similar beneficial effects upon people suffering from various psychological difficulties. Some therapists relied on a single administration of a large dose to induce dramatic changes in the patient's view of himself. In some ways, it was meant to resemble a mystical experience or the process of religious conversion. Although this form of therapy rested on very doubtful theoretical foundations, it had been linked to the work of a psychologist, Abraham Maslow, on peak experiences.

Peak experiences are moments of pure, positive happiness when the individual is free from all their normal doubts, anxieties and tensions, when they lose their sense of self-consciousness. Maslow regarded peak experiences as being therapeutically beneficial in the sense that they led to a symptomatic improvement in people who suffered from various forms of psychological disorder and, more generally, in that they had a positive influence upon people's lives. Many people who have taken LSD have described it in precisely these terms. LSD was also used in psychiatry through the repeated administration of smaller doses of the drug in conjunction with psychoanalytically oriented psychotherapies. By the middle of the 1960s, there were 18 treatment centres in Europe which used LSD in this way.

In practice, various combinations of drug administration and psychotherapy evolved. These were used to treat virtually every form of disorder to which the psychiatrist is exposed: anxiety disorders, depression, sexual problems, alcoholism, schizophrenia and even drug addiction were treated this way. LSD was also used with dying patients. Aldous Huxley was so profoundly impressed by his spiritual experiences after taking mescaline that he asked to be given the drug as he was dying. His wife gave him two doses of mescaline during the day and as he lay in bed he said little but gazed at his wife with an expression of love and happiness. His wife wrote of his death, 'Is his way of dying to remain for us, and only for us, a relief and a consolation, or should others also benefit from it? Aren't we all nobly born and entitled to nobly dying?'

Several research studies have looked at the uses of LSD in this context. The final months of life for someone dying of cancer are often marked by depression, psychological isolation, anxiety and pain. Even the efforts of doctors and nurses to keep the person alive can contribute towards the patient's unhappiness. LSD was originally given to cancer patients to discover if it relieved their pain. Although it had some success in this respect, its psychological effects were of far greater significance. These were explored in some detail at the Spring Grove Hospital in Maryland during the 1960s by Dr Pahnke, who was a doctor of divinity as well as a psychiatrist.

Of the patients who were given LSD, none were harmed even though some were physically in poor condition at the beginning of the trial. About a third of them were unmoved by the experience, and a third reported some benefit. More interestingly, the remainder appear to have experienced dramatic gains after taking LSD. As a result of what Dr Pahnke describes as a 'psychedelic mystical experience', these patients became more able to tolerate their physical pain: psychologically they showed an increase in their peace of mind and a decrease in their anxiety and depression. But most striking of all was the change in their attitudes towards death. After the LSD experience, they showed less fear of death.

Many of these investigations that were carried out into the therapeutic uses of LSD can be criticized from a scientific point of view, and few should be regarded in any way as conclusive. However, all available surveys suggest that the use of LSD in therapy is not especially dangerous, and although most of the early expectations about the therapeutic potential of the hallucinogenic drugs remain unfulfilled, it is surprising to find that these drugs are almost never used in psychological medicine today. There is no longer even an experimental interest in them. The reasons for this have more to do with the irrationality of human psychology than with any process of scientific or medical evaluation. The LSD crusades (both for and against the drug) have made it all but impossible to hold a rational discussion about the possible benefits associated with these drugs.

Ecstasy MDMA

> The drug takes away all your neuroses. It takes away the fear response. There is an overwhelming feeling of peace. ... You feel open, clear, loving. I can't imagine anyone being angry under its influence, or feeling selfish or mean, or even defensive. You have a lot of insights into yourself, real insights, that stay with you after the experience is over.

This is not a 1960s statement about LSD. It is from the *New York Magazine*, 1985, and it is about 'ecstasy', a later arrival on the drug scene which revived many issues from the LSD saga.

Actually, ecstasy is not a new drug. It was first synthesized and patented in Germany in 1914 and was developed as an appetite suppressant, though it was never marketed. It is synthesized from molecular components of methylamphetamine and safrole from either sassafras or nutmeg. It is otherwise known as MDMA and is similar in its chemical structure to MDA, though the two drugs have different effects.

Ecstasy is a difficult drug to categorize. Like LSD it leads to changes in states of consciousness, but unlike LSD it does not produce hallucinogenic effects, nor does it usually lead to any disturbances in the person's grasp of reality. The changes in consciousness that occur after taking ecstasy tend to be more associated with emotional states. Many users find that the experience is very sensual. Ecstasy has sometimes been described as an 'entactogen'. Such drugs occupy an intermediate position between stimulants and hallucinogens. As well as causing stimulation similar to that of amphetamines, they usually induce a pleasant, easily controllable emotional state with relaxation and feelings of happiness. In higher doses they can have hallucinogenic effects though they lead to less distortion of normative consciousness than classic psychedelics, such as LSD.

Doses are generally in the range of 75–150 milligrams and the effects start within about half an hour of taking the drug by mouth. The peak effects tend to occur over the next hour or so, and then fade over the next two hours. In the same way that arguments about LSD were polarized, views about ecstasy have also tended to present it either as a sort of miracle drug which has vast psychotherapeutic potential or simply as one more drug of abuse.

The drug has been used in psychotherapy for purposes that have somewhat lyrically been described as 'the untying of psychic knots'. It has been given with some success to patients with long-term or terminal illnesses such as cancer, to help them come to terms with their impending death and to help them communicate their feelings to family and friends. In marital therapy it has helped to break down long-standing destructive barriers between husbands and wives. Those therapists who have used it claim that ecstasy has low abuse potential when used in clinical doses and under supervision.

One of its main uses has been as a 'dance drug'. From about 1988, and directly following the media promotion of the drug under the guise of publicizing the dangers of ecstasy, there developed a strong youth culture involving ecstasy and House music centred around night clubs and all-night 'raves'. The supporting music was fast and accompanied by flashing lights. Ecstasy was hailed as the drug that 'could make a white man dance'. Recent surveys in the UK and the US have estimated that between 5 and 13 per cent of young adults have tried ecstasy. Estimates taken in clubs and raves have found prevalence rates of up to 80 per cent.

Among the more common side effects of ecstasy are tension in the jaw and grinding of the teeth. Anxiety, heart palpitations and, in a few cases, paranoid delusions have been reported. As with 'bad trips' on LSD, 'talk down' methods have generally been sufficient to deal with these adverse effects. The drug also produces increases in blood pressure, and anyone with high blood pressure or heart problems would be well advised not to use it, as would people with a history of diabetes or fits. Also, the pharmacological effects of ecstasy may be compounded by the exertion that follows hard and fast dancing. Rave dancers have been advised to wear loose clothing, to drink plenty of water or non-alcoholic liquids, and to stop dancing when feeling exhausted. Some club owners provide 'chill-out' rooms with seating and air conditioning to help cooling. Among the complications that have been recorded are extremely high body temperatures, collapse, convulsions and acute kidney failure.

A small number of deaths have occurred after taking ecstasy. Two mechanisms can lead to fatal responses. The best known is hyperthermia – overheating due to a combination of the drug's effects on the temperature-regulating centres in the brain during high levels of exertion in overheated environments. Equally dangerous but less well-known is the body's reaction to excessive intake of water (hyponatraemia). Most ecstasy users are so aware of the risks of overheating and dehydration that they can fatally overdo the drinking. Where deaths have occurred, these have received a huge and disproportionate amount of media attention, with the consequent misperception that ecstasy carries a high risk of fatality. Such misperceptions are also held in high places: the Home Secretary chose to reject the recommendation of the Runciman Report that ecstasy should not be included with Class A drugs such as heroin and crack cocaine by asserting that 'ecstasy is a killer'.

One of the concerns lurking in the shadows behind ecstasy is the suggestion that it may cause long-lasting damage to the brain. Many research studies which have been conducted with animals have shown that ecstasy can cause damage to specific neural pathways in the brain that may lead to impairments of memory and learning. These effects have been most commonly linked to reductions in the release of the important brain chemical, serotonin.

This claim ('drugs cause brain damage') is one area where researchers and others have cried wolf so often that it can be difficult to provide a clear interpretation of the research. The animal studies have often made no attempt to duplicate the typical conditions under which ecstasy is used. So, animal studies have used very much higher doses than those which would be taken by humans, more frequent dosing schedules, and different routes of drug administration (for example, by injection, sometimes directly into the brain). There are also important differences in response to ecstasy between different types of animals. Rats, for example, respond to ecstasy quite differently from mice. There are even strain differences in drug response within the same animal type (some laboratory rats are highly sensitive to the effects of ecstasy whereas others are much less so).

The relatively few studies that have been done with human ecstasy users have not clarified whether adverse neurotoxic effects are found only among excessive users of the drug or whether they can also occur among occasional users. Human studies have often failed to control for other factors which could be directly relevant to any such adverse effects (for example, the purity and strength of illegally synthesized ecstasy, the general health status of the user, diet, or even use of alcohol and other drugs). Several studies have uncritically reported neurobiological changes as if these were synonymous with 'damage'. And there has been surprisingly little research into the critical question of the extent to which the neurobiological changes that may be detected by extremely sensitive brain imaging techniques may be reversible. Many of the long-term abnormalities that have been found in animal studies even after exposure to repeated high doses of ecstasy have been only subtle.

Nonetheless, the research from the animal studies does show clear and often persistent changes to the neurochemistry of the brain, and these findings raise serious anxieties about the potential for damage to users of ecstasy. Recent scientific reviews have tended to use phrases such as 'alarming but not conclusive' or 'patchy and partly contradictory' or, more worryingly, 'not yet proven, but highly likely' when trying to summarize the evidence. This issue may not be fully clarified for some years.

As with other illicit drugs, there is the danger of buying a drug with unknown constituents. Some of the 'ecstasy' being sold contains ecstasy-amphetamine mixtures, amphetamines only or LSD-amphetamine mixtures. An occasional substitute for ecstasy is ketamine: an anaesthetic with analgesic and hallucinogenic properties. Ketamine was first synthesized in 1962 and is widely used as a veterinary anaesthetic. Its use as a recreational drug dates back to the 1960s. Some users take it as a dance drug and for its hallucinatory effects, which are shorter-acting than for LSD. Ketamine also has some similarities to phencyclidine ('angel dust' or PCP). Some unpleasant acute reactions have been recorded and the long-term effects of ketamine are not known. Because of its respiratory depressant effects, and its unpredictability when used with other drugs, it is unsafe to take it at the same time as alcohol, Valium or opiates. For the user who thinks they have taken ecstasy, the side effects of these substitutes can be unpredictable and alarming. For many ecstasy users their most pressing drug problem may be how to buy the genuine product rather than a more dangerous substitute.

Chapter 9

Archetypal Drugs of Abuse

Heroin and the Opiates

Morphine (named after Morpheus, the god of dreams), was first derived from opium in 1803. In 1843, Alexander Woodin invented the hypodermic needle, thereby laying the necessary foundation for the drug addiction that is often thought to be such a typically 20th-century problem. The history of opiate addiction stretches back over thousands of years, but it is only very recently that the problem has assumed its current form.

Interestingly, wars have played a central part in the historical development of the current problem. Both the Crimean War (1851–56) and the American Civil War (1861–65) contributed towards the development of opiate abuse. But whereas the Crimean War made little lasting impact on Europe, the Civil War left a permanent impression upon America. The troops had free access to morphine and opium which they carried so that they could give some relief to their wounded colleagues during the fighting. The Surgeon General, in his contemporary *Medical and Surgical History of the War of the Rebellion*, commented: 'Opium … was used almost universally in all cases of severe wounds and was found particularly useful in penetrating wounds of the chest. … When used with discretion, there can be no question of its great utility.'

The front-line soldier, famed for his brutality and licentiousness, is less often credited with a remarkably inventive turn of mind. It is, perhaps, hardly surprising that he found other uses for his drugs. Whether administered for the relief of pain or for other less official purposes, opiate addiction grew to such proportions that it became variously known as 'the soldiers' sickness' and 'the army disease'. At this time the drug was legally available in the US, and after the war many physicians encouraged soldier addicts to buy their own hypodermic syringes so that they could continue to inject themselves with opiates.

It is always difficult to put any reliable figure on the incidence of drug addiction. One estimate relating to the period between the end of the Civil War and the Harrison Act of 1914 estimated the number of US opiate addicts at about 200,000. Another estimate suggests a minimum of 264,000 addicts by 1920. Whatever the precise numbers, by this time the problem had assumed alarming proportions. In 1921, the Chief Medical Officer of New York City noted that Americans were consuming 12 times as much opium as any other people in the world. More than 750,000lbs were being imported every year, even though legitimate medical uses of the drug accounted for only 70,000lbs.

The year 1898 saw a further significant development. A new drug which had first been synthesized at St Mary's Hospital, London, was introduced. This new preparation was widely held to be both safe and non-addictive. The new miracle drug was used in the treatment of morphine addiction. It was given a name which reflected the high expectations that everyone held about it – heroin (from 'hero', meaning someone of superhuman strength, someone favoured by the gods). As with so many other miracle drugs, the miracle turned out to be sadly tarnished. The drug certainly helped morphine addicts to stop taking morphine: with some speed, they switched to heroin addiction. It is surprising that there should have been so few initial reservations about the value of heroin in the treatment of morphine addiction, since heroin is derived from morphine. (Its pharmacological name is diacetylmorphine.)

The next major event took place during the Second World War. A new opiate-type drug was synthesized by German chemists. Originally named Dolophine, in honour of Adolf Hitler, the new drug was uncovered after the war by an intelligence group of the US Department of Commerce during an investigation of the Axis pharmaceutical industry. This drug, methadone, was later to play an important role in the search for a medical cure for drug addiction.

These, then, are the three main opiates. Among their lesser known cousins are pethidine and dipipanone (Diconal). Although the different opiates differ somewhat in their relative strength and in their overall duration of effect, they have broadly the same effects. Each produces an initial stimulation of the central nervous system, followed by a more marked depressant effect. This shows itself in drowsiness, changes in mood and mental clouding.

In their legitimate role, the opiates are mainly used to relieve pain, though it is not clear how much this pain-relieving property owes to physiological and how much to psychological effects. A standard experimental technique that is used to measure the effects of drugs on pain is to apply a small heat stimulus to the skin. The temperature can be gradually increased until the subject reports that it is painful. After taking morphine, the pain threshold is only slightly altered. If these drugs were used only for their physiological effects, they would be of little use as analgesics. Their advantage as pain relievers is that, although the person can still feel the pain, they are no longer afraid of it – and it is this fear and anxiety that is associated with pain which causes so much distress. Rather than blocking out the pain directly, heroin and morphine relieve the anxieties which are associated with pain.

The use of heroin to treat severe and intractable pain is not regarded as controversial within the UK. Heroin is carried by GPs and is used to treat patients who have had heart attacks. It is also is used to treat people who are in severe pain as a result of serious illnesses such as cancer. In this role, almost all UK doctors see the drug as a useful adjunct to their pharmacopoeia. If a patient is facing a terminal illness and heroin can be used to ease their suffering, it seems both stupid and callous to refuse to take advantage of any drug which can help.

Some patients who receive potent opiates to relieve their pain may become addicted. In the case of fatal illnesses, this is often a relatively minor and secondary consideration. One case of a patient who received opiates to relieve the pain of a wound received during battle (in the First World War) was Hermann Goering. He became addicted to morphine and continued to use it throughout the 1930s and 1940s. It was not until the Nuremberg trials after the Second World War that he was withdrawn from opiates.

The popular view of heroin use and especially of heroin addiction almost exclusively associates it with the act of injecting the drug into a vein. Intravenous injection gives an almost instantaneous effect – the rush or flash – which is much prized by the drug taker. The intensity of the rush is something difficult to describe: the nearest analogy for the non-user seems to be that of sexual orgasm. The dramatic initial effect is extremely pleasurable to many (though not all) first-time users. However, it soon dies away, to be replaced by the drug 'high', which is usually described as a feeling of calm, detached and dreamy relaxation.

There are important reasons to separate the use of heroin from the way in which the drug is used. There have been many times and many situations in which heroin has been used by other routes of administration. In the Far East, heroin has been smoked in the form of granules on the tip of a cigarette (called 'ack ack'). In many parts of South-West Asia (such as Pakistan and India) heroin is usually smoked. But even in Western countries, heroin has often been used in ways other than by injection. In the US, up to 1930, heroin was most often sniffed. Even when it was injected it was usually injected into muscle tissue (with a slower onset of the drug effect) and addicts deliberately tried to avoid injecting into a vein because they believed it to be dangerous. The spread of intravenous injection seems to have spread during the 1930s, and by 1945 it was the predominant pattern. This pattern of intravenous use is still very common among heroin addicts in many Western countries, but since the late 1970s another pattern of use has emerged: heroin smoking, or 'chasing the dragon'.

Chasing the dragon usually involves heating the heroin on a piece of tinfoil and inhaling the fumes through a small tube. Smoking heroin in this way gives an effect which is just as rapid but generally less intense than injecting it. The act of inhaling the drug, however, seems far less dangerous than pushing a needle into a vein and, for this reason, it has proved to be a seductive pathway into heroin use for many people.

In London, the percentage of heroin users who took their first dose of heroin by chasing the dragon steadily increased from less than 10 per cent before 1974, through about 60 per cent between 1980 and 1984 and reached 94 per cent in the period after 1990. Within a relatively short period of time the predominant pattern of *initiation* into heroin use had changed from injection to chasing. Virtually all new heroin users in London now take the drug for the first time by chasing the dragon and not by injection. In some other parts of the world, chasing the dragon or other forms of heroin smoking provide the dominant technology of heroin administration. Heroin smoking has been common in Hong Kong since the beginning of the twentieth century and in Pakistan and India it has been estimated that there are currently more than a million heroin smokers.

The difference between injectable and smokeable heroin can be found in the chemical composition of the drug. Drugs such as heroin can exist in two forms – as a base or as a salt – with the core part of the drug (the heroin) being pharmacologically identical, as are its effects. However, the salt dissolves in water and has a high melting point, which makes it suitable for injection but not for smoking. The base chemical, on the other hand, is fat-soluble. It does not dissolve in water, but is more volatile and on heating the substance forms a vapour which can be inhaled. Base forms of the drug need to be transformed (usually by the addition of some sort of acid, like lemon juice) before they can be dissolved and injected.

Many heroin chasers falsely believe that heroin is not addictive if it is smoked, but people who regularly use heroin by chasing the dragon are at risk of becoming psychologically and physically dependent upon the drug. However, recent research has suggested that chasing heroin may produce less severe dependence problems than injecting it, though many chasers also become severely dependent upon heroin. Chasing the dragon may also be risky if it serves as a 'gateway' to injecting. As the user becomes more severely dependent upon smoking heroin and the costs begin to mount, the temptation to switch to the more efficient method of injection may also increase.

Heroin may also be taken by snorting (intranasally). Heroin snorting has been an occasional though rare means of using heroin by early experimental users in the UK for many years. Those who wish to continue using the drug tend to move fairly quickly to other routes of administration, typically becoming chasers or injectors. Ominously, the US has seen increasing signs of heroin snorting in recent years. As with chasing, the apparently lesser risks of this route can attract experimenters from those who would be repelled by the idea of injecting and, as a result, heroin snorting can also be a seductive new path into heroin use.

In principle, and also in practice, heroin users may change their main route of administration between snorting, chasing and injecting. However, the likelihood of such transitions are biased towards more efficient (and more risky) routes of administration. In a study of such transitions among heroin users in London, we found that users were twice as likely to switch from snorting to chasing or to injecting as to make the reverse transition. Similarly, chasers were twice as likely to move on to injecting as to switch back to chasing. However, it is still interesting that some heroin users do move back from intravenous use of the drug. Most heroin users are well aware of the health risks associated with injecting and, for those who switched from injecting to chasing, concern about the risks of HIV and other health problems were amongst the most common reasons for making this change. Indeed, one of the very first health problems to be linked with heroin injection occurred when an epidemic of malaria broke out among American injectors who were sharing infected equipment in New York City during the 1930s.

It is doubly unfortunate that chasing the dragon appeared on the UK scene at the same time as the drug became more easily available. Greatly increased quantities of heroin began to be smuggled into Western Europe during the late 1970s and early 1980s. Heroin is currently more widely available in the UK, and used by more people, than ever before. Its cost (allowing for inflation) has dropped by almost half since 1978. Using heroin is no longer a bizarre and dangerous habit confined to a small number of junkies in central London. The drug and those who use it are spread throughout the country and throughout all sections of society, and the casualties of heroin are becoming more obvious. At one time, few people in the UK knew anyone who had ever seen a heroin addict. Now, too many people know a friend or family member who has or has had a heroin problem.

The opiates have had a powerful influence upon our attempts to understand drug dependence. Indeed, opiate addiction has served as a yardstick by which other forms of drug dependence have been measured. The two most characteristic features of physical addiction to drugs both apply to the opiates: the development of tolerance to the drug effects, and the withdrawal syndrome.

Tolerance

Tolerance shows itself in the need to increase the dose of the drug to obtain the effects that were previously obtained with a lower dose. For the first-time user, or when it is used medically, an effective dose of heroin would be in the region of 5–10 milligrams, and for the non-tolerant user a dose of 200mg would probably be fatal, though non-addicts have survived overdoses in excess of 350mg. As the regular user increases their tolerance, they can take ever-increasing doses of the drug. Among the addicts at London clinics during the 1970s who received prescriptions for pharmacologically pure heroin, some were taking daily doses of up to 900mg. This was the dose of a Canadian man who had been a heroin addict for more than 40 years. He had reduced his intake of drugs to this level from more than 1,600mg, and when he first attended one of the London drug clinics there was some doubt among the staff as to whether he could really be using such a large amount. Because of this he was asked to inject his drugs under supervision. After his first injection of 160mg of heroin he said he felt 'less fidgety' and went off to have lunch. During a four-hour period he injected himself seven times with a total of 1,000mg of heroin and 600mg of cocaine. In the recent Dutch heroin trial, addicts were given up to 1,000mg per day, with a maximum single administration of 400mg.

In countries where heroin is manufactured, some users have developed tolerance to astronomical doses of heroin. In some parts of Pakistan, daily doses in excess of 4 grams (4,000mg) are typical and doses of 10 grams per day are not unknown. The highest dose user that I have seen was a man in Pakistan who was smoking 16 grams per day. Even when this dose is adjusted for the presence of adulterants (the average purity level at the time was 30 per cent) this is a remarkable daily dose of 4,800mg per day. There seems to be no known limit to the amount of opiates that the body is capable of tolerating.

Tolerance to some effects of the opiates occurs after even a single dose of the drug; other effects are partially resistant to tolerance; and yet other effects are almost completely resistant to the development of tolerance. Most textbooks of pharmacology and most addicts are in agreement that the euphoria produced by opiates disappears fairly rapidly with repeated use of the drug. At one time it was thought that all opiate addicts would inevitably take larger and larger doses of drugs in order to compensate for this tolerance to the euphoria of the initial injection. This does not always happen. Many addicts stabilize their daily intake of drugs at a particular level and, provided that they are able to obtain a regular supply, seem to be happy to go on using that amount. Because of this, the tendency to increase the amount of drugs used is better thought of as satisfying some sort of psychological need rather than merely as a reflection of physical needs.

The Withdrawal Syndrome

Above everything else, this is the most distinctive feature of physical addiction: it is certainly the most visible and the most dramatic manifestation, and it has had a profound influence on almost every theory that has been put forward to explain drug addiction. Despite this, few people have understood the nature of the opiate withdrawal syndrome, and the myths surrounding it could fill a whole book. A few of these are discussed in Chapter 11.

The withdrawal syndrome begins to show itself within hours of the drug effects wearing off. During the early stages, the addict may feel drowsy and be subject to frequent bouts of yawning. After about 24 hours they become anxious and apprehensive: they are restless and find it difficult either to sleep or to rest comfortably. Glandular secretions increase; the eyes and nose run, and salivation and sweating are increased. As the process develops, the bones, muscles and joints ache, and the addict may also suffer from vomiting and diarrhoea. Stomach cramps are another common symptom at this stage.

Two phrases of junkie slang are derived from the symptoms of withdrawal. 'Cold turkey' refers to the appearance of the skin. The sweating, hot and cold flushes, and piloerection (gooseflesh) can make the skin look very much like that of a cold turkey. As a response to drug deprivation, there is often a slight tremor in the limbs, with occasional twitches of the legs. This produces a sudden kicking movement, hence 'kicking the habit'. Among the more esoteric withdrawal symptoms that have been reported are involuntary ejaculation in the male and spontaneous orgasms in the female addict. With the exception of these curious symptoms, opiate withdrawal is comparable to a bad dose of influenza – very unpleasant but certainly not intolerable.

If left untreated, the acute phase of heroin withdrawal peaks at 48–72 hours. Usually, the withdrawal syndrome is treated by various sorts of drugs to make it less uncomfortable. Addicts commonly treat their own withdrawal by using tranquillizers. These may also be used as part of medically supervised withdrawal treatments. However, heroin withdrawal does not necessarily require drug cover. Many addicts manage to detoxify themselves without using any other drugs, especially if they have sufficient psychological and social support to help them through withdrawal.

Although the withdrawal syndrome has an obvious physiological foundation, it also has strong psychological and social determinants. The degree of discomfort that addicts experience during withdrawal can be significantly reduced by providing them with accurate information about what will happen and with simple reassurance about the course of withdrawal. Most addicts can successfully complete withdrawal within a week or two. This is true even of the highest dose users. In Pakistan, I have seen addicts who were withdrawn abruptly from massive doses of heroin with only 'symptomatic' treatments of tranquillizers and anti-diarrhoeal drugs and who were feeling better within 10 days of starting treatment.

However, during the 1930s and 1940s, some doctors who were treating opiate addicts began to suspect that the withdrawal effects lasted very much longer. Since then, researchers have confirmed that it can take months for the body to return to a completely normal level of functioning. In an experiment where volunteers took a small dose of heroin on three consecutive days, there was evidence of sleep disturbance for up to two months. This study involved normal, non-addicted subjects. In studies with addicts, physiological abnormalities have been found as long as six months after the drugs have been withdrawn, though these are generally detectable only with sophisticated measuring equipment.

The Dangers of Heroin

Few people have any doubt that heroin is a killer drug. After all, the newspapers never tire of bringing us new examples of 'drug deaths' and the most dramatic recent examples of these have involved AIDS deaths (see below). In the same way, the medical journals report the range of diseases 'caused' by heroin addiction, of which liver disease and blood poisoning are the two most common. Yet the facts of the matter are quite different. Rather than being a particularly dangerous drug, heroin itself is comparatively safe; it is safer, for instance, than alcohol. One of the few adverse effects of addiction to heroin and the opiates (apart from constipation) is that they reduce the user's sexual capacity. In the male, this usually shows itself as impotence. In the female addict, the drugs interfere with her menstrual cycle: sometimes the periods become irregular; often they stop altogether. In both sexes, opiates reduce the sexual drive, the level of sexual activity and the user's enjoyment of sex. Strangely, the effects of the drug during the early, experimental phase, may increase the level and the pleasure of sexual activity. I have even seen cases where men have become addicted to opiates after taking them in the first place to treat their impotence. But after a short period in which the user gains some benefit from the drug, there almost inevitably follows a period of sexual suppression. This is probably due to the drug's effect on the body's biochemistry, and as a direct drug-related effect it usually disappears after the person has stopped taking opiates.

The dangers of heroin addiction owe far more to the psychology of the addict and the ways in which addicts use the drug than to any property inherent in the drug itself. Yet, for most people, this conclusion seems to run contrary to the vast weight of evidence. How can such an assertion be supported? The death rate among opiate addicts, for instance, is much higher than that of the general population. Several estimates have suggested that addicts may be 20 times more likely to die than comparable groups of non-addicts. In order to understand why this happens we must again look at the psychology of the addict. Many addicts show a remarkable lack of concern for, if not deliberate disregard of, their own physical welfare. Some openly express their wish to die, and sometimes their behaviour reflects this. The analogy between opiate addiction and death has been a recurrent theme of the addict literature. Jean Cocteau, himself an opium addict, wrote in his *Diary of a Cure*, 'Death separates completely our heavy waters from our light waters. Opium separates them a little.'

It is important not to lose sight of the fact that the injection procedure is a separate feature of drug taking from the direct drug effects themselves. Many complications of drug taking can be traced to the injection rather than to the drug. Addicts often use unsterile or even downright dirty equipment to inject themselves. This deplorable habit can lead to septicaemia (blood poisoning) and to such other infections as endocarditis (infection of the heart valves) and viral hepatitis. Each of these infections seriously weakens the sufferer's health, and can even lead to death. But none is directly caused by the drug itself. They are consequences of the dangerous and ill-advised ways in which the addict takes drugs, and are specifically linked to the route of drug administration.

Many drug injectors become infected with one or more of the hepatitis viruses. The forms that most affect drug injectors are the hepatitis B, hepatitis C and hepatitis D forms. In many parts of Europe and North America, more than half of all drug injectors are infected with hepatitis B, and in many countries there is also a serious problem among drug injectors with hepatitis C infection. These are serious infections: they can lead to cirrhosis and liver cancer and they can be fatal. Hepatitis infections can be spread both by sharing injecting equipment and by sexual contact. Many drug users are exposed to a high risk of infection when they first start to inject drugs since they are more likely to share injecting equipment with the person who introduced them to the habit at that time. A UK report in 1991 observed that in later years we may come to regard the hepatitis infections as 'the great overlooked epidemic'.

There are other complications associated with persistent injection into a vein, especially when done clumsily. The formation of scar tissue and other vein damage can eventually lead addicts into the position where they find it increasingly difficult to discover any further sites to inject themselves. When this happens, a minority may reconsider the wisdom of continuing their use of drugs. Some others adopt alternative routes of administration, perhaps by injecting into muscle tissue. Least sensible of all are those addicts who continue to search for more and more hazardous injection sites. Some of the more bizarre and dangerous examples that I have seen include injecting drugs into veins in the breast, ankles, fingers (I have known several cases of addicts needing amputation of a finger) and even the jugular vein. Some addicts resort to injecting themselves in the femoral vein in the groin. This can be dangerous through the increased risk of blood clots forming at this site. These could either cut off blood supply to the leg or even break away and be transported to the brain, with disastrous consequences. There is the further danger that the injection could easily penetrate the femoral artery by mistake.

AIDS and HIV Infection

Probably the single most alarming development since the first appearance of *Living With Drugs* has been the appearance of the virus leading to AIDS (Acquired Immune Deficiency Syndrome). At the time of writing this sixth edition, more than 40 million people worldwide have contracted HIV infection. More than 25 million people have died of AIDS.

AIDS was first identified as a new syndrome in 1981 and by 1984 the Human Immunodeficiency Virus Type 1 (HIV1) had been identified as the cause of AIDS and its associated clinical conditions. HIV is a type of retrovirus which has the ability to cause a range of diseases some years after infection. HIV is spread through blood products, semen or vaginal secretions. In almost all cases the virus has been transmitted in one of three ways: these are by sharing blood or blood-contaminated instruments, for instance syringes and needles, through heterosexual or homosexual intercourse, or from a pregnant woman to her foetus.

HIV infection can have several consequences. Some people show no symptoms: some become slightly unwell, often with swollen glands. Some develop a number of symptoms with varying degrees of disability. Most serious of all are those cases in which people go on to develop the syndrome known as AIDS that often includes pneumonia and a rare form of cancer. If left untreated, AIDS is almost always fatal. Probably all who carry the virus are infectious to others.

Every drug taker who shares needles or syringes is at risk, even from the very first injection. Although less obvious, there are also risks attached to sharing spoons or other pieces of equipment that have been used to prepare injections. One of the first parts of the UK to be badly affected was Edinburgh, where a 1986 survey of injectors found that more than half of them had HIV infection, a rate higher than in any previous European study, and similar to that reported in New York City.

The circumstances and events surrounding the development of Edinburgh's AIDS problems are now better understood. During 1982–83, a small family group of Edinburgh users had lived in Oxford, where they shared needles with Oxford undergraduates, US Air Force personnel and a drug-using haemophiliac. The family returned to Edinburgh in 1983 and played an active role in the local drug scene; two were later found to be HIV-positive. Also, in 1982, the football World Cup was staged in Spain and many local drug users travelled to Spain where some of them injected drugs with Spanish users. HIV infection was also established and spreading rapidly among drug injectors in Spain at that time. One of the main local circumstances which made Edinburgh so vulnerable to the spread of HIV was the restricted availability of injecting equipment and the willingness to share needles.

Injecting equipment may be shared because of the limited availability of sterile equipment, at places where drug injectors meet socially or to obtain drugs, and as a result of drug taking or bonding rituals. In Edinburgh, the low availability of needles was largely due to an anti-drug campaign to prevent drug users from having access to injecting equipment. It is a tragic irony that the same anti-drug campaigns which have made it harder to obtain needles and syringes have also caused injury and death to drug takers as well as creating increased public health risks by encouraging them to reuse and to share their equipment. From the experience of New York, Milan, Edinburgh and Bangkok, it is known that HIV infection can spread among drug injectors with alarming speed.

During the 1970s, Poland developed an increasing problem with the use of a home-produced Polish heroin called 'kompot'. This crude product was made from poppy straw. Polish users injected this drug and often shared injecting equipment or used a drug solution which had been contaminated by the blood of previous users. As a result, HIV infection spread rapidly among the Polish heroin users and infection rates of 20–40 per cent were soon reported in Warsaw.

In Europe, the earlier phases of the epidemic saw high percentages of drug abusers among the total cases of AIDS in Italy, Spain, Ireland, Poland and to a somewhat lesser degree in France, Austria and Switzerland. Many of the countries with a relatively high prevalence of HIV seropositivity formed a geographical belt stretching roughly from Spain along the south of Europe through southern France, Switzerland and northern Italy to the former Yugoslavia. The countries with a relatively low percentage of drug abusers among total AIDS cases were predominantly in northern Europe. However, all statements about HIV seroprevalence within countries tend to be generalizations, since there may be local areas where HIV infection is more prevalent (as is currently the case, for instance, in parts of Italy, Spain and the Netherlands).

During the past few years, the newly independent republics of the former Soviet Union and other post-socialist countries of Eastern Europe have experienced some of the most rapid increases in HIV/AIDS, and the majority of HIV infections are among drug injectors. Prior to the mid 1990s, fewer than 9,000 cases of HIV infection had been recorded throughout the whole of Central and Eastern Europe. By June 2001, there were more than 200,000 officially recorded cases. New HIV infection incidence rates in some Eastern European areas are now among the highest in the world.

Central and Eastern Europe has seen massive political, social and cultural changes in recent years. Before the break-up of the former Soviet Union, drug injection problems were not widespread, and anti-drug policies were aggressively enforced by the state. Since then, drug availability and demand have increased, and there have been dramatic increases in the number of drug injectors. Russia, for example, is estimated to now have at least three million drug injectors, and there are estimated to be at least 650,000 drug injectors in Ukraine. At the same time, the social changes have often included the collapse of the public health infrastructure, which has further hastened the rapid spread of HIV. Both Russia and Ukraine already have advanced HIV epidemics, and in several of the post-Soviet countries, the HIV epidemic is rapidly accelerating and is already largely out of control.

Some of the earliest HIV outbreaks occurred among drug injectors between 1994 and 1996 in Kaliningrad and Moscow in Russia, and in Odessa in Ukraine. Two-thirds of the drug injectors in Odessa are currently infected with HIV. Drug users in the former Soviet countries also tend to be very young. In St Petersburg, almost one-third of drug injectors are under 19 years of age, and as a consequence many HIV infections are among young people. In other Eastern European countries, the epidemic is still in its early stages. The Baltic region, for example, had relatively low HIV rates during most of the 1990s.

Many drug injectors have now learned to reduce their risks of HIV infection by not sharing, by sterilizing injecting equipment, or at least by sharing less often and with fewer partners. The spread of HIV infection among drug users may also be linked to the sexual transmission of the virus.

Most drug takers are young and sexually active, and HIV infection among drug takers may be spread by either sexual activity or drug injection practices. HIV infection among drug injectors can pose a serious risk to their sexual partners, whether or not they themselves are drug injectors. Indeed, many drug abusers who do not themselves inject drugs are likely to mix socially and sexually with drug injectors. It would be unfortunate if an emphasis upon avoiding risky injecting behaviour were allowed to draw attention away from avoiding the risks associated with HIV transmission through sexual behaviour. In some cities in North America with a high prevalence of HIV infection among drug injectors, many cases in which HIV has been acquired heterosexually can be traced to sexual contact with a seropositive drug user. HIV can also be transmitted from a seropositive mother to her baby and this problem is also increasingly linked to drug injection, whether by the mother or by her sexual partner.

If HIV infection manages to become established in the general population it will tend to spread in the same 'epidemic' fashion as other sexually transmitted diseases. At present there is no preventive vaccination nor any cure.

The Mysterious Case of the Heroin Overdose

Another well-publicized form of drug-related death, of course, is the overdose. Until the recent increase in the numbers of young people addicted to opiates, there were relatively few fatal overdoses. By the 1970s, this had changed and overdoses had become a major killer of young people. Since the 1970s, thousands of deaths, particularly in New York, have been attributed to opiate overdoses. This is a most peculiar observation, for several reasons.

In the first place, the quality of street heroin in New York was, for many years, extremely poor. The purity of street heroin was often less than 10 per cent, and one analysis of a range of street drugs taken from Brooklyn dealers revealed a heroin content of only one part in a thousand. This analysis found 16 different adulterants, of which quinine was the most common. In London, the quality of street heroin was somewhat better, with a heroin content of about 50 per cent, though this still leaves the addict using a mixture with half of its ingredients unknown.

Between the late 1960s and the mid-1970s, the most widely available heroin in the UK was 'Chinese' heroin. This came from a variety of South-East Asian sources and was sold in two forms, 'rice' and 'elephant'. Rice owed its name to its appearance: it was light-coloured and granular. The other form was named after the picture of an elephant that appeared on the large packets of heroin that were smuggled into the country. 'Elephant' was a mid-brown in colour and was the stronger of the two. Oddly enough, many addicts described Chinese heroin as stronger and superior in the quality of its effects to UK heroin, even though Chinese usually contained only about one-third of the amount of heroin in the pharmaceutically pure UK heroin. The reasons for this strange preference may have something to do with the adulterants used in Chinese heroin, or, more probably, the preference may be yet another example of the potency of attitudes, beliefs and other psychological factors in determining a person's response to drugs.

Chinese heroin virtually disappeared from the UK's streets in the late 1970s, after a number of successful police raids. Its place was immediately filled by 'Iranian' heroin and, at the time of writing the first edition of this book, most of the street heroin available in the UK was Iranian. Iranian heroin was a dark-brown powder: pharmacologically, it was a fairly crude preparation, probably because of some fault or faults in the preliminary process of cleaning up the morphine.

At the time of preparing this sixth edition of *Living with Drugs*, almost all of the illicit heroin available on the streets of the UK comes from the Afghanistan/Pakistan area. During the early part of the 1980s, the purity of heroin at the point of import was sometimes as high as 70 per cent. When sold on the street its purity had dropped to about 50 per cent, with a range of 30–60 per cent. Forensic laboratory analyses carried out on 1991 seizures showed a very similar picture, with purity levels of street heroin between 35 and 55 per cent.

Like the Chinese and Iranian heroin that preceded it, 'Pakistani heroin' is cut with various adulterants. In UK street heroin, unlike that of the US, quinine is seldom used as an adulterant. Instead, the user may be privileged to pay for heroin which has been cut with anything from bicarbonate of soda or sugar powder to brick dust or talcum power. Even strychnine has been used. (In small doses, strychnine acts as a stimulant. In larger doses it is a poison.) Street heroin has sometimes been found to contain other sedative drugs such as barbiturates or methaqualone (Mandrax) which have been added to the drug prior to export. The addition of these drugs will certainly alter the subjective 'buzz' that the user experiences. They may help to persuade the users that they are being sold a good quality product, but they also increase the risks both of overdosing and of certain medical complications such as abscesses if the drug is injected.

One theory about opiate overdoses is that they are really caused by the impurities in the street drugs. Quinine, for instance, can cause death in a way that matches up almost exactly with the symptoms described in cases of heroin overdose. Another theory, and one to which many addicts subscribe, suggests that overdoses are the result of unexpectedly pure samples of the drug. Although not impossible, there is little evidence to support this. Packets of heroin that have been found near to the bodies of dead addicts have been analysed and found to contain heroin of the same strength and sort as ordinary packets. In any case, if street heroin were of such unpredictable strength, the non-tolerant experimenter would be most at risk. In fact, it is usually the experienced, long-term addict who dies in this way.

Another, and more plausible, hypothesis is that alcohol (or, more precisely, the joint effect of alcohol and the opiates) is the real villain of the piece. Even an ordinary, safe therapeutic dose of an opiate such as morphine or heroin can be fatal when administered to someone who has already been drinking. Many deaths might have been avoided in the past, and more could be avoided in the future, if addicts were clearly warned of this danger. What masquerades as a heroin overdose may actually be due to the interaction of alcohol and heroin. The two drugs do not mix. (The same is true of heroin and both benzodiazepines and barbiturates, which are also injected by addicts.)

Overdoses are a much more common event among heroin users than is usually acknowledged. Some studies have found that most regular heroin users will, at some time, take an overdose. Our own research at the National Addiction Centre found that two-thirds of a sample of heroin users had overdosed at least once, and that the users who are most at risk are those who take several drugs (particularly alcohol or sedative-type drugs) at the same time as the heroin. Not surprisingly, it is those who use heroin by injection who are at highest risk. In one study of heroin users we found that only 2 per cent of the heroin chasers had overdosed, compared to 31 per cent of the heroin injectors.

Since most overdoses take place when other drug users are present, it may be possible to introduce innovative measures to reduce the risk of death. Such measures could include educating drug users to recognize the signs of overdose and showing them how to lay the unconscious person in the recovery position, and encouraging them to call an ambulance without delay. A more radical suggestion has been to provide drug users with instant access to the drug naloxone, an opiate antagonist which can be injected to provide an instant reversal of the effects of a heroin overdose.

Cocaine

Sigmund Freud, the founder of psychoanalysis and, for better or worse, probably the most influential psychological thinker of the 20th century, had a considerable personal involvement with drugs. He was always an extremely heavy smoker, consuming 20 cigars a day. Indeed, his tobacco intake was so great that in 1894 he suffered from an attack of what was diagnosed as 'nicotine poisoning', and there can be little doubt that he was dependent on tobacco. In his letters to Wilhelm Fliess, he described his efforts to reduce or give up the habit. These all failed, and he commented that he would rather have the pleasure of smoking, even at the risk of his health, than lead 'a long and miserable life' without it.

Freud also became very interested in cocaine after reading about the way Peruvian Indians chewed coca leaves to increase their endurance and their capacity for work. He himself was troubled with what he referred to as 'nervous exhaustion', and decided to try cocaine as a remedy. He tried the drug both orally and by injection, and found that it gave him a quite remarkable sense of well-being. He gave it to his friends; he sent some to his fiancée; he gave it to his sisters and to his patients. He wrote several articles in praise of it, describing 'the exhilaration and lasting euphoria which in no way differs from the normal euphoria of a healthy person'. He also wrote that 'this result is enjoyed without any of the unpleasant after-effects that follow exhilaration brought about by alcohol'. In a letter to his fiancée, he described one of his articles as 'a song of praise to this magical drug'. After using cocaine for three years, Freud gave it up without any difficulty (in direct contrast to his dependence upon tobacco). His friend Ernst von Fleischl, on the other hand, had developed such a taste for the drug that he felt himself to be hopelessly dependent upon it.

At this time, there was general agreement among the medical profession that cocaine was a most valuable drug. Freud had called it an instrument of almost unbelievable curative power, and an editorial in *The Lancet* (1885) commented:

> The therapeutical uses of cocaine are so numerous that the value of this wonderful remedy seems only beginning to be appreciated. Almost daily we hear of some disease or combination of symptoms in which it has been tried for the first time and has answered beyond expectation.

One sickly young man who was given cocaine at this time was Robert Louis Stevenson. Stevenson hardly enjoyed a single day's relief from illness during his entire life and spent much of his time confined to the sickbed. After taking cocaine for his respiratory condition, Stevenson seems to have shown a quite remarkable response to the drug. He wrote 60,000 words of his novel *The Strange Case of Dr*

Jekyll and Mr Hyde within six days. It is not clear precisely what role cocaine played in this. It is probable that the mental and physical energy released in him by the drug enabled him to do the actual writing, but it is equally likely that its effects inspired the theme of the book itself – that of a man completely transformed by a strange potion.

Conan Doyle's creation, Sherlock Holmes, was another regular user of the wonder drug. In *The Sign of Four*, Holmes describes his 'seven per cent solution' as being 'transcendingly stimulating and clarifying to the mind'. At the end of the book, Dr Watson comments that it seems unfair that everyone except Holmes should have received some credit for solving the case; he asks,

'What remains for you?'

'For me,' said Sherlock Holmes, 'there still remains the cocaine bottle.'

And he stretched his long, white hand up for it.

Cocaine was sold in cigarettes, in soft drinks, in nose sprays, in chewing gum and various patent medicines. One hundred per cent pure cocaine could be freely bought over the counter from the local chemist. It was also commercially available in wine which was first introduced to the public in the 1860s and was produced by Angelo Mariani. Mariani's goods became so well established that Pope Leo XIII is said to have been 'supported in his ascetic retirement by a preparation of Mariani's coca', and later he presented Mariani with a gold medal, citing him as a benefactor of humanity.

In 1885, America saw the introduction of another interesting preparation which eventually came to symbolize the American way of life itself. This contained extracts of the African kola nut (caffeine) as well as cocaine; hence its name, Coca-Cola. The cocaine was taken out of the drink in 1906, and by 1909 the American Bureau of Food and Drugs was able to initiate a legal action against the company producing the drink. It was alleged that the name was likely to mislead the customer because it contained no coca and very little kola.

Coca comes from a flowering shrub which is indigenous to the eastern slopes of the Andes and can be found from the southern tip of Chile to the northernmost part of the range. For centuries coca has played a central part in the life of the Peruvian Indians who use it to increase their physical strength and endurance, and to lessen fatigue. Coca increases heart rate, arterial pressure and the number of breaths per minute. All these effects are useful for the special requirements of high-altitude living. Typically, coca leaves are chewed together with a little lime powder made from crushed shells. The lime helps to extract the cocaine and its related alkaloids from the leaves. Obviously, there are wide variations in the daily intake of cocaine, but it is probable that an average amount is in the region of 350–400mg. This constitutes a sizeable dose of the drug.

Despite the invasion of the Incas and the Spaniards, both of whom tried to suppress the use of cocaine, the Andean Indians have never stopped using it. Various estimates suggest that the region still contains between 8 and 15 million users. In Bolivia, cocaine is currently one of the mainstays of an extremely shaky economy. The distribution of the drug is largely in the control of the army, and in 1980, just prior to the military coup that overthrew the government, an aircraft belonging to a general was reported to have been discovered with 1,500lbs of 90 per cent pure cocaine on board.

The majority of all coca cultivation takes place in Colombia, Bolivia and Peru. Whereas Peru was the largest producer of coca during the early 1990s, it has since been overtaken by Colombia. More than half of the world's coca production currently takes place in that country. The peak year for production was 2000 when more than 220,000 hectares of Colombian land was devoted to growing coca, with a potential yield of about 350,000 metric tons of dry coca leaf. Farmers in these countries are working hard to improve their cultivation techniques both to increase yields and to hide crops. As a consequence of their hard work, cocaine availability throughout the world has increased and retail prices have dropped. In Europe, for example, the street price for a gram of cocaine has fallen steadily since 1990, and street prices in 2002 were about half those in 1990. The world's main cocaine trafficking route runs from Colombia to the US, and the greater availability of the drug in the US has been associated with a correspondingly greater price reduction. US street prices for cocaine in 2002 were about one-third of the levels in 1990. In 2002 it was estimated that almost 6 million people used cocaine in the US, which is, not surprisingly, the world's largest market for cocaine. The 3.3 million cocaine users in Europe now consume about a quarter of the world's cocaine.

There is some doubt as to who first isolated cocaine. This seems to have occurred during the middle of the 19th century. By 1883, German army physicians were giving the drug to Bavarian soldiers during the autumn manoeuvres. The effects were similar to those reported by the Andean Indians – increased levels of physical energy and reduced fatigue. The value of the drug as a local anaesthetic was also demonstrated at this time.

Cocaine is regularly and mistakenly described as a narcotic, a term which has no precise meaning but is usually applied to the opiates, such as heroin and morphine. Cocaine has next to nothing in common with the opiates except that in the UK it shares the same legal status as those drugs. Heroin, morphine and the other opiates are classified together with cocaine under Schedule 2(1) of the 1973 Misuse of Drugs Act, and it is possible that this legal quirk encouraged people to assume that cocaine is the same sort of drug as the opiates.

There has always been disagreement about whether cocaine is or is not an addictive drug. This issue reached the level of hysteria as a result of the problems with crack cocaine that the US experienced during the 1980s in some of its large cities. The media presentation of crack cocaine (supported by some unfortunate and ill-advised comments by 'drug experts') emphasized its supposed addictiveness: ' "Crack is the most addictive drug known to man" says Arnold Washton' (*Newsweek*); this drug is 'instantly addictive and absolutely deadly' (*The Observer*). However, this argument is not worth pursuing since it is based upon one of the central misunderstandings which this book aims to correct, namely that addictiveness is an intrinsic property of the drug itself. Cocaine is not physically addictive in the same way as heroin or alcohol. The important feature of cocaine is that it can produce what many people regard as a powerfully attractive experience, and the intensity of the rewarding effect is greater when the drug is smoked. Cocaine is a central nervous system stimulant and the first site of action is the cortex. Among its effects, users describe euphoria, laughter, talkativeness and excitement. Along with many other pills and potions, it also has a reputation as an aphrodisiac.

At low doses there is an increase in activity levels, and bodily movements are well coordinated. At high doses, the excessive stimulation of lower centres of the brain leads to tremors and convulsive movements. Overdoses produce anxiety, depression, headache, confusion and fainting; occasionally, they lead to convulsions and respiratory arrest due to over-stimulation of the lower brain. It is very difficult to say what constitutes an overdose of cocaine because of the wide range of individual differences in sensitivity to the drug. A few individuals are so sensitive to its effects that even a small amount can produce the symptoms of an overdose. Shortly after cocaine was introduced as a local anaesthetic, it was found to produce dangerous toxic reactions in some patients. It is not clear why some people should show what seems to be a sort of allergic reaction to the drug.

Until the 1970s there was little concern about the use of cocaine. Certain adverse effects were well known but there was a broad if non-specific agreement that for most users cocaine was neither especially harmful nor likely to lead to dependent patterns of use. This may have had much to do with the manner in which the drug was used. When taken by sniffing, the effects tend to be milder and the impact is slower than if the drug is either injected or smoked. In recent years there has been a trend towards using purer forms of the drug, higher doses and techniques of administration that lead to a more rapid onset of action, such as crack smoking and freebasing.

Freebase cocaine and crack are the same drug; they are both forms of cocaine which have been prepared for smoking. This is done by separating the base form of the drug from its hydrochloride salt. The preparation of freebase is often done by chemically treating cocaine hydrochloride by dissolving it in a solvent such as ether to obtain a purified cocaine base in crystal form. Crack is reputed to be the gift to mankind of a Los Angeles backroom chemist who discovered a way to transform a gram of cocaine into a dozen little 'rocks' by combining it with bicarbonate of soda in a microwave oven. Crack is now the predominant type of cocaine use in many countries. However, the use of crack and freebase cocaine was preceded by coca paste smoking in several Latin American countries.

As early as 1971, doctors in Peru began to see young people who were experiencing a range of problems as a result of smoking cocaine paste. These problems appeared to be powerfully related to the fact that the drug was being smoked. Although at least

13 per cent of the population in Peru chewed coca (and this percentage was much higher in the mountain areas), hardly any of these coca chewers reported serious psychological or health problems as a result of their using coca. Cocaine paste can be regarded as a less sophisticated version of freebase or crack.

Cocaine paste is the first extraction product in the process of refining cocaine from coca leaves. The leaves are mashed up and mixed with such chemicals as sulphuric acid and paraffin. Laboratory analyses have shown that paste can have a cocaine content ranging between 40 and 90 per cent. Unfortunately, cocaine paste also tends to contain traces of all the chemicals that have been used to process the leaves and these can cause serious damage to the lungs.

It is often the case that patterns of drug use in producer countries differ from those in countries to which drugs are smuggled. One such difference can relate to the amounts of drugs used. It is not unusual for heroin users in Pakistan to take up to 10 grams a day (in contrast to users in London, who might typically use three-quarters of a gram). Similarly, in the coca-growing Andean countries, cocaine is often consumed in very large quantities. In a recent survey of cocaine users presenting for treatment in Peru and Bolivia, we found that the majority of these users were smoking cocaine in the form of *pasta, pitillo* or *basuco*. On average they reported using a massive 16 grams per day. This is well in excess of the amount used in Western countries and is probably one of the main reasons for the high levels of dependence and other adverse effects experienced by the South American users.

The effects of smoking paste, crack or freebase cocaine resemble those of intravenous cocaine injection. The blood concentration rises as fast, if not faster, causing a sudden 'rush' of pleasure. This pleasant effect soon subsides, to be followed usually by a 'down' of depression, irritability and craving.

One of the more common types of problem associated with cocaine is that some users find themselves locked into a compulsive need to take the drug, and find that their psychological dependence upon the drug is very difficult to handle. This problem is often associated with cocaine 'binges' in which the users take the drug continuously over a period of days until either the supply is exhausted or they are. The binge usually ends with the person falling into a disturbed sleep.

A telephone information service for cocaine users established in the US in 1983 received more than a third of a million calls in its first year. A random survey of callers revealed that they were spending an average of $637 per week on the drug. Most of them said they would use more if the price went down. Most of them said they used sedative drugs to help them calm down after using cocaine, and the majority described such adverse effects as sinus headaches, nasal problems such as cracked, ulcerated or bleeding nasal membranes, or sexual problems such as impotence. More than two-thirds of them complained of insomnia, anxiety, depression, irritability and difficulties in concentrating, and a quarter said they had had fits or loss of consciousness. More than one in ten Americans has used cocaine.

Alcohol and cocaine are frequently used together and, when taken together, the two substances interact to produce cocaethylene, an active metabolite which is longer-acting and is more toxic than cocaine alone. The combined use of alcohol and cocaine produces an increased and prolonged feeling of subjective euphoria compared to the use of either substance on its own. The combined use of the two substances may also offset some of the sedating effects of alcohol as well as reducing the discomfort when coming down from cocaine. However, the heavy drinking of some cocaine users can create its own problems as well as aggravating the effects of cocaine use.

A great deal of attention has been paid to the severity of cocaine problems among users in some parts of the US and in some of the South American countries where it is the most common type of drug problem among people seeking help with drug addiction disorders. However, not all cocaine smokers become compulsive users of the drug. A survey carried out in Miami (a city which is reputed to be as badly affected as any in the US) found that, although nine out of 10 of the young people in the survey had used crack at least once in the previous three months, only a third were using it daily, with another third using it no more than once or twice a week. Although the frequent use of cocaine presents a number of risks to the psychological and physical health of the users, studies in Canada and the Netherlands have concluded that the risks of cocaine use have been exaggerated by the media and that many cocaine users manage to avoid the more serious consequences.

Continuous consumption of high doses of cocaine carries its own special dangers. The user may become irrational and start to develop feelings of persecution; in extreme cases, they may develop a toxic psychosis. Another curious side effect of immoderate use that is sometimes seen revels in the title of 'formication'. The word can usually be relied upon to get a laugh, but for the victims the symptoms are no laughing matter. They have the delusion that ants or insects are crawling about on or under their skin. In their distress the victims may pick at their skin and produce open wounds in an attempt to free themselves from this imaginary infestation. Such catastrophic reactions, however, are comparatively rare.

The arrival of crack has taken cocaine very much downmarket. In the US, crack is frequently a problem of the most socially deprived inner city ghettos. The days when cocaine was in vogue as a recreational drug in artistic and intellectual circles have rapidly come to an end. Through most of the 20th century cocaine held an elitist aura which was reflected in its black-market price, and in the silver cocaine spoons and various related drug paraphernalia which could be obtained from the most expensive shops in the capital cities of Europe and America. The new street image of crack seems to have profoundly changed the image of cocaine.

The Amphetamines

The amphetamines[1] are another central nervous system stimulant. Their most common oral forms are dexedrine and benzedrine. Methedrine is also available as an injectable preparation. Amphetamines were first introduced in the form of a benzedrine inhaler as a treatment for asthma, but, as with virtually every other drug described in this book, there was an immediate rush to extend their therapeutic applications, and amphetamines were promoted as a treatment for such diverse medical conditions as schizophrenia and migraine, alcoholism and epilepsy.

In the Second World War, amphetamines were widely used. The German army found them 'very useful in modern battle conditions when used in mass attacks'. Presumably, others found them equally useful: 72 million tablets were distributed to the UK's armed forces, and the Japanese were reported to use even greater amounts of the drug. In the decade after the war, the old war stocks of amphetamines were dumped on the open market in Japan. As a result, there was an unprecedented increase in the use of these drugs – mainly methedrine, and often in an injectable form. The use of amphetamines seems to have reached a peak in Japan around 1954, when up to a million people were estimated to be using these drugs.

It is not entirely clear what are the current military attitudes towards amphetamines. During the 1960s the US army was consuming millions of amphetamine tablets (mainly dexedrine). The military values of amphetamine would appear to be obvious enough. It creates a temporary increase in energy, in alertness and in confidence. This would be good, except that it can also cause edginess, panic and errors of judgement. The use of amphetamines by the US Air Force was banned by the Chief of Staff in 1992. However, amphetamines were quietly reintroduced during the war in Afghanistan. At this time, the US Air Force generously gave its pilots $30 million F-16 fighter jets, laser-guided munitions, and amphetamines, referred to as 'go pills'. The Air Force described these as a 'medical tool' but, more ominously, put pressure on its pilots to take the drugs, suggesting that pilots might be found unfit to fly unless they took the pills. One of several incidents which may reflect the effectiveness of this particular medical tool took place in a friendly fire incident over Kandahar. After sighting a group on the ground, and despite clear advice to hold fire from the mission controllers in an AWACs plane, the speeding pilot was convinced he was under threat and attacked. This incident led to the deaths of four Canadian soldiers, and wounded eight others.

It is not generally known that Adolf Hitler regularly used drugs. Many of these were taken to relieve his various physical symptoms (for he was not a well man), but others were taken without any proper medical rationale. In 1938, his physician began to give him occasional intravenous injections of Eukadol and Eupaverinum for abdominal pain. These synthetic opiates have the same sort of effects as morphine. It

---

1   There are also a few non-amphetamine stimulants included in this discussion, notably Ritalin (methylphenidate) and Kethamed (pemoline). Although these drugs are chemically distinct from the amphetamines, their effects and the ways in which they are used are for all intents and purposes identical.

is unlikely that Hitler became addicted to them if they were administered on only an occasional basis. Throughout the war Hitler also took barbiturates for his insomnia: again there is no evidence that he used these except as a night sedative, though this pattern of daily use may well have established both a physical and psychological dependence upon them. It is possible that his insomnia and his need for sedatives were themselves caused by other drugs.

From about 1941, Hitler received daily morning injections of what seems to have been methedrine. By 1943, he needed more than just the one injection – sometimes as many as five a day. Witnesses at the time described how these made Hitler instantly alert and talkative. In addition to the injections, Hitler also took methedrine tablets. Such prolonged and progressive use of amphetamines takes its toll, and it has even been suggested that Hitler's unrealistic optimism and his fixed, rigid thinking during the Battle of Stalingrad and on subsequent occasions may have been due to the adverse effects of his amphetamine abuse. This sort of speculation is interesting but inconclusive, though the irrationality, outbursts of rage, obsessional thinking and persecutory ideas that Hitler showed at that time are known symptoms of excessive use of amphetamines.

Curiously, Hitler and the Nazis had other interesting associations with drug use. During the 1930s, Nazi scientists 'proved' that smoking caused lung cancer. They even identified the dangers of passive smoking decades before the issue became a matter for concern in the modern world. Once a chain-smoker, the Führer gave up the habit and condemned tobacco as 'one of man's most dangerous poisons'. Nazi propaganda gloated over the fact that, unlike Churchill with his cigars and his heavy drinking, Hitler was a non-smoker and a teetotaller. His use of amphetamines, barbiturates and other drugs does not appear to have featured in the propaganda.

Hitler may have been a uniquely horrible political leader, but the prospects of any powerful figure acting under the influence of powerful psychoactive drugs is not reassuring. During the brief fiasco of the 1956 Suez War, the UK's Prime Minister Anthony Eden has described how he was 'living on benzedrine'.

It is not only the armed forces that have seen the potential of these drugs. As a source of artificial energy, they are not without their appeal to athletes. Some sports, such as cycling, have gained quite a reputation for their involvement with stimulants, but it is clear that the performance of athletes in many different sports can be improved by amphetamines. Swimmers, runners and weight-throwers all perform better on amphetamines than on a placebo, and this enhancement occurs both when the athlete is rested and when he or she is tired. Weight-throwers showed the most gain in performance after taking stimulants – between 3 and 4 per cent.

Medically, it is far from clear what value the amphetamines have. Most of the original claims for their therapeutic powers have been discredited. They are still occasionally used in the treatment of obesity because of their appetite-suppressant effects, though other, safer alternatives are now available. Something like 20 million people in the US are obese, so there is no shortage of potential customers for such drugs. However, it is very doubtful whether obesity can be effectively treated by drugs of this sort. The causes of obesity are usually social and psychological, and it is these factors that need to be dealt with if the patient is to lose weight successfully. In view of the potential hazards of prolonged amphetamine use, it would be unwise to keep any patient on these drugs for more than a short period of time.

One of the most surprising uses of Ritalin and the amphetamines is in the treatment of hyperactive children. Although it is a stimulant, amphetamine has a paradoxical calming effect on such children. Many hyperactive children who have been treated in this way show a marked reduction in their restlessness, coupled with an improvement in their ability to concentrate. Some children maintain their improvement even after the drug has been withdrawn. However, there are problems. In the first place, somewhere between 10 and 40 per cent of hyperactive children show no improvement when given amphetamine. More worrying, perhaps, is the potential for misusing drugs to control difficult children. Hyperactivity (hyperkinesis) is far from being a unitary or properly understood phenomenon, and the label is often wrongly applied. It would be mistaken to regard any disruptive child as necessarily being hyperkinetic. Nonetheless, it is tempting and convenient to dismiss unacceptable behaviour as 'sick' and to treat what is really a social and psychological problem as if it were a medical one.

All the ambiguities inherent in the concept of addiction come to the fore in any discussion of the amphetamines. Some authorities are convinced that amphetamines are definitely not addictive. Others are equally certain that they are physically addictive, and that statements to the contrary are dangerously inaccurate.

What is certain is that some people are so impressed by the elation produced by amphetamines that they feel a powerful need to go on using them. And with prolonged use, some individuals take progressively larger doses of amphetamines. However, this does not necessarily reflect the tolerance-producing properties of the drug itself. In the strict sense of the term, tolerance to the stimulant effects of the drug does not occur. Patients with narcolepsy (a rare disorder in which the sufferer suddenly falls asleep) can be maintained for years on a fixed dose of amphetamines. In terms of their response to stimulants, the difference between the speedfreak and the patient with narcolepsy can be found in the reasons why they take the drug. The psychological needs of chronic amphetamine abusers which led them to become dependent upon the drug in the first place make them increasingly dissatisfied with the effects from a given dose. So they take more. In so far as tolerance occurs with the amphetamines, it reflects the body's capacity to cope with the progressive increases that are taken to achieve some psychological reward. It is not an inevitable process. Certainly, not all amphetamine users escalate their dose, as might be expected if a true tolerance were present.

Similarly, when the regular user stops taking amphetamines, several withdrawal responses may occur. Some of these appear to be rebound-type effects which are opposite to the drug effects. These may include lethargy, tiredness and depression. However, the withdrawal responses are often more complex. For instance, the apparent sleep rebound includes a period of marked sleep disturbance with difficulties in sleeping at night and drowsiness during the day. It is not clear whether these responses should be regarded as evidence of physical addiction to the drug or merely of the body's reaction against a prolonged chemical over-stimulation that has suddenly been removed. In some respects, the argument about whether the amphetamines are really addictive can be seen as a semantic rather than a medical issue.

Amphetamines are relatively easy to manufacture and 'kitchen' laboratories have been able to provide large amounts of the drug, often in the form of amphetamine sulphate. The US has recently had problems with methamphetamine, which began in the western states and moved east, often particularly affecting small towns in rural parts of the West and Midwest. In these areas methamphetamine-related emergency visits have increased in recent years, with methamphetamine being responsible for more emergency department visits than any other drug. The use of amphetamines is also widespread in Australia, Japan, Ireland, and in some Scandinavian countries (in Sweden, for instance, amphetamine is the most common drug taken by injection).

In recent years there has been a marked increase in the numbers of people using amphetamines in many countries throughout the world, and its geographical spread is also increasing. The UN report for 2004 noted seizures of amphetamines in 58 countries, an increase of 25 per cent since 2001. It has been estimated that more than 38 million people use amphetamine-type stimulants, with 60 per cent of the users in East and Southeast Asia. China, Myanmar and the Philippines have been identified as major sources of the drug in the Asian region.

One of the most worrying forms of amphetamine use to appear (or more precisely to reappear) in recent years, has involved methamphetamine. Like amphetamine sulphate, methamphetamine can be easily manufactured in kitchen laboratories using ingredients purchased from local stores. Much of the world's methamphetamine comes from large, industrial scale 'superlabs'. Some of the superlabs that have been detected in the Far East have had the capacity to produce 400kg per week. The purity of the finished product, especially from small kitchen labs, is, understandably, extremely variable. In some samples, it can be as high as 80–90 per cent: in others it may be as low as 10 per cent. Seizures of methamphetamine laboratory equipment in the US doubled between 1999 and 2004, but meth labs can be portable, and can be dismantled and moved to avoid detection. Many of the chemicals that are used are toxic, corrosive and highly flammable, and fires and explosions are a constant threat in the labs. In the US, 694 fires or explosions were directly attributable to illicit methamphetamine production in 2002.

Crystal methamphetamine (also known as ice, LA glass, and meth) typically looks like small fragments of colourless or blue-white glass. Methamphetamine can be smoked, injected, snorted or eaten. Crystal meth is usually smoked in pipes similar to those used to smoke crack cocaine. It can also be injected. It produces an intense rush followed by a high that may last for 10 hours.

Amphetamine users are a varied group in terms of age, social background and patterns of use. Some amphetamine users take the drug in an 'instrumental' fashion because the extra wakefulness and confidence enable them to do other things (such as staying up all night dancing or driving long distances). Crystal methamphetamine is often used as a club drug, and has considerable popularity in the gay scene in the US and other countries. Where high doses of amphetamine are used over prolonged periods, this can lead to various difficulties. Although some users of amphetamine sulphate become psychologically dependent upon the drug, it is unclear whether or not this is a common problem. A recent study carried out among drug takers in south London found that the majority of amphetamine users reported having experienced no feelings of dependence upon the drug; only a small minority reported dependence problems rated as moderate or above. The risk of dependence is undoubtedly greatly increased among users of methamphetamine.

Amphetamine users may have short-term problems with anxiety, tension and irrational fears. The likelihood of such problems increases with the use of repeated doses or unusually high doses of the drug. There is no longer any doubt that the amphetamines can produce one of the more dramatic examples of the hazards of drug taking. With prolonged heavy use, or after a sudden increase in the dose, the user may develop persecutory symptoms which resemble those of paranoid schizophrenia. For many years, cases of amphetamine psychosis were mistakenly diagnosed as schizophrenia. It was not until the publication of Philip Connell's research monograph on the topic in 1958 that this toxic state was properly identified. Most commonly, sufferers believe that others are trying to harm them in some way; occasionally, they have visual or tactile hallucinations. These delusions are often accompanied by intense fear.

Amphetamine psychosis seems to be a true toxic reaction which can develop in individuals whose personality does not predispose them to such feelings. The risk of psychosis appears to be greatly increased among users of methamphetamine. No special treatment is needed. If a person is kept drug-free the psychotic state can be expected to disappear within a matter of days.

Barbiturates and Benzodiazepines

The barbiturates (otherwise appropriately known as barbs) are probably the most dangerous of the drugs discussed in this book. They depress activity in the central nervous system, and in small doses they act like tranquillizers to relieve anxiety and tension. In larger doses their depressant action causes drowsiness, laziness and sleep. Until the discovery of the barbiturates, alcohol, opium and belladonna were the only soporific drugs available to doctors and it is in this role of sleep-inducing drugs (hypnotics) that the barbiturates are most often prescribed.

The first barbiturate was produced in 1903 under the trade name Veronal (named after a Munich waitress); in 1912 it was followed by Luminal. Since then, more than 2,500 derivatives of barbituric acid have been synthesized. Tuinal, Seconal, Amytal and Nembutal are among the more common barbiturates currently available. Since 1954, more than 350 tons of the barbiturates have been manufactured in the US every year. During 1968, more than 17 million prescriptions were issued for over 1,000 million tablets of these drugs in England and Wales. Since then, there has been a considerable reduction in the overall levels of prescribing for barbiturates, partly as a result of the introduction of better alternative drugs, and partly because of the increased awareness by doctors of the dangers associated with barbiturates.

Very soon after the introduction of the barbiturates, cases of fatal poisoning began to be recorded. These drugs have been widely used as a means of committing suicide, and for many years barbiturate poisoning has been a major cause of death. In 1965, barbiturate overdoses accounted for half of all cases admitted to the Edinburgh poisoning treatment centre. In the US, barbiturates are still the drugs most commonly mentioned in coroners' reports into drug-related deaths.

With the development of physical tolerance to barbiturates, the user is tempted to take higher doses. There are special dangers involved in this, since the proportional difference between the effective dose and the lethal dose decreases as the dose level goes up. Because of this, the chronic high-dose user is particularly vulnerable to the risks of overdosing.

Despite their toxicity, the barbiturates have been dispensed on a massive scale as a remedy for sleeplessness. But although they once seemed to be highly efficient sleep-inducing drugs, there is increasing doubt even about their value in this role. Some people experience a definite hangover the morning after, and some of the long-acting barbiturates (such as phenobarbitone) have more serious dangers since the user might be quite obviously intoxicated and drowsy the next day.

Most sleeping tablets produce marked changes in the type of sleep the person gets. Sleep consists of several different stages, and one of the most important of these is the lighter level of sleep during which we have dreams. Everyone goes through this stage of dreaming sleep. When people say that they never dream, they are really saying that they never remember their dreams. Most barbiturates reduce the amount of dreaming sleep that occurs during the night, and this is a worrying sign that normal sleep is not occurring. Some experiments have found that, when deprived of this stage of sleep, people become more irritable and suspicious, and occasionally they show signs of emotional disturbance. When someone stops taking barbiturates as sleeping tablets, there is an immediate rebound increase in dreaming, as if the body needed to make up for being deprived of this part of sleep.

In any case, the initial advantages of sleeping tablets often wear off. When people first start taking barbiturates to help them sleep, the drugs usually work well and they fall asleep quite quickly. But with continued use, the drug seems to lose its effectiveness and they begin to take just as long to fall asleep as they did before they took the drug. If they continue taking the drug or even increase the dose, they risk becoming addicted to it. On the other hand, the real problems are likely to begin when they stop taking it. The period immediately afterwards is marked by considerable difficulty in sleeping, disturbed sleep, many body movements and nightmares.

During the 1960s a new, non-barbiturate sleeping tablet was being promoted as a safer alternative to the barbiturates. It was not until about 1970 that the medical authorities began to suspect what the sophisticated drug taker had known for some time: that the new drug was just as attractive as the barbiturates in terms of its intoxicating effects. This drug, Mandrax (otherwise available as Quaalude and Dormutil), had almost exactly the same effects as the barbiturates; it was misused in the same ways and its withdrawal effects were so similar to those of the barbiturates that for most purposes it can be regarded as the same sort of drug. Its attractions were so considerable that, within a few years of its appearance, a 'Mandrax problem' was being described in the US, the UK, Japan, France, Germany and many other countries around the world.

Barbiturates act in many ways just like alcohol. In small doses they remove anxiety; at high doses they produce slurred speech and encourage displays of heightened emotional behaviour. Whether this emotion turns out to be of the maudlin or aggressive variety will depend upon the user and the circumstances. Pharmacologically, the barbiturates are another way to get drunk, and it is hardly surprising that they should have lent themselves so readily to abuse. As with alcohol, excessive use of barbiturates causes a hangover the next day; and, as with alcohol, prolonged use of barbiturates establishes a physical dependence on the drug, complete with a full-blown withdrawal syndrome. Their resemblance to alcohol is sufficiently close for the two sorts of drug to combine in their effects. Anyone who takes barbiturates after drinking a large amount of alcohol puts himself or herself at risk of overdosing, and many suicides have been due to the combined effects of both drugs.

Because there have been such vast quantities of barbiturate drugs available, they have been used by a large proportion of the population, and there is little doubt that many people who are leading perfectly ordinary 'normal' lives are both psychologically and physically addicted to the barbiturates they take under the label of sleeping pills. Despite their addiction, they would be outraged by any suggestion that they were drug addicts. At the other end of some social scale of drug involvement are those deviant and disorganized barbs addicts who present such an obviously unacceptable face of drug taking.

At the time that barbiturates were easily available, the casualty departments of London hospitals close to the West End were seeing a steady procession of barbs addicts in various stages of overdose. Although some overdoses were accidental, most belonged to a peculiar category halfway between accidental and suicidal. Certainly, a sizeable number of the overdose cases were regular customers of the emergency services and many were known to the ambulance staff by name. They were not, however, much appreciated. Some cases were simply a nuisance, staggering about being drunkenly abusive. Others had passed beyond that stage and were comatose. Of this latter group, many recovered, discharged themselves and returned on some future occasion (or even later on the same day). A few joined the pathetic and anonymous statistics for drug-related deaths.

The risks of overdose are greater among barbs users than among other drug users and, obviously, they are greater for the addict who is seeking oblivion than for those who take the drug under medical instructions or with some degree of restraint. But there are other, special dangers associated with the injection of barbiturates. This is one of the most hazardous of all forms of drug abuse. Some addicts argue that they have been forced to use barbiturates because they have been unable to get hold of the heroin they really need. In fact, a considerable number of drug takers prefer the effects of the barbiturates, and will choose them in preference to the opiate drugs.

Most of the barbiturates used by addicts are chemically unsuitable for injection. They form an acidic mixture which can cause inflammation if it is not injected properly into a vein. Also most barbiturates dissolve very poorly in water, especially since the street addict often grinds up chalk-based tablets which were manufactured for oral use only. As a result, many barbiturate abusers inject themselves with an unsterile acid containing lumps of chalk, and abscesses are a frequent medical complication of this most ill-advised form of drug taking. Such abscesses are smelly, nasty, unpleasant for the nursing staff to treat, and generally leave a disfiguring scar. Occasionally, they set up complications which require surgery. This danger is increased by another side effect of the barbiturates. These drugs reduce blood flow and, as a result, users may develop blisters and ulcerations of the skin. This is often caused by users being overcome by their injection of barbs and lying heavily on some part of their body in a semi-conscious condition. By cutting off their blood circulation in this way, several addicts have had to have limbs amputated, and some have even died as a result.

Even the process of withdrawing the barbiturate addict from their drugs is more complicated than for most of the other drugs of dependence. The barbiturate withdrawal syndrome is a serious condition and, unlike heroin withdrawal, which is comparatively trivial, it can have fatal consequences. The first symptoms of withdrawal are usually restlessness and anxiety coupled with irritability and insomnia. Body temperature rises slowly, sometimes reaching levels as high as 105°F in the most advanced stages of withdrawal. The pulse rate goes up and the person begins to feel a muscular stiffness. This may be followed by vomiting, delirium and convulsions, and occasionally, if untreated, by coma and death. These symptoms can be alleviated by using a gradual withdrawal schedule in which the person is given progressively smaller doses of phenobarbital (a long-acting barbiturate which is seldom chosen by addicts). Nonetheless, barbiturate withdrawal remains a serious medical problem and, even at the end of the most gradual withdrawal, the person may still have fits.

The commercial success of the benzodiazepines (see Chapter 4) was partly due to these drugs being introduced as a safer alternative to the barbiturates. The benzodiazepines are more effective in reducing anxiety, they have fewer and less severe side effects and they are safer in overdoses. However, their attractions have not been overlooked by drug takers. Diazepam has had many high-profile users, including Elvis Presley and Andy Warhol. Elvis Presley was mixing Valium with other prescription medicines when he was found dead in his bathroom at Graceland. Liz Taylor mixed her doses with Jack Daniels.

Since 1984, there has been a growing problem with the injection of these drugs. Between 1988 and 1991, the percentage of heroin addicts admitted to the Maudsley Hospital inpatient treatment unit who were also regularly users of benzodiazepines doubled. By the beginning of the 1990s, about one-third of all admissions were using benzodiazepines and about half of these were also physically dependent upon them and required treatment for benzodiazepine withdrawal symptoms. Reports from Scotland and the north of England have also indicated that these drugs are widely misused.

Many of the benzodiazepines have been misused in this way, but the two most commonly used drugs have been diazepam (Valium) and temazepam. Temazepam was originally available as a soft capsule containing a clear liquid. These were known as 'eggs' and the liquid was drawn out with a hypodermic needle and injected. Concern about the risks of this practice led the manufacturers to change the formulation of the capsules to a hard gel (like candle wax) in the hope that this would prevent people from trying to inject them.

Some users continued to inject the new hard capsules. One method consisted of warming the capsules in an oven until the gel was sufficiently soft to be able to inject. Attempts to inject the hard gel led to even more severe physical complications. A letter to the *British Medical Journal* from Glasgow reported 15 cases of drug takers who had been admitted to hospital with severe complications following the injection of temazepam. In some cases these required amputation of the leg, arm or fingers. Although the introduction of the hard gel capsules was done with the best of intentions, this is another example of a preventive measure which, for some users, has been a direct cause of harm.

A recent addition to the pharmacopoeia of street drugs is GHB (gamma-hydroxybutyrate). Although neither a barbiturate nor a benzodiazepine, GHB is a central nervous system depressant. It was first synthesized in 1960 and was used as an anaesthetic in surgery. However, it was not effective because it had little analgesic effect, and often provoked seizures.

GHB was initially marketed as a dietary supplement in health food stores and later was promoted as a 'safe' agent for use by bodybuilders (as a 'growth hormone stimulator'). It is also part of the chemical repertoire of 'club drugs' and is often used by teenagers and young adults at bars, clubs, and parties to produce altered states of consciousness. It has also been used as a date rape drug. GHB is available through illicit sales and home manufacture, and recipes are obtainable on the Internet.

GHB is known by many names on the street, including G, liquid ecstasy, grievous bodily harm, wolfies and blue nitro, and many countries have experienced problems in recent years due to the use of GHB. Although serious adverse effects are not common, use of GHB has been reported to cause coma and death. In Sweden, for example, deaths related to the use of GHB are as frequent as those for heroin. Adverse effects related to GHB ingestion are highly variable among individuals. This variability combined with the variations in purity due to home manufacturing, makes GHB an unpredictable and potentially dangerous drug.

Chapter 10

The Control of Drugs

One of the most comprehensive and systematic works dealing with the relationship between the individual and the society in which they live is John Stuart Mill's essay *On Liberty*. It was Mill's thesis that individual liberty was the primary principle which should govern relations between the individual and society, and that there were large and important areas of human conduct which should be beyond the control of the state. Mill was worried by the tendency of the state, like some malign octopus, to take over more and more of the individual's freedom of action.

> The disposition of mankind, whether as rulers or as fellow citizens, to impose their own opinions and inclinations as a rule of conduct on others is so energetically supported by some of the best and by some of the worst feelings incident to human nature that it is hardly ever kept under restraint by anything but want of power; and as the power is not declining, but growing, unless a strong barrier of moral conviction can be raised against the mischief, we must expect, in the present circumstances of the world, to see it increase.

Mill felt that 'the only purpose for which power can be rightfully exercised over any member of a civilised community, against his will, is to prevent harm to others. His own good, either physical or moral, is not a sufficient warrant.'

Things have changed since Mill's essay was first published in 1859. As he feared, the state has increased the extent of its influence and control over the individual. Some of the legislation and government intervention has sought to promote economic security or material welfare or racial equality; and, while some might find fault with this, most of us would not. On the other hand, there are more doubtful areas in which the state has tried to exert its influence over individuals in matters affecting their moral welfare, such as sexual practices, pornography, obscenity and, of course, the use of drugs.

Prohibition

The major systems that can be used for the control of drugs involve prohibition, decriminalization or legalization. Decriminalization and legalization are sometimes discussed as if they were synonymous. They are not. In decriminalization, the drug remains illegal but penalties for use are reduced, or waived. With legalization, the possession and sale of a drug is legal but is generally regulated, as with the laws regarding the sale or availability of cigarettes or alcohol.

National drug control policy in the UK, in the US and in most countries throughout the world, is heavily committed to a model of prohibition backed by punishment. Prohibition is the most coercive and paternalistic of the policy options, and ought to require the strongest justification in a free society. The current approach to the prohibition of drugs in the UK is based upon the Misuse of Drugs Act 1971 which places drugs into three classes. The classification system is used by the courts to determine what scale of penalties should be applicable to offences involving different drugs. The classes are supposedly linked to their comparative harmfulness and are related to maximum penalties, with the highest penalties for Class A drugs and the lowest for Class C.

One major problem with this system is that it mistakenly presumes that 'harmfulness' can be understood as an intrinsic property of the substance itself. One of the central themes of *Living with Drugs* is that the harm that can follow in the wake of drug taking is seldom directly attributable to the substance itself. Much more often it can be understood only in terms of a complex interaction between the substance, the user, the route of use and of the circumstances in which drugs are used. Another problem is that the UK classification system operates on the basis that people who are caught taking what are supposedly the more harmful drugs should also be punished most severely (thereby increasing their misfortune). Presumably this approach is based upon the old-fashioned and naïve assumption that harsher punishments serve as a deterrent to the use of drugs.

But even allowing for that, the UK classification system is pretty strange. For example, among the most harmful Class A drugs, the system lumps together heroin, crack cocaine, magic mushrooms and ecstasy. Until the 2004 reclassification, it also included cannabis derivatives such as cannabinol as Class A drugs (see later in this chapter). Yet methylamphetamine, which is a powerful and potentially very risky drug (certainly on a par with crack cocaine), has been classified as Class B (only after questions were asked in Parliament was this reconsidered, with the recommendation that it be moved up to Class A). And temazepam and other benzodiazepines which can cause many problems, especially when injected, are classified as C. Since the system was first established, and despite advice to the contrary, very few changes have been made. Where changes have been made, these have not always been sensible. One such change (in 1977) involved the promotion of ecstasy to Class A so that it was now included with what are supposedly the most dangerous drugs.

Different countries take different approaches to this issue. Most other European countries divide commonly misused drugs into classes though none uses the same system as the UK, and only three (Italy, the Netherlands and Portugal) relate the classes to maximum penalties. However, many countries (among them, Germany, Greece, Denmark, Finland and Ireland) continue to put heroin and cannabis into the same legal class.

Although different countries appear to adopt different policies towards the control of drugs, the differences are relatively minor compared to the similarities of approach. The one thing that unites them is the overwhelming reliance upon the tools of prohibition – enforcement and supply reduction. This is mostly clearly seen in those countries like the US or Sweden which like to be seen as 'tough' on drugs. More surprisingly, it is also true of the countries which are sometimes described as being 'soft' on drugs (such as the Netherlands).

In Sweden, enforcement takes up about three-quarters of the total financial resources. Out of the total annual expenditure for 1997–98 which was devoted to tackling drug misuse in the UK (about £1.4 billion), law enforcement and customs/interdiction accounted for 75 per cent of the expenditure, with about 13 per cent spent on treatment. In the US, the National Drug Control Strategy allocated two-thirds of the entire 1999 annual federal drug control budget to supply reduction measures. In that year, the sum provided by the federal government for drug control was just under $18 billion. This was backed up by a further expenditure of about 70–80 per cent of the tens of billions of extra dollars spent on drug control by state and local governments. All of this goes towards policing, prosecution and punishment of illicit drug users. The amount to be spent from the federal allocation during 1999 on domestic law enforcement measures alone was a staggering $9 billion (about half of the entire budget). The amount allocated in 1999 to treatment (one of the only areas in which there is strong scientific evidence of effectiveness) was just over $3 billion (about one-sixth of the budget).

However, as in virtually all other countries, the Netherlands also spends much more on enforcement than on prevention, treatment and harm reduction together. Despite the widely stated opinion that drug policy in the Netherlands is moving towards legalization of drugs, the reality is a long-standing emphasis on prohibition and drug control measures. The number of coffee shops fell from about 1,200 in 1997 to 805 in 2001, and special enforcement units have been set up to target the production and the trafficking of illegal drugs. The major public sentiment and political stance in the Netherlands has always been 'antidrug', with perhaps a partial exception for cannabis, and enforcement activities have taken up most of the financial resources allocated to drug policy in the Netherlands for decades.

In return for the huge sums that are spent on prohibition and repression, the usual indicators of 'success' are the numbers of arrests, or quantities and hypothetical 'street values' of drugs seized. Such indicators are used without evidence to show how (if at all) these are related to levels of drug use. In stark contrast to the money so freely spent on supply reduction measures, any money which is spent on treatment is linked to strict requirements to demonstrate both effectiveness and cost-effectiveness. Although there is good evidence of the benefits of the treatment of drug addiction, most of the available money is poured down the bottomless drain of prohibition. There are few points of general agreement with respect to the control of drugs. But one thing which should no longer be in doubt is that laws do not stop the use of drugs.

In fact, there is hardly any consistent relationship between the prevalence of drug taking and the types and severities of drug policies in different countries. Some countries have extremely harsh prohibitionist policies and high rates of illegal drug use. Others operate the same sorts of policies and have low rates of use. Some countries apply relatively tolerant and liberal drug policies without experiencing high rates of use. Even where national drug laws have been relaxed (as with cannabis in the Netherlands and Australia) there have been no corresponding increases in use.

The earliest record of prohibitionist thought can probably be credited to an Egyptian priest who, in 2000 BCE, wrote: 'I, thy superior, forbid thee to go to the taverns. Thou art degraded like the beasts.' By the 16th century, a German prince was offering financial rewards to anyone who gave information leading to the conviction of coffee drinkers; and a century later, the czar of Russia executed anyone found in possession of tobacco.

In the UK during the First World War, Lloyd George laid the basis for the UK's system of 'opening hours'. Lloyd George felt that one of the most serious obstacles to increasing the output of munitions was heavy drinking by the workforce. The factory owners who made so much profit out of the war were in complete agreement with this opinion. The Ship Building Employers Federation asked for the closure of all public houses and clubs in the area of any munitions factory. The king himself offered to give up alcoholic drink if it would provide an example to the workers. This gesture, which became known as 'The King's Pledge', was not a success, partly, one feels, because of a conspicuous unwillingness on the part of certain politicians and other public figures to adopt the same extreme measures that they urged upon everyone else. After trying various other ideas, Lloyd George produced the Defence of the Realm Act. This drastically reduced the availability of alcohol, and introduced the UK system of opening hours.

Whether as a result of this or of other factors, there was an immediate and dramatic change in the nation's drinking habits during the war. Between 1914 and 1918, the consumption of spirits was reduced by half, and that of beer was cut even more drastically, from 1,200 million gallons to 460 million gallons. Drunkenness convictions were reduced by almost 80 per cent and death from liver cirrhosis dropped by more than 60 per cent. For various reasons, these changes seemed to occur mainly in the large towns and cities; the new licensing regulations had little effect on country areas. It is also apparent that what effects the new laws did have were short-lived. Within a year or two, the initial effects seem to have been swamped by other more important changes that were taking place at the time. Quite apart from the massive social disruption that was a result of the war and the post-war economic depression, there was already a clear national trend towards reduced consumption of alcohol prior to the war.

This UK system of control was primarily geared to restricting the overall levels of alcohol consumption. It did not prevent (indeed it may have encouraged) 'binge drinking'. As closing time approached in the UK's pubs, it was typical to find an increased tempo of drinking and an increased number of drunks. The laws relating to opening hours in England and Wales were dramatically changed in 2005. The new Licensing Act represented a significant change in alcohol control policy in that it permitted flexible opening hours. This included the possibility of 24-hour licences with round-the-clock drinking in pubs and clubs, and 24-hour sales in supermarkets. A spokesman from the British Beer and Pub Association welcomed the changes: 'At last .... Adults are going to be treated like grown-ups and given a little bit of choice about having a social life beyond 11 o'clock at night'. In one pub chain, 90 per cent of the pubs immediately applied for extensions to their licensing hours. The government argued that the new law would help to tackle the problems associated with fixed closing times. The police, however, feared that this would aggravate the problems of drunkenness and public disorder during the early hours of the morning. This represents an extremely interesting natural experiment. Time will tell.

The most dramatic efforts to control alcohol, however, have attempted to prevent any use of it. Finland and Norway have both tried this approach. Both subsequently abandoned it when it failed. But the best-known example of prohibition occurred in the US between 1920 and 1933. During this period, America provided a convincing demonstration of what can go wrong with efforts to legislate drug taking out of existence.

Among the pressure groups which worked to achieve the Act of Prohibition were the temperance societies. Variously appalled both by drinking as a form of pleasure in its own right and by the wide range of social ills that they attributed to the effects of drink, they were firmly convinced that alcohol itself was sinful; and they were determined to enforce their beliefs on the rest of American society. To this end, they applied their considerable political influence.

As in the UK, part of the rationale behind the US legislation was also linked to the war effort. The Anti-Saloon League declared alcohol to be 'un-American, pro-German, youth corrupting, and treasonable'. The Eighteenth Amendment (otherwise known as the War Prohibition Law) was introduced partly to prevent the alcoholic subversion of the war effort, though by the time it was introduced the war had been over for a year. It attempted to remove alcohol from the American culture without providing any alternative form of satisfaction. The legislators were strong in their moral certainty that alcohol was a bad thing, but weak in their psychology. Drug taking should not be regarded merely as some trivial fault in human behaviour that can be easily corrected. Those whose business it is to pass our laws are deluding themselves if they believe that a law can achieve things that people themselves cannot.

The weight of public opinion was not behind Prohibition. Throughout the country, illicit alcohol was produced and distributed to meet the popular demand It has been estimated that, during a one-year period, the citizens of America consumed 200 million gallons of malt liquor and 118 million gallons of wine. By 1930, more than half a million Americans had been arrested for drink offences and sentenced to a total of more than 33,000 years' imprisonment. More than a quarter of a million stills were confiscated, but the bootleg liquor continued to flow. The black market that was necessary for the manufacture and supply of illegal alcohol encouraged the involvement of organized crime: there were more than 700 gangland assassinations during Prohibition. At the same time, many public officials showed an obvious disregard for the prohibition law. Respected public figures, including many politicians in Washington, routinely broke the alcohol laws. Al Capone commented on this state of affairs:

> I make my money by supplying a public demand. If I break the law, my customers, who number hundreds of the best people in Chicago, are as guilty as I am. The only difference between us is that I sell and they buy. Everybody calls me a racketeer. I call myself a businessman. When I sell liquor, it's bootlegging. When my patrons serve it on a silver tray on Lake Shore Drive, it's hospitality.

As with other attempts to prohibit a particular drug, the black-market alternatives are frequently of poor quality. Some of the illegal alcohol that was manufactured may have been as good as the original product; some of it can only be regarded as poisonous. The consumption of illicit alcohol was responsible for 35,000 deaths, and many more were permanently incapacitated. Such was the deterrent effect of Prohibition that, in Chicago, deaths related to the use of alcohol rose by 600 per cent during that period.

Prohibition is still with us. It no longer applies to alcohol in Western societies, but to drugs; and most people accept this as a completely natural and desirable state of affairs. As with the prohibition of alcohol, the laws prohibiting drugs were passed, not so much on the basis of reasoned argument or scientific evidence, but more often as the result of some moral crusade. It is not so long since heroin, LSD, cannabis and the amphetamines were all legally available. In the US, heroin and the opiates were outlawed at the same time as alcohol.

At the end of the 19th century, American newspapers 'discovered' a new scandal. Lurid tales of crime and debauchery emerged, all centred on the sinister oriental menace of the opium den. Anti-Chinese feeling, which had been endemic in America throughout much of its history, was translated into a fear and hatred of one of the most characteristic habits of this group, opium smoking. Feeling at this time reached a peak of hysteria culminating in the Harrison Act. This made it impossible for the hundreds of thousands of opiates addicts in America to go on obtaining their drugs by legal means. The people who were dependent upon opiates were appalled. They wrote to the Treasury Department in their thousands, asking for 'registration permits', but no such permits were available. In 1918, a number of clinics were opened to treat the addicts. Within a year the government had forced them all to close down. The addict was forced to become a criminal and to associate with criminals if they wanted to go on using drugs. As a result, the myth that all addicts were criminals became a self-fulfilling prophecy: the laws had made it a criminal offence simply to be a heroin addict.

The approach to this issue in the UK was less harsh. Throughout most of the 19th century, opiates had been freely available, and there is little evidence that this led to any dramatic increase in either the amount of the drug that was consumed or the rate of deaths from opiates. As laws were introduced to restrict the availability of specific preparations of these drugs, the public switched to other, unrestricted, forms. The influence of the recently passed Harrison Act, and the increasing pressure applied by the medical profession to limit this form of self-medication, furthered the trend towards legal control. If any final impetus was needed, it conveniently appeared in the form of scare stories about the use of morphine and cocaine by Allied troops. (This was during the most severe period of the First World War.) The use of cocaine by soldiers on leave in the West End of London was rumoured to have reached alarming proportions. Respectable London stores (including Harrods) had been fined for selling morphine and cocaine to the troops: one store advertised them as a 'useful present for friends at the front'.

These and other incidents were inflated by fears about the potential threat that such drugs might pose to national security, and they too were prohibited under the Defence of the Realm Act. In *The Lancet*, Sir William Collins confidently but mistakenly predicted that the new laws would eliminate the use of these drugs.

There is a widespread belief in the existence of a thing called 'The British System' which has been applied to control the heroin problem in the UK. Belief in 'The British System' tends to become stronger with increasing distance from the UK. This is often, and quite falsely, described as consisting of the widespread medical prescription of heroin to addicts. In fact, heroin was only ever used in this way during the first half of the 20th century when a very small number of (mainly middle-class and medical) addicts were provided with heroin or morphine prescriptions by private and family doctors. Since the radical changes during the 1960s, and with the vastly increased numbers of opiate addicts since that time, heroin has only rarely been made available to addicts on prescription. Current estimates suggest that there may be about a quarter of a million heroin users in the UK. Probably less than a quarter of these are in contact with treatment services, and only the smallest proportion of those (perhaps about 1 per cent) is receiving a prescription for heroin. In 1990, the total number of addicts receiving injectable heroin was approximately 200. Even though heroin prescribing receives a disproportionate amount of international attention, the prescribing of heroin or other injectable drugs is numerically of small significance within the overall UK response.

The latest round of the 'war against drugs' was first declared by President Nixon in 1971, by President Ford in 1976, by President Reagan in 1982 and by other drug warriors on repeated occasions since then. The war was originally intended to be a war against supply. Gradually, it turned into a real war involving the US Customs Service, Coast Guard, Border Patrol, Department of Defense, Federal Aviation Administration, the intelligence agencies and even NASA. National Security Agency satellites tracked shipments of chemicals to processing laboratories in South American countries. American military teams went into the front lines in foreign countries where they destroyed coca crops and cocaine-manufacturing laboratories. Drug Enforcement Agency personnel went off to do their work in more than 40 foreign countries. Many people were assassinated or put on hit lists.

In 1986, President Reagan's Commission on Organized Crime reviewed the progress of the war on drugs. The conclusion was obvious: 'Despite continuing expressions of determination, America's war on drugs seems nowhere close to success.' The Commission's report noted that, after three-quarters of a century of federal effort to reduce drugs supplies, there had been no reduction in the social, economic or criminal problems related to drugs. The conclusion that was drawn was that the war should be redirected against demand, against the drug users themselves. Now there would be 'zero tolerance' for drug takers. One anti-drugs video showed an egg ('your brain'), a simmering frying pan ('this is drugs') and a fried egg ('this is your brain on drugs'). An anti-drug poster offered advice for employers: 'Help an Addict. Threaten to Fire Him.' Demands were made for compulsory testing for drugs through the screening of blood or urine samples. But despite the war against drugs and drug users, drug taking continued.

Where there is a demand for drugs, prohibition does not work. It does not work whether it is alcohol, tobacco, cannabis or heroin that is being forbidden. But worse than that, it is too often forgotten that any law has certain social costs which must be endured by society. The most serious of these is that the drug prohibition laws encourage and maintain a black-market economy and a criminal subculture. Prohibition may actually increase the likelihood that those who continue to take drugs will be damaged by them, either as a result of the impurities and adulterants that are sold with street drugs, or because the user who has suffered physical or psychological harm is afraid to seek help because of the illegality of drug taking. Anti-drug laws may lead otherwise law-abiding citizens into direct confrontation with the police, as a result of which they may suffer considerable social harm. Many students who have been caught experimenting with drugs have been expelled from universities and people have been dismissed from their jobs after a drug conviction. Nor are the police themselves left untouched by the prohibition laws. There have been various cases over the past few years in which members of police drug squads have been convicted on corruption charges after accepting bribes and even reselling confiscated black-market drugs. Society pays a heavy price for retaining these laws, yet there is a surprising reluctance to take account of these costs.

There were 86,000 drug seizures by police or Customs in the UK during 1993 (it is usually estimated that these represented 10 per cent or less of the total). During the same year nearly 5,000 people were imprisoned for drugs offences, almost one-third of whom were serving sentences of two years or more. Despite the trend in many countries towards increased tolerance of cannabis use, a vast amount of time, money and other resources in the UK continues to be directed towards cannabis, with more than 80 per cent of all drugs offences being related to this drug. More than 50,000 people were arrested for and convicted of unlawful possession of cannabis during 1993.

In the US, where the 'war against drugs' has been fought more intensely, the unforeseen consequences of using the law to regulate drug use are greater. The anti-drug laws have been made increasingly strict. In 1993, more than 1.1 million people were arrested for drug law offences and the increase in the number of people arrested for drugs offences is directly related to the growth of the prison population. Between 1986 and 1991, the proportion of people in US prisons for drugs offences more than doubled, from less than 9 per cent to more than 21 per cent. It is striking that the increase was largely due to the incarceration of black and Hispanic drug users. For black drug users, imprisonment rates increased by 447 per cent; for Hispanics, rates went up by 324 per cent. In 1994, for the first time ever, the US prison population exceeded one million. In California, which has proportionately the largest prison population in America, there are 126,000 prisoners occupying spaces intended for half that number of people. The California prison system alone costs $3 billion a year to run.

Efforts at social control do not always have predictable consequences. If architects fail so often to design successful urban living spaces, those who aspire to regulate and control our social behaviours would be well advised to show a little more humility. The efforts of police, doctors, the Pharmaceutical Association and others to restrict access to needles and syringes in Edinburgh during the early 1980s led to addicts stealing from hospital dustbins and buying injecting equipment from other users. The last retail supplier who was willing to sell injecting equipment was forced out of business in 1982, when local doctors withdrew their trade and the police put pressure on him to change his practice. This restricted access was one of the reasons for the needle sharing that led to such an explosive growth in HIV infection and hepatitis among Scottish injectors. Surveys in some areas of Scotland (notably Edinburgh and Dundee) found that up to 65 per cent of some samples of drug injectors were HIV-positive. These HIV rates were as high as anywhere in the world and Edinburgh became known as the AIDS capital of Europe.

The drug prohibition laws have established cocaine as a central part of Florida's economy. An estimated 60–80 per cent of all the cocaine that enters the US enters through Miami: this may be more than 20 metric tons of the drug. Although this may have increased the growth rate in the standard of living by up to 5 per cent per year, the social costs, as with alcohol prohibition, include some of the worst gangland battles for many years. Local police have described their attempts to enforce cocaine prohibition laws as impossible. Whenever there is a gangland killing, or some similarly shocking episode hits the headlines, the predictable reaction is to blame the drug. In fact this crime and violence is a direct product of the prohibition laws. The organized criminal is involved because they can make huge amounts of money out of the black market. It is immaterial to them whether they deal in diamonds, paintings, illegal immigrants, heroin or alcohol. The most direct measure of the failure of the prohibition of drugs can be gauged by the fact that the international trafficking in drugs is now a business on the same scale as the international petrochemical industry or global tourism.

The situation in Afghanistan is even more dramatic. Opium cultivation in that country has increased steadily since the early 1980s and the US-led war against the Taliban appears to have only briefly interrupted it before producing a further stimulation of the trade. Opium production has now spread to all of Afghanistan's 32 provinces and is the largest in the world. Afghanistan now produces very nearly 90 per cent of the world's opium stock. As of 2004, the opium/heroin industry represents more than 60 per cent of the entire national income and has become the main engine of national economic growth.

Not surprisingly, any illicit trade that is so lucrative creates its own trails of corruption, violence and instability. As a consequence, this market in opium disrupts the social and political fabric of Afghanistan, and the United Nations has suggested that 'the fear that Afghanistan might degenerate into a narco-state is slowly becoming a reality'. Far from helping the situation, the 'war on drugs' has made matters worse. Even that most fanciful of UK prime ministers, Tony Blair, was forced to recognize that despite the hundreds of millions of pounds that have been poured into this effort to eradicate the opium trade, there has been little progress since the fall of the Taliban.

The Icelandic laws against alcohol are among the most strict in the Western world. The sale of beer is forbidden and alcohol is only available from state shops under very restricted conditions and at an extremely high price. There are no pubs or bars and alcohol can only be drunk publicly in restaurants. The familiar result of all this is that there is a thriving black market. Most drinkers use spirits rather than wines or beer, and, unlike the regular daily consumption of alcohol that is often found in wine-producing countries like France, the pattern of heavy drinking typically involves episodes of drunkenness followed by periods of sobriety. The Icelandic system of control is associated with one of the highest rates of alcoholism in Europe.

A different social cost of the prohibition laws lies in the waste of social resources that is involved. The Mexican government directed 70 per cent of its Federal Law Enforcement Budget into a campaign against the opiates, even though narcotics-related offences accounted for only 7 per cent of the criminal prosecutions in the country. The most significant result of this was that the purity of street heroin in Mexico dropped from 40 per cent in 1976 to a mere 3 per cent. Mexican addicts paid more for their heroin and injected a more impure solution into their veins.

But if prohibition of the opiates does not prevent people from using heroin, as a law it is not disregarded by any significant proportion of the population. Only a comparatively small number of people use such drugs. The laws prohibiting cannabis, however, are more questionable.

The Prohibition of Cannabis

The laws that prohibit the use of drugs have not usually been conspicuously based on scientific evidence or even on rational thought. The Eighteenth Amendment was carried onto the statute books largely as a result of the political pressure exerted by temperance societies; the laws against narcotics owed much to xenophobia (in the US) and to fears about the threat to national security (in the UK). The laws against cannabis are of equally doubtful parentage.

The UK's laws against cannabis are almost entirely a product of the Geneva International Convention of 1925. More specifically they owe a great deal to an emotional outburst by the Egyptian delegate in the discussions preceding the conference. This led to cannabis being included among the opiates and addictive drugs needing control. The UK's delegates were content to legislate against cannabis through their lack of interest in a drug that was hardly ever used in Europe at that time, and the Act was ratified by Parliament almost without comment.

Unlike the UK, which adopted its anti-cannabis laws more or less by default, there was no such disinterest behind the US laws. Paradoxically, the prohibition of alcohol had stimulated interest in cannabis as an alternative drug. In New York City, 'tea pads' appeared. These smoking parlours were similar to opium dens, and sold cannabis very cheaply either for consumption on the premises or to take away. Such places were tolerated by the city in much the same way as the speakeasies (illicit drinking houses), and during the early 1930s New York City alone had about 500 of them. However, the use of cannabis was not particularly widespread, and following the legalization of alcohol in 1933 it might well have gradually faded back into obscurity had it not been for the reawakening of interest inspired by Commissioner Anslinger.

In 1932, Harry J. Anslinger was appointed Commissioner in the Federal Bureau of Narcotics. Cannabis held an intense fascination for Anslinger, who was committed to the extinction of this 'lethal weed', and in his enthusiastic zeal he promoted the most misleading and ridiculous drug myths, some of which are detailed in the next chapter. But whether they were myths or not, these stories made a powerful impact both on the general public and on the legislators.

Medical authorities at the time were less impressed by the value of a further act of prohibition. One medical expert who spoke against the new bill pointed out that the case against cannabis was not based on any satisfactory scientific or medical evidence, but rested upon a few, mostly sensational, newspaper stories. And not only was the case against cannabis very weak, but there was no reason to believe that a new law would work. An editorial in the *Journal of the American Medical Association* at the time (1937, vol. 108) commented:

> The best efforts of an efficient bureau of narcotics, supplemented by the efforts of an equally efficient bureau of customs, have failed to stop the unlawful flow of opium and coca leaves and their compounds and derivatives ... What reason is there, then, for believing that any better results can be obtained by direct federal efforts to suppress a habit arising out of the misuse of such a drug as cannabis?

Other opposition was voiced by birdseed distributors who complained that canaries would not sing as well (or might even stop singing altogether!) if they were deprived of their diet of cannabis seed. Congress was sufficiently impressed by this argument to exclude sterilized cannabis seed from the bill. The opposition of the American Medical Association, on the other hand, was disregarded.

As soon as the new law had been passed, Anslinger extended his campaign against the drug. Even the medically authorized use of the drug was so energetically discouraged that it rapidly ceased altogether. Penalties against the drug increased in severity. Indeed, as recently as 1970, a first conviction for selling cannabis in Georgia could lead to a life sentence: a second conviction was punishable by death. In Louisiana, mere possession of the drug carried a minimum sentence of five years' hard labour, though the judge could sentence such vicious criminals to as much as 15 years' hard labour at their discretion. Despite the savagery of these laws, they did not stop people from using cannabis.

In most Western countries, the current trend is towards a relaxation of penalties. Many of the American states now regard possession of cannabis as a trivial offence, comparable to a minor traffic violation. In Denmark, Italy, Norway, Sweden, Switzerland and Germany, people who have been caught in possession of small amounts of cannabis are usually let off with a warning or a small fine. The UK remained one of the few European countries that retained the laws to send people to prison for up to five years merely for possessing cannabis. In 1992, more than 40,000 people in the UK were taken to court and convicted of cannabis-related offences (compared to 1,400 for heroin) and 1,700 people were serving prison sentences for cannabis offences (compared to 350 for heroin). The number of cannabis arrests continued to climb ever upwards having increased by almost two-thirds in the five years since 1988. By 1997, the number of people convicted of cannabis offences had doubled to more than 86,000 and more than 1,900 people were in prison for cannabis offences. In 1999, there were more than 110,000 recorded cannabis offences, with 76,769 offences for possession. The cost of policing cannabis during that year was estimated at £350 million. This is a wasteful and misguided approach to the control of drugs.

Various attempts had been made to correct this situation. The 1979 Report of The Advisory Council on the Misuse of Drugs suggested that cannabis be reclassified (from B to C). No action was taken. More recently, in 2000, the Runciman Report of the Police Foundation concluded that, despite its extremely widespread use, cannabis was a relatively safe drug with extremely low acute toxicity and with no deaths directly attributable to its recreational use. Their view that there was no justification for the inclusion of cannabis in Class B, nor for the inclusion of other cannabis preparations in Class A, provoked a casually dismissive response from the government which claimed that any reclassification would 'send the message that … drug taking is in some way acceptable'.

However, in 2004, the UK government (or more precisely, David Blunkett, the Home Secretary) finally acted to reclassify cannabis by moving all cannabis products to Class C. But almost immediately, the new Home Secretary who had replaced Blunkett got cold feet about the reclassification, and started to consider moving it back again to class B. After some dithering, and following the advice of the national drugs advisory committee that told him this would be a bad move and was not justified by the data, the Home Secretary finally backed off in 2006 and left cannabis in Class C. After this game of 'will he, won't he?', the Home Secretary noted that many people have been 'confused' by the debate.

But even with this welcome reclassification of cannabis, it remains illegal to possess cannabis. The guidance issued to police by the Association of Chief Police Officers recommended that police should not automatically make an arrest where users had only small amounts of cannabis in their possession, with the implementation of this guidance being left to the discretion of individual police officers and the policing priorities of particular forces. Examples of circumstances in which people might be arrested if their actions were seen as going beyond 'simple possession' include smoking in public (as at a music concert), or if the user was aged 17 or under. Possession of a Class C drug carries a maximum sentence of 2 years in prison, and offences involving supply or trafficking carry a maximum sentence of 5 years in prison.

Irrespective of how harmful cannabis may (or may not) be, legal prohibition of the drug works no better than the Eighteenth Amendment. The prohibition of alcohol produced men like Al Capone. The prohibition of cannabis has already enticed organized criminals into this area and gun battles between them and the police have been seen in the US, in Europe, and now in London.

Most actions have unforeseen as well as intended consequences (as with the restriction in availability of needles in Edinburgh). The prohibition of cannabis has had many unforeseen consequences. At the personal level users have been placed in situations in which they are at greater risk of becoming involved with other, potentially more harmful, substances and patterns of use. Similar unforeseen consequences can be found at the national level.

In 1969, Operation Intercept was launched in the US. This led to the arrest of 493 people carrying cannabis at the border with Mexico, but only small quantities of the drug were seized. Soon afterwards the name of the operation was changed to the more politically sensitive Operation Cooperation and the Mexican police were invited to destroy marihuana fields in northern Mexico. Following this, the cannabis smugglers moved further south, where they found more potent varieties of the drug. Because of the reduced supply of Mexican cannabis, other (also stronger) types were imported from Thailand and North Africa. The average THC content of cannabis in the US rose sevenfold as a result of these supply reduction campaigns and US consumers of the drug acquired a taste for the better quality product.

In order to meet this new demand, an industry in home-grown marihuana began to flourish in the US. In 1978 the US conducted dangerously misguided paraquat spraying programmes on Mexican marihuana crops, thus providing even more incentive for domestic cultivation. One outcome was the development and cultivation of *sinsemilla*, a high-potency seedless variety of marihuana. Soon, American home-grown marihuana and its farmers had become the best in the world.

The heartland for domestic cultivation was a 10,000-square-mile area of northern California – The Emerald Triangle. Indoor cultivation involving halide growing lamps, hydroponic tanks and all the latest high-tech growing methods became very popular because it was more difficult to detect. By 1987, the US home-grown marihuana crop was estimated to be worth $33.1 billion, a 150 per cent increase from 1981. Supplies had gone up and demand appeared to be insatiable. By 1988, NIDA (the US National Institute on Drug Abuse) estimated that one-third of the US population aged 12 years or over (that is, 66 million people) had used cannabis at least once. Anyone who wants to know how effective prohibition laws are when set against popular demand should look no further than this fact.

There are countries where the use of opium has been incorporated as a normal, or at least tolerated, social behaviour. In the austere but beautiful Indian state of Rajastan, opium is quite widely used in rural areas. The drug is used in many social gatherings; it is used by men and women; its use crosses boundaries of caste and religion. In many respects, the use of opium appears to occupy the same place as alcohol in most Western countries. In such circumstances it can be extremely hazardous to introduce laws of prohibition. When this was done in Pakistan, it was almost immediately followed by the introduction of heroin powder and the rapid development of heroin smoking. Thailand had a very similar experience. In 1960, the opium prohibition law was introduced and was immediately followed by the rapid growth of a national heroin problem.

Like it or not, the tendency to use drugs would appear to be an important part of the human condition, and it is one that will not be eliminated by external restraints. Physical, fiscal and statutory means have been used at various times and in connection with various different drugs. Sometimes, they have discouraged some people from using a particular drug. Occasionally, they have failed in the most conspicuous way.

But whereas governments cannot prevent people from using certain drugs, they are capable of making it extremely convenient for people to use them. As laws of prohibition represented the least subtle means of preventing drug taking, so the Opium Wars stand as one of the least subtle examples of the promotion of drug taking.

The Opium Wars

During the 18th century, England was in the grip of what the newspapers would fondly call a 'drugs epidemic'. The consumption of tea had increased by more than 20 times during the century, and the UK government was worried about the strain imposed upon the economy by this drug which was imported mainly from China. If the Chinese had been prepared to buy the UK's manufactured textiles there could have been an exchange of commodities between the two countries. Unfortunately, trade with foreign powers had been restricted by the Chinese government. In any case, the only commodity for which there was any demand was opium. Supposedly, this could only be imported under licence, but, because of the demand for the drug, opium was smuggled into China in some quantity.

Although it is generally assumed that opium smoking has always been part of the Chinese cultural tradition, it seems to have been introduced to China as late as the end of the 17th century. The commercial interest behind this was the East India Company, who cynically suggested that opium was 'a pernicious article of luxury, which ought not to be permitted except for the purposes of foreign commerce'. So successful was this commercial enterprise that, by the end of the 18th century, the regular use of opium was an established part of the Chinese way of life, with perhaps as many as 10 per cent of the population using the drug; in some provinces the majority of the population seems to have been addicted. The unfortunate social effects of the drug became more widespread and the abuses associated with it more unacceptable to the Chinese authorities. Opium smoking was rife among the Chinese soldiery. Out of a thousand troops sent to put down a rebellion in the province of Canton, the commanding officer was forced to reject 200 as unfit for service. When the rebels defeated the imperial forces, opium was blamed. Every part of Chinese society was affected. Three of the emperor's sons were addicts and the drug was again blamed for their deaths.

Prohibition had been completely unsuccessful, despite the fact that it was reinforced by flogging, exile, imprisonment and finally death. In the end, the emperor sent Imperial Commissioner Lin to Canton to suppress the illicit traffic in opium. After making various appeals to the UK, including a letter which was sent to Queen Victoria (but was never delivered), Lin confiscated and destroyed almost 2,500,000lbs of British opium. It was mixed with lime and salt, dissolved in water and flushed into the sea.

Angered by this affront to British dignity, no less than by the considerable loss of revenue involved, Lord Palmerston and the government decided that China must be compelled to pay compensation for enforcing its own laws against smuggled drugs. It was also to be compelled to extend the UK's right to import opium. A naval force of 16 warships backed up by 7,000 troops was sent to enforce this arrangement, which it duly did. Imperial policy, however, remained the same in its attempt to enforce the ineffective laws against opium smuggling. In 1856, more than 10 years after Commissioner Lin's confiscation of opium in Canton, the new emperor sent another commissioner to resume Lin's policies. As a result, the *Arrow*, was seized. The *Arrow* was a Chinese-owned smuggling ship which had been registered as a UK vessel in Hong Kong. Again Palmerston sent out the gunboats. The commissioner's official residence was shelled, and a UK expeditionary force occupied Peking and burned down the emperor's Summer Palace. As before, the military contest was one-sided, and as part of the settlement China was compelled to accept unlimited imports of opium on payment of a duty. Afterwards, there was a massive increase both in the amounts of opium imported into China and in the corresponding economic benefits to the UK government.

So successful was the opium trade that, in many Asian countries, good agricultural land was turned over to the cultivation of the poppy instead of food crops. Whole communities became dependent upon the production of opium, and the local warlords found it a reliable source of revenue. During the Japanese occupation of these territories in the 1930s and 1940s, opium was used to provide revenue for the occupation forces and morphine factories were set up. Throughout Asia there are many communities that rely upon the opium crop for their survival. The same is true in a number of Middle Eastern countries where the poppy is the staple of village life. Its oil is a base for cooking, its leaves can be used to make a salad, its seeds to enrich the bread, and the pods to feed cattle. And there remains the gum itself, which can be sold to many interested parties. Once the poppy has become an established crop, it is very difficult to eradicate it. Once the opium is available, the temptations for the drug smugglers are enormous. The Opium Wars were a comparatively trivial incident in history, but their consequences are still very much with us.

Alternative Methods of Control

Somewhere between total prohibition (which is ineffective) and the promotion of drugs by the state (which is undesirable) there remain a number of less dramatic alternatives. These may include state rationing, state-run monopolies, restriction of outlets for the sale of drugs, licensing hours and limited forms of prohibition which may apply to children (or other stigmatized groups, possibly including women or ethnic minorities).

Undoubtedly, there is a need for better information to be made available about drugs and their effects. A better informed public might use drugs more sensibly and suffer less harm from them as a result. However, it would be naïve to imagine that to provide the public with such information would necessarily lead to any dramatic decrease in drug use. Indeed, it is possible that unrealistic fears about drugs may sometimes serve as a deterrent to drug use.

The early abolitionists believed that teaching children 'the evils of alcohol' would lead to abstinence, but it did not. Since anti-drug propaganda does not prevent the use of drugs, there is little reason to expect impartial drug information to do so. Psychologists have found little evidence that knowledge and behaviour are directly related. A person may know that riding a fast motorcycle is extremely dangerous and still continue to do so; equally, knowing that air travel is one of the safest forms of transport does not stop many people from being terrified of flying.

A good deal of drug education has been an anxiety-stricken enterprise which has tried to 'innoculate' children with 'preventative' information that will keep them safe from drugs. This approach has not worked. All too often it has failed because the educational material has purveyed an alarming but completely unrealistic picture of drugs and drug taking. The 'facts' have simply not been true, and they have not deterred children from experimenting with drugs. Most of the studies that have looked at the effects of drug education have found that it makes little impression upon attitudes and has no consistent effect on subsequent behaviour. For years, health education programmes have emphasized the risks associated with cigarette smoking. Cigarette packets carry government health warnings. No one who smokes can have avoided exposure to this deluge of information, yet millions of people continue puffing away.

In 1988, California increased the excise tax on a packet of cigarettes from 10 to 35 cents. Of the expected $600 million revenue, 20 per cent was earmarked for health education purposes. Much of this was spent on a campaign that was designed to undermine the credibility of the tobacco industry. One anti-smoking advertisement carried the message, 'Warning: the tobacco industry is not your friend.'

There is an urgent need to reassess what drug education can realistically be expected to achieve. It is vital that everyone realizes that it cannot eliminate drug taking. What it could do is to reduce the amount of harm that people suffer as a result of their drug taking. If the quality of information about drugs was better, and if it was more widely available, it might help people to use drugs more intelligently. If the relative hazards of the different drugs were fully appreciated, those who chose to take drugs might avoid the more obviously dangerous ones.

Fortunately, attempts to direct drug prevention activities towards reducing the harm suffered by users are now, at last, gradually becoming respectable and acceptable. It is sad that it took something as threatening as AIDS to produce this change of direction, but at least late is better than never. There are still committed abolitionists who remain opposed to harm-reduction initiatives and who expect prevention campaigns to present drug taking as dangerous, unpleasant and totally unacceptable. For some, anything less than zero tolerance reeks of collusion.

Few of us are in favour of people systematically harming themselves; it is, nonetheless, legally permissible to eat yourself to death, or indeed to smoke and drink yourself to death. Since the Suicide Act was passed, you can deliberately kill yourself by taking an overdose of legally available drugs or of a legally available poison. Yet we retain laws prohibiting the recreational use of certain drugs. These laws have comparatively little to do with the intrinsic dangers of the drugs involved (though this issue is always one of the first to be cited by proponents of the existing prohibition laws): for instance, the available evidence suggests that cannabis is a less harmful drug than alcohol, yet this provides little impetus towards changing the legal status of these drugs.

A more central principle in this issue is that of society seeking to protect the individual from the consequences of their own actions. This principle was first stated by Plato who argued that the state must save its citizens from the corruptions that are intrinsic to the masses; it is based upon a belief that the general public lacks the intelligence, discipline and motivation to protect or even to know what is in their own interests. Unfortunately, drug taking may well be something from which people do not want to be saved.

Among the other factors behind the drug prohibition laws is the desire of certain sections of society to suppress anything that upsets or offends them. It is interesting that the Third Reich was committed to the drive against smoking and sponsored many anti-smoking campaigns. Cigarettes were banned in many public places and from Luftwaffe premises. SS officers were forbidden to smoke when on duty, and cigarette advertising which featured sportsmen, attractive women and fast cars was banned. In recent years, the view that the state has every right to ban behaviour which is deemed to be offensive was vigorously expressed by Lord Devlin, who argued that the law is a legitimate means of forcing the individual to adopt conventional moral codes of conduct. Devlin's argument turns on the point that anything which offends the community may justifiably be made against the law.

John Stuart Mill had anticipated each of these paternalist arguments and found them repugnant:

> So monstrous a principle is far more dangerous than any single interference with liberty; it acknowledges no right to freedom whatever, except perhaps to that of holding opinions in secret, without ever disclosing them; for the moment an opinion which I consider noxious passes anyone's lips, it invades all the social rights attributed to me.

However, the way in which we are to separate the rights of the individual and the notion of harm to others is not entirely straightforward. Many drugs, and especially those such as tobacco and alcohol which are most widely used, impose a considerable burden upon others in society who must pick up the costs of health care and economic loss through accidents, industrial inefficiencies and so on. Although these costs are impossible to quantify with any accuracy, it is clear that they are very high. The economic costs to the US of alcohol problems alone are estimated at over $100,000 million per year. In addition, there are other incalculable costs, such as the misery caused by friends or relatives being injured by drunk drivers.

We are increasingly aware of the many costs of drug taking. However, John Stuart Mill was not unaware of these issues and he did consider an alternative form of restriction: that although the state should permit such forms of behaviour as drug taking which might be against the best interests of the individual, it could also indirectly discourage such behaviour. One way of doing so is through taxation.

This system is already used for alcohol and tobacco, both of which have carried a high excise duty for so long that this is accepted as a fact of life. (The actual cost of a bottle of whisky is only about one-fifth of its retail price.) For some years now, there has been a growing acceptance of the notion that the incidence of drug-related problems in society is closely related to the average consumption levels in that society. As a result there has developed a preference for tackling such problems by using legislative controls. The comments of the advisory committee to the UK government in 1977 reflect a good deal of common sense in this matter:

> We do not recommend, for example, that alcoholic drink should, by the increase of taxation, be priced out of the reach of many people. We consider that this step would unfairly penalize the vast majority of unaddicted drinkers, and do nothing to reduce the incidence of alcoholism amongst those who could still afford it, whilst tempting those who could not toward dangerous alternative sources of intoxication.

It is still not clear precisely how taxation affects consumption. Detailed analyses show that, whenever there has been an increase in the cost of alcohol or tobacco, there has been a short-term fall in consumption (or the rate of consumption has increased less sharply). It has been suggested that a 10 per cent increase in the price of cigarettes produces a reduction in consumption of about 10 per cent among teenagers, and of about 4 per cent among adults. There are links between the price of a drug and levels of consumption, but these relationships often moderated by other factors, and are sometimes rather weak. Between 1960 and 1990, there was a steady decline in the use of tobacco in the UK. During that time, the real (inflation-adjusted) price of tobacco also fell. The principal factor affecting demand during that time seems to have been not price, but changes in attitudes towards smoking possibly related to health warnings and health education programmes but more probably associated with the complex and unquantifiable shifts that occur in social belief systems over time. Similarly, in Ireland, where alcohol is expensive as a result of high taxation, this had led to a large proportion of income being devoted to the purchase of drink, rather than to any fall in consumption. Since most of the studies of the link between price and consumption have been done with the legal drugs such as alcohol and tobacco, it is unclear what sort of link might exist for other types of drugs.

If legalization or some form of state regulation of what are currently illegal drugs is ever to take place, the economic regulation of drug consumption will become important. It has often been assumed that the demand for illegal drugs is likely to be independent of the cost of the drug; that is, relatively large increases in price would leave demand unchanged (in the jargon of economists, this sort of demand is elegantly described as being 'price-inelastic'). When this is the case, supply reduction efforts tend not only to be ineffective, they are also frequently counterproductive. For example, users may turn to crime to obtain money, and the use of adulterated drugs may increase. Heroin users switch from chasing the dragon to the more cost-efficient but more dangerous method of injecting heroin because of the high cost of their habit. At present, very little is known about the effects of price upon demand for different types of illegal drugs by users at different stages of their drug-taking careers.

In any case, there are problems involved in using taxation as a way of controlling the use of drugs which are currently only available from illicit sources. If these drugs were legally available, but taxed heavily enough to deter consumption, there would be an incentive to evade paying the tax by using the illegal channels of distribution that already exist. This problem is already evident with the growth of cigarette and tobacco smuggling which has established itself across Europe within the past decade. Conversely, if prices were reduced to sufficiently low levels to cut out any profits for black-market supply networks, there would be a risk that the low price of the drug would increase availability and increase the numbers of people who would take the drug. Other problems to be addressed in any consideration of the state regulation of drugs might include the details of how retail sales might be organized, age limits and restrictions in the circumstances in which drug taking would be permitted.

Another way in which the state can attempt to influence the consumption of drugs is through advertising. It remains an intriguing but unanswered question whether advertising really does affect the amount of drugs that people take. The companies that advertise cigarettes and alcohol have argued that advertising does not turn non-users into users, but that its major purpose is to change brand preferences. The manufacturers would like us to believe this was true. The cigarette and alcohol-control lobbies would wish us to believe otherwise. In fact, there is little evidence one way or the other. No one knows to what extent cigarette and alcohol advertising contributes towards the consumption or abuse of these drugs.

One of the few occasions on which a government has prohibited the advertising of alcohol and tobacco occurred in British Columbia from 1971 to 1972. This was done in the hope that it would reduce smoking and drinking, especially among young people. The ban proved to be generally unpopular: six months after it was introduced almost two-thirds of the population was opposed to it, and after only 12 months the ban was lifted. The Addiction Research Foundation of Toronto, which examined the effects of the ban as it related to the consumption of alcohol, found no evidence that it led to any reduction in drinking. Ultimately, the control of drug taking always remains in the hands of the individual, and the best chance of achieving effective control lies in helping each person to make a responsible choice.

Chapter 11

Junkie Myths

The Slavery of the Drug Fiend

At the very heart of the twilight world of drug addiction is the archetypal junkie, a nebulous figure misunderstood both by drug takers and by others. To the straight world, the addict is variously seen as a depraved criminal and as a sick person in need of help; but the addict is often a fiction even to themselves. The fascination of the addict attaches not to the person who is dependent upon drugs, but to their fabulous shadow.

One of the most powerful of the drug myths is that of the dope fiend. This has had a crucial influence upon our understanding of drug addiction. Its great popularity during the early years of the 20th century owed much to the efforts of Commissioner Anslinger. The remarkable Harry J. Anslinger, former US Commissioner of Narcotics, has already appeared briefly in these pages. It is worth returning to him because he was such an influential force in establishing certain drug myths. In setting up the myth of the drug fiend, one of Anslinger's successful ploys was to attach to cannabis the thread of xenophobia that runs through the US's cultural tradition. Not only was cannabis a foreign drug, but almost certainly it was an un-American drug. Mexicans and blacks smoked it. An article published in the *New York Times* (15 September 1933) described how Mexican drug peddlers had been seen distributing cigarettes containing marihuana to school children. Not surprisingly, foreigners were affected in a particularly awful way by this drug. A Colorado newspaper of the time commented obliquely, 'I wish I could show you what a small marihuana cigarette can do to one of our degenerate Spanish-speaking residents.' The reader is not shown, but is encouraged to muse upon, the worst sorts of atrocities. Violence, sexual frenzy and homosexuality are the most common themes that turn up in the discussions of the cannabis threat.

It was no accident that such stories came to be linked with cannabis. During a conference on the drug, a government official is on record as asking Commissioner Anslinger for details of how cannabis affected the user: 'Have you lots of cases on this? Horror stories – that's what we want.' Anslinger was happy to oblige with descriptions of the total moral and physical degradation produced by the drug. The smallest dose, he told his eager audience, was likely to cause fits of raving madness, sexual debauchery, violence and crime: it was one of the most dangerous drugs known to man. In his book, *The Traffic in Narcotics*, he spares none of the lurid details that were requested, offering several revolting case histories which describe in the sort of detail familiar to certain Sunday newspapers how cannabis had caused rape, violation of a 17-month-old baby, berserk violence, murder and even mutiny. As an example of the quality of this evidence, there is one case history that describes how a man shot two women and then committed suicide by 'slicing himself to bits about the abdomen, heart and throat'. Anslinger was convinced that this was directly caused by cannabis because 'law enforcement officers believed that G. was under the influence of marihuana at the time'. If that 'evidence' were not enough to convince the reader, he adds: 'It was the opinion of the doctor who saw G. just before he died that … the only thing … that would produce such a condition, to such a degree, is marihuana.' Some evidence!

The myth of the dope fiend clearly satisfied some profound need in the citizenry. It became more and more widely accepted. By the 1930s, it was firmly established in popular literature. In *Bulldog Drummond at Bay* (1935) the villains are torturing a man to make him talk: after a whispered conversation, the deadly cannabis is produced and administered.

That drug; what is that ghastly drug? moaned the prisoner.

Haven't they told you?' asked Veight. 'It is not a nice one, Waldron, and its result in time is to send you mad. It is … a Mexican drug called Marihuana … It instils such fear into the mind of the taker that he ceases to be a man. He is mad with terror over nothing at all; his brain refuses to function; his willpower goes. And finally he finishes up in a suicide's grave or a lunatic asylum.

In the years prior to the 1937 anti-cannabis legislation, Anslinger and his Bureau on Narcotics spearheaded the propaganda campaign linking the drug with various atrocities. Anslinger had read what he was pleased to refer to as 'a very unfortunate report released some years ago by the LaGuardia Committee. In its wisdom, the Bureau immediately detected the superficiality and hollowness of its findings and denounced it.' Like so many drug myths, the notion of the dope fiend was immediately adopted as incontrovertible fact. In some strange way, it provided a psychological satisfaction too profound to give way easily in the face of more considered evidence, and it has proved remarkably resilient.

The myth of the dope fiend is still with us. Every so often it thrusts its way back into the public consciousness to mobilize our deepest fears and to provide a scapegoat for our anger and hatred. Anslinger did not restrict his mudslinging to cannabis users. His righteous anger was exercised even more by those who indulged in the use of opiates. *The Traffic in Narcotics* (which might lay legitimate claim to the title of the worst book written about drugs) is packed with little gems. One of his 'acknowledged experts' on drugs is Judge Michelsen of San Francisco: 'the dope fiend in his every activity should be recognized and indexed for what he is … In the world of crime we find him standing in the front ranks of the most subversive and anti-social groups in the country.' Also quoted in the book is a more recent decision of the Supreme Court of the US which described addiction in the following terms:

> To be a confirmed drug addict is to be one of the walking dead ... The teeth have rotted out, the appetite is lost, and the stomach and intestines don't function properly. The gall bladder becomes inflamed; eyes and skin turn a bilious yellow; and in some cases membranes of the nose turn a flaming red; the partition separating the nostrils is eaten away – breathing is difficult. Oxygen in the blood decreases; bronchitis and tuberculosis develop. Good traits of character disappear and bad ones emerge ... Nerves snap; vicious twitching develops. Imaginary and fantastic fears blight the mind and sometimes complete insanity results. Often times too, death comes – much too early in life.

Most people would like to believe that this was an accurate and objective description of the consequences of drug addiction. It is not.

There are individuals who have used heroin or other potentially addictive drugs (and this includes alcohol) throughout their lives without suffering any of the physical and mental damage described in this statement. I have seen several people who have been addicted to huge amounts of heroin for more than 40 years, yet even this had produced none of the horrifying effects supposedly linked to drug addiction. Two addicts, both men in their sixties at the time of writing the first edition of *Living with Drugs*, had used heroin in large doses, sometimes as high as 1,600 milligrams a day, since they were teenagers. By any normal standards, they were in reasonable mental and physical health; certainly, they had suffered none of the appalling consequences listed above. Nor are these just two isolated cases.

Since the setting up of the London drug clinics, there has been a sizeable number of 'stable' addicts who have not been involved in crime, who have not involved themselves with the black-market drug scene and whose physical health has been generally satisfactory; many have been regularly employed. Despite the fact that these addicts are in many respects the most 'normal' group within the addict population, they have been prescribed larger amounts of heroin than other, more chaotic, addicts. The drug itself does not cause the social and psychological, nor even the physical, deterioration that is so often attributed to it. The reasons for such deterioration must be sought in terms of the psychological characteristics of individual addicts and in the social meaning that drug taking has for them. Descriptions of addicts that merely reiterate Anslinger's stereotype of the 'parasitic', 'depraved', 'vicious', 'dangerous' drug fiend are worse than useless. Not only do these descriptions present the most misleading of stereotypes, but they also construct an imaginary type with which the addict can identify. This is not as far-fetched as it may sound. The myth of the dope fiend is just as firmly entrenched in the junkie subculture as it is in straight society.

Indeed, addicts are often the most fervent believers in their own total and irreversible slavery to drugs. Jean Cocteau's book, *Opium: The Diary of a Cure*, is based on a set of notes written in 1929 and 1930; in it he writes how 'one always speaks of the slavery of opium'. This theme runs through most of the junkie literature.

Few writers have put the position more forcefully than William Burroughs. In his book, *The Naked Lunch* (1968), he wrote:

> Junk is the ideal product ... the ultimate merchandise. No sales talk necessary. The client will crawl through a sewer and beg to buy ... The junk merchant does not sell his product to the consumer, he sells the consumer to his product. He does not improve and simplify his merchandise. He degrades and simplifies the client.

Later in the same book he amplifies this point: 'Beyond a certain frequency need knows absolutely no limit or control ... lie, cheat, inform on your friends, steal, do anything to satisfy total need ... Dope fiends are sick people who cannot act other than they do.'

In recent years, the myth of the drug slave has been exhumed with the American 'discovery' of the horrors of crack. In April 1989, Special Agent Stutman of the US Drug Enforcement Agency (and very obviously a man after Commissioner Anslinger's heart) addressed the British Association of Chief Police Officers. He told them that crack 'has taken over our society and changed the face of our society'; that 'the last vestiges of family ... in New York and in most other major cities in the United States, are beginning to disappear'; that 73 per cent of fatalities in child battering cases were children of crack-abusing parents; that crack 'is a drug unlike any other drug that we have ever seen'; that 'of those people who tried crack three or more times, 75 per cent will become physically addicted at the end of the third time'; that 'crack is considered a virtually incurable addiction' [*sic*]; and finally that 'I will personally guarantee you that two years from now you will have a serious crack problem.'

This ill-informed nonsense had a predictable impact upon the good folks of the UK press, who did their best to whip up a lather of consternation. Two years later, Stutman's guarantee seemed to have been lost, and whenever the media reported upon cocaine problems no reference was made to their previous predictions.

The slavery and helplessness of the drug user occurs regularly in junkie conversation: such comments are both a celebration of, and an apology for, the junkie life. They excuse any fault, on the grounds that, as a helpless slave to their addiction, the addict is not responsible for their own behaviour. It is a view of drug taking that combines the perverse satisfactions of martyrdom with a powerful rationalization about why it is pointless to try to give up drugs. Such beliefs are both a justification and a trap. They give meaning and significance to the addict's lifestyle, but because they attribute such invincible power to the drug effects, they create a barrier to change. The world that addicts invent for themselves hardens and imprisons them. Instead of freeing them from the demands of reality, the junkie identity has a nasty habit of turning into a cage that traps them, and from which escape seems only the most remote possibility.

In fact, the addict, like anyone else, faces choices between different options. The decision to give up may be a difficult one. Turning that decision into reality is even more difficult but it is far from impossible, and sooner or later most addicts do give up. Many will also give up without any formal treatment. Many people with alcohol problems (including alcohol addiction) give up without treatment, and the vast majority of cigarette smokers who give up do so without any sort of treatment. Many people who use drugs such as heroin and cocaine also give up without treatment. Indeed, some of the most interesting clinical treatments for addictive behaviours have incorporated principles of self-change.

Contrary to junkie myths about the irreversible and inescapable decline into addiction, some drug takers stop using precisely because they become aware that they are drifting into physical dependence. For the addict, as for many drug users, the balance sheet of costs and benefits gradually tends to shift away from an overall benefit to increasingly heavy costs. Some of these costs provide the most important reasons why addicts decide to give up. One epigrammatic summary of the reasons why alcoholics choose to stop drinking can be neatly summarized as *livers, lovers, livelihoods and the law*.

Withdrawal, the Torment of the Damned

The addict's exaggerated fear of withdrawal fulfils a similar role, offering a powerful justification for not coming off drugs. A good deal is made of 'the sickness', both by addicts and by non-addicts. Indeed, a good deal too much is made of it. The idea that heroin withdrawal involves unbearable pain has proved to be a most convenient fiction for the media. It provides exactly the right sort of voyeuristic titillation for which the general public has shown itself to be so eager. *The Man with the Golden Arm* was one of the first films to linger over the agonies of withdrawal. More recently, *French Connection II* showed the tough-guy hero reduced to a grovelling animal as he tried to kick the habit that had been forced on him by the gangsters. John Lennon's record 'Cold Turkey' is a celebration of the torments of withdrawal, culminating in Lennon's screams of pain and anguish. And in the magazine *New Society* (6 March 1980), an article, 'Cold Turkey in Harlem', tells the same story. An addict 'has endured the withdrawal tortures … and pulled through'. This is described as 'miraculous' and 'unbelievable'. The hyperbole of these accounts bears little resemblance to what might more realistically be compared to a dose of flu: certainly withdrawal can be unpleasant and distressing, but it fails by some considerable distance to match up to the myth.

Although the opiate withdrawal syndrome is one of the accepted criteria of physical addiction, it has a very large psychological component. For most addicts, withdrawal and craving are inextricably linked: each one produces the other. According to the principles of Pavlovian conditioning, if an addict regularly associates a particular place or event with their injection of drugs, that place or event will acquire some of the rewarding properties of the drug itself. As a result, things that are of no special significance to other people can provoke a powerful need for drugs in the addict. Craving and conditioned withdrawal symptoms can be triggered off by the sight of a regular scoring place such as Piccadilly Circus or Times Square, or by music that has strong drug-related memories for the addict. After giving up heroin, Anthony Sharples (1975) wrote:

> In practice I had to avoid the company of other addicts, for their presence and conversation was … the strongest stimulus of all … Equally there were whole areas, geographical and social, financial and cultural, which overlapped with the junk community and which I had to avoid.

Conditioning processes can also have the opposite effect. When an addict is badly in need of a fix but has no drugs, they can obtain some relief from their craving by injecting water, or even by just pushing the needle into a vein. This event has come to provide a small part of the drug experience with which it has been so often associated.

For most forms of drug taking, the actual process of withdrawing from drugs presents few medical problems and can be managed easily and with the minimum of discomfort for the addict. Using a gradual inpatient withdrawal scheme, an addict can be withdrawn from any dose of any drug within a short period of time. The time taken to complete withdrawal will vary according to the preferences of the doctor and the user, but for heroin it can be completed in anything from a couple of days to two or three weeks. The time that I spent in the drug treatment clinics in Pakistan showed me how even heroin users on doses of up to 10 grams could be withdrawn with only moderate discomfort and be symptom-free within as little as 10 days.

There are different problems for different drugs. Withdrawal from alcohol, for instance, carries some of the more serious medical risks, and it can lead to some of the most distressing withdrawal problems for the individual. In comparison, the opiate withdrawal syndrome can be reduced to minimal proportions by a carefully regulated withdrawal regime, yet almost all opiate addicts are terrified of withdrawal. This exaggerated fear makes more sense if it is reinterpreted as a fear of living without drugs. What terrifies the addict is not the symptoms of withdrawal, distressing though these may be, but the yawning emptiness beyond, the prospect of learning to live without a chemical crutch.

In this context, it is futile to look for objective causes of addiction, or to talk of whether or not the addict can really give up drugs. The attitudes, beliefs and expectations of the addict are of paramount importance. If the addict believes that they are totally helpless before the power of heroin, or whatever drug it might be, then they are indeed helpless. But the origins of the helplessness lie in the psychology of the addict and not in some chemical property of the drug.

The clearest and most convincing evidence against the addict's need to remain addicted is that large numbers of people abandon their addictions through their own efforts. People can and do give up tea and coffee if they are convinced that it is important and necessary for them to do so; they give up cigarettes and alcohol; and they give up other supposedly more addictive drugs such as heroin. In her studies of American servicemen, Lee Robins (1974) found that, although the use of drugs was rife in Vietnam, the numbers who became re-addicted to drugs on their return to America was extremely small.[1] Even among those who had been addicted to opiates (mainly heroin) in Vietnam, only 7 per cent became re-addicted after going home. More than nine out of every 10 addicts were able to give up. Admittedly, the circumstances in which these studies took place are very unusual, but even among the ordinary street addicts it is not generally known that many successfully give up drugs.

In 1995, we started the National Treatment Outcome Research Study (NTORS). This was a prospective follow-up study of over 1,000 people (almost all of whom had heroin problems) who attended 54 treatment agencies throughout England. The study showed that the majority of the NTORS clients managed to achieve substantial and important improvements in most of their drug-related problems. Two years after starting treatment, almost half of the clients who attended the residential treatment programmes were abstinent from heroin. Even among the clients who attended the community methadone programmes, which were aimed primarily at harm-reduction rather than abstinence, one-third had managed to stay off heroin. These levels of recovery rates are impressive and they have also been found in many other studies. These findings show, without any question, that drug addiction is far from being the irreversible condition that has sometimes been assumed.

The Serpent

> Now the serpent was more subtil than any beast of the field which the Lord God had made (Genesis 3:1).

Clearly, the serpent was too clever for Adam and Eve, who were expelled from the Garden of Eden after succumbing to temptation.

One of the recurrent spectres of drug mythology is the pusher. Society is haunted by a stereotype of the pusher as a totally evil and unscrupulous figure, the serpent who corrupts the young and innocent by forcing drugs on them (he, of course, does not use drugs, being fully aware of their terrible powers). Once his victims are enslaved by their addiction – which is presumed to occur immediately and irreversibly – he assumes command of their very existence, leading them into a life of crime, vice and degradation.

Although this picture bears virtually no resemblance to reality it is one of the most popular and enduring of all the drug myths. Its appeal is that it allays primeval fears about our own vulnerability. There is always a temptation to construct outside enemies as convenient objects for us to blame when things go wrong. When confronted by the threat of serious internal opposition, politicians have traditionally sought for, and even invented, some common external enemy to unite the faithful. In George Orwell's *1984* this fear of the danger outside has been elevated to one of the central pillars of state power. The same fear underlies one of the most widespread views of physical illness. This is based upon an idea that the world is full of hostile

---

1   The social significance of these studies is described in greater detail in Chapter 3.

germs designed expressly to attack us (a fear that the deodorant and disinfectant manufacturers are careful to ensure that we should not overcome).

When faced by some threat to our cherished social and moral order, we look for the menacing stranger. When young people became dependent upon drugs, we want to blame the pusher, the demon that takes possession of their souls. Any explanation seems preferable to the prospect that the drug addictions may be due to properties of ourselves and of the social structures we believe so blameless. Addiction reawakens that ancient dread reserved for the omniscient and utterly evil corrupter.

The idea that there was a drugs problem in the UK developed quite suddenly during the 1960s and it seems to have been provoked largely by a sudden change in the numbers of heroin and opiate addicts who were known to the Home Office. Throughout the earlier years of the century, the numbers had been uniformly low: there were 367 addicts in 1945 and 335 in 1955. Most were either therapeutic addicts who had become addicted to opiates while taking them for medical reasons, or doctors and nurses whose access to drugs puts them at risk. During the 1950s, the number of non-therapeutic addicts had remained extremely low, fewer than 100. But during the 1960s, the number of young people who were addicted to heroin suddenly began to increase at an alarming rate. In the four years prior to 1968 the number of non-therapeutic addicts known to the UK Home Office quadrupled. From a mere 68 in 1958 it had reached almost 2,500 10 years later. At the time, these figures caused considerable alarm. Indeed, the hysteria that greeted the new drug problem would not have been inappropriate if the Devil himself had appeared on the streets of London.

The inevitable search for a scapegoat soon bore fruit. Several popular newspapers made a great deal of capital out of this new sensation. Pushers were sighted everywhere. One apocryphal story told how pushers had been seen masquerading as ice cream salesmen, lurking outside schools to entrap their innocent victims. Paradoxically, the child who is brought up to believe in the pusher is least well-prepared to cope with the actual offer of drugs. In reality, almost all drug dealing goes on between users. The attempt to draw some hard-and-fast line between users and pushers is based upon a misunderstanding of the drug subculture. The first time a person is offered drugs, this is most likely to involve a casual offer in a relaxed, social setting such as a party, and the offer is most likely to come either from a friend or from someone who is already known to the person. As a result, the offer is evaluated, not in terms of the conventional morality tale about the evil pusher, but in terms of the current situation and the normal rules of social behaviour. Having been prepared to resist the inveiglings of a sinister stranger, the person is taken by surprise that they should be offered drugs in such a familiar and ordinary manner.

The myth of the pusher can also take on different guises. At the time, a new angle to the pusher scare was found in the behaviour of a small number of London doctors who were prescribing what appeared to be alarming amounts of heroin and cocaine for addicts. The Brain Committee's 1965 report to the UK government identified a small group of junkies' doctors as the major source of supply for the new addicts.

During the intervening years, this story has been repeated so often as an explanation of how the heroin problem arose in the UK that its plausibility is very seldom re-examined.

Six doctors in particular were said to have acted irresponsibly. One of these was Lady Isabella Frankau, who ran a private practice in Wimpole Street, one of the most fashionable and prestigious medical addresses in London. In order to keep her patients away from the black market, Dr Frankau was prepared to prescribe whatever they asked for. During 1962, she was said to have prescribed almost 600,000 tablets of heroin. On one occasion she prescribed 900 tablets of heroin to an addict and then, only three days later, she issued a further prescription for another 600 tablets 'to replace pills lost in an accident'. Two other doctors each issued a single prescription for 1,000 tablets. Stated in such bald terms, these figures suggest malpractice. However, without knowing how many addicts were being treated, nor how heavily addicted each patient was, the figures can be misleading. In the absence of this sort of information, it is impossible to make any exact interpretation of each doctor's prescribing habits. For instance, I know of addicts attending the junkies' doctors at that time who were heavily addicted to heroin and who needed more than 1,000 tablets of heroin each week. If this is taken into account, the Brain Committee's figures lose something of their initial shock value.

By 1967, two new doctors had emerged on the drug scene. One of them, Dr Petro, had no surgery but would meet addicts in pubs, or on stations in the London Underground, where he charged £3 for each prescription. After he was arrested for failing to keep proper records of the narcotics in his possession, hundreds of his addict patients turned to other agencies for help. Petro is remembered with genuine affection by some of the addicts he treated (and not merely because he provided them with a ready source of drugs). Eventually, he was struck off the Medical Register, but even as a sad and broken old man, he was occasionally to be seen in the Underground station at Piccadilly Circus, tending the sores of the addicts.

In fact there was never a single group of just six junkies' doctors. Although the number of doctors involved rarely fell below six or rose above 12, the group was not always made up of the same people. It is too easy to vilify these doctors. Without doubt, some of them were corrupt and deliberately exploited the addicts for financial gain or for other, more sinister, purposes. One of them was later declared to be mad and was committed to an institution for the criminally insane. But others were compassionate and well-intentioned, even if their actions now seem naïve. Those who are so ready to condemn these doctors conveniently forget that most other general practitioners refused to have anything to do with drug addicts, and that there were no specialist drug dependence clinics in the UK until 1968.

Addiction as Sin and Sickness

In view of the muddled thinking that surrounds the addictions, it is hardly surprising that there should be even greater confusion about how we should treat people who become addicted to drugs. This confusion is epitomized in the inimitable Commissioner Anslinger's view of the problem. On the one hand, he wants to regard the person's dependence on drugs as an illness which can be cured by medical treatment; but, at the same time, he cannot really bring himself to believe it.

After talking of the addicts as 'unfortunates' who need treatment, Anslinger reverts to contemptuous references to 'so-called patients' and their dreadful vice; and he cites with approval a report stating that 'addiction is simply a degrading, debasing habit ... it is not necessary to consider this indulgence in any other light than an anti-social one'. In the end, Anslinger calls for a form of treatment which is indistinguishable from imprisonment. The addict must be hunted down, 'plucked out of the community and quarantined, forced to undergo a cure' (though he does not specify how this cure is to be achieved). The essence of Anslinger's idea of treatment is long-term, forcible control of the addict's behaviour; the addict must be deprived both of their freedom of movement and of their freedom of choice: 'the development and utilization ... of legal methods of restraining the personal liberty of the addict ... is highly desirable'. Some addicts, Anslinger suggests, will need this control for the rest of their lives.

It is no great surprise that Anslinger, as Commissioner of Narcotics, should have thought that this was an appropriate way for society to respond to drug taking. What is more alarming is to find an editorial in the *American Journal of Psychotherapy* (1972) not only agreeing with most of Anslinger's opinions, but proposing even more extreme solutions to the problem. Among its proposals was that any heroin addict with a criminal record predating their addiction should be permanently imprisoned on a work-farm if they committed any other crime while addicted to drugs. Also suggested were the compulsory sterilization of all opiate addicts, and the removal of children from the homes of any parent addicted to heroin. These extraordinary suggestions are based on the unsupported and erroneous assumption that addicts are by definition unable to bring up children properly: 'While this programme may sound cruel, it is far less so than to leave a child to the mercy of an addict.'

The essence of the dope fiend myth is the dehumanization of the addict. They are no longer regarded as a person who has become dependent upon drugs, but they are reduced to a robot, lacking emotion and morality, whose only desire is to obtain drugs at any cost. Provided the addict is kept at this level, the need to extend to them the usual human rights can easily be withheld; and what more basic human right than that to bring up one's own children?

The inevitable moral, physical and social decay that has so often been attributed to the use of drugs turns out to be another myth, a moral judgement masquerading as an impartial medical observation. One of the curiosities of the Wootton Committee's 1968 report to the UK government is the main appendix, written by Aubrey Lewis, Professor of Psychiatry at the University of London. Lewis was firmly of the opinion that continued use of cannabis leads to the individual's moral and social decay. This degradation was said to be shown by the way the addict becomes irritable and impulsive, by their self-neglect and inability to sustain any effort, by their refusal to accept responsibility for their family, by their homosexuality or other sexual abnormalities. 'His unkempt and prematurely aged appearance, inflamed eyes, tremor and malnutrition … make up a fairly characteristic picture.'

When doctors talk like this, it is time to withhold any easy credibility. In all discussions of drug taking there is a danger that moral attitudes may eclipse scientific judgement. It is not so long since masturbation was well-known to both the medical profession and the general public as the cause and the symptom of a variety of illnesses. Benjamin Rush, the father of US psychiatry, knew that solitary sex caused impotence, pain on urination, a lack of coordination, tuberculosis, indigestion, dizziness, epilepsy, loss of memory and many other disorders. In France, the great psychiatrist Esquirol stated that masturbation 'is recognized in all countries as a common cause of insanity'. From our smug contemporary omniscience we can laugh at this hopeless tangle of medical science and puritan morality. It was not so funny, however, for the victims of this error. In the mid-19th century, the president of the Medical Society of London created a surgical procedure to remove the clitoris in order to prevent the female version of this disease. In 1891, the Royal College of Surgeons advocated amputation of the penis as a treatment for masturbation. The final accolade for this new disease was Sigmund Freud's recognition that masturbation is the 'primal addiction'; all others, whether to alcohol, morphine or tobacco, were merely a substitute and a replacement for it. This curious episode in the history of medicine is seldom mentioned in the medical and psychiatric textbooks, though it provides an instructive example of how behaviour that offends accepted morality may be mistaken for an objective medical disorder.

It is no more logical to suppose that drug addiction, any more than masturbation, should in itself cause the sorts of deterioration described. We no longer expect addiction to tobacco or coffee to cause these changes (though they were once widely believed to do so); why then should heroin or any other illegal drug have such magical effects? There is no reason, for instance, why a drug addict should not work productively. Sigmund Freud, who was a regular and enthusiastic user of cocaine, found that it enabled him to think more clearly and to work more intensely when he was under its influence.

Another successful medical addict was Dr William Stewart Halstead, one of the greatest surgeons in the US, and a founder of the prestigious Johns Hopkins Medical School. For most of his life Halstead never used less than 200mg of morphine a day (a large dose by today's standards) and on this he was able to work efficiently. Because of his morphine addiction, he was at first offered only a junior position in the hospital, but his work was so impressive that he was soon made senior surgeon, and as such went on to earn national and international renown. While on morphine he married the head nurse in the operating room at the Hopkins and they lived happily until Halstead's death at the age of 70. There has always been a sizeable number of doctors and nurses who are addicted to drugs. A considerable number of them continue to work effectively without detection, leading otherwise ordinary lives.

Prior to the passage of the Harrison Act in 1914, the average US addict had little or no involvement with the criminal world. He or she carried on their job, keeping their home and their family life much as anyone else. A study published in 1928 showed that, out of 119 US morphine addicts, 90 had good work records. The same was true of the UK addict until as late as the 1960s. The present-day picture of drug addiction as a chaotic and criminal activity is largely due to the different people who are now attracted to this subterranean world of drugs. Probably about half of the opiate addicts today have a record of criminal convictions (sometimes an extensive record, and sometimes for serious crimes). Yet it is unwarranted to jump to any simple conclusion that the addiction caused the criminal behaviour. Many addicts become involved in crime *before* they become addicted to drugs. The crime and the drug addiction may sometimes reflect a more general social deviancy that led the person to reject a more conventional life. On the other hand, the need to maintain a regular drug habit places the drug user in the difficult position of having to find huge sums of money or other (generally criminal) ways of obtaining drugs.

In the NTORS project, more than 1,000 addicts were admitted to treatment programmes across England. These addicts were involved in a massive amount of criminal activity. They had committed more than 70,000 crimes within a 90-day period before starting treatment. Most of this involved either drug-selling offences or crimes of theft. These offences were closely related to the need to obtain drugs of dependence (usually heroin). But, within this group, 75 per cent of all the crimes were committed by only about 10 per cent of the addicts. After treatment, those addicts who managed to stay away from regular use of heroin were more than 10 times more likely also to stay away from crime than the addicts who went back to regular heroin use.

The moral view of addiction as a form of depravity is no longer as fashionable as it once was. It is sometimes felt to be more acceptable to say that the addict is sick. As a result of the latest neurobiological research studies, it has again become fashionable to talk of addiction as 'a brain disease'. But, in itself, drug addiction is neither sickness nor moral depravity. Addictions are acquired habits. They undoubtedly can become extremely powerful habits which can be driven by repeated and potent chemical reinforcers acting directly upon the central nervous system. Nonetheless, as habits, they may be regarded as being good or bad according to what they help us to do or what they interfere with our doing.

The idea that addiction was a sickness developed partly as an alternative to the punitive approach. For most of the 20th century, the US opiate addict was left completely untreated, except by punishment and imprisonment. In this context, it seemed more humane to try to help the addict to escape their dependence upon drugs than simply to punish them. As a result, addiction was redefined as an illness. More humane it may have been, but in the end this view may be no more helpful, and it actually perpetuates many of the misconceptions that so bedevil our understanding of addiction. Dr Marie Nyswander, whose work was largely responsible for the establishment of the methadone maintenance clinics in the US, begins her book

The Drug Addict as a Patient: 'Drug addiction is a distinct medical entity which ravages the patient, destroys the entire fabric of his life.' In some respects, this view of addiction as a sickness may even be positively harmful. In so far as it perpetuates the myth that the drug addict is a passive and helpless victim of their addiction it contradicts any expectations that the addict can, through their own efforts, learn to live without drugs. Nyswander states: 'As in every other major disease, the patient is helpless before its destructive inroads. Struggle as he may, the ... inexorable process overwhelms him.'

Methadone maintenance is the epitome of the medical approach to heroin addiction, and it deserves special mention among the drug myths if for no other reason than the fact that it has now generated a multimillion-dollar industry to back it up. In 1975, the annual budget for the New York methadone maintenance treatment project alone was as high as $20 million. Methadone maintenance embodies several of the more traditional misconceptions about addiction, as well as fostering some new ones.

The search for a drug to cure drug addiction, for instance, is not new. Heroin was once thought to be a safe and non-addictive drug to be used in the treatment of morphine addiction; in its own time, morphine had been used to treat cocaine addiction. Dr Halstead, after being dependent upon cocaine, 'cured' himself by taking morphine. On the other hand, in 1878, a Dr W.H. Bentley announced that cocaine could be used to cure morphine addiction. By the 1960s, methadone had replaced them all as the new wonderdrug. Now this drug in its turn was being lauded as the definitive treatment for heroin addiction: yet again, the new drug was hailed by the medical profession as 'the safest narcotic drug yet produced'.

The rationale behind the use of methadone was that addiction to heroin or morphine was a medical disorder, a fault in the addict's metabolism induced by the repeated use of opiates. It was a disease much like diabetes; and just as the diabetic could be treated by the daily administration of insulin, so the heroin addict could be treated by the daily administration of methadone. Provided that the heroin addict was maintained on their methadone, the proponents of this new treatment saw no reason why they should not lead an otherwise normal life. Yet this is the same mistake as that made by those who believe in the drug fiend myth.

The drug addict is not an evil, vicious and depraved monster; nor is he or she a perfectly normal person suffering from a metabolic disease. Addicts are individuals. Some are friendly, others are hostile; some are law-abiding, many are not. There is no such thing as a single addictive personality. Nor is there a single addict lifestyle. People become drug addicts for many reasons. A considerable number of people who become addicted to drugs have extensive problems in their personal and social lives; many were involved in crime prior to using drugs. There is no reason why such people should suddenly experience radical psychological and social changes merely because they have switched from heroin to methadone. Equally, some addicts become addicted to drugs, not because of their personal and social problems, but simply because of the availability of drugs. Their access to drugs put doctors and nurses at a much greater risk of addiction than the general population. In such cases, there is no necessary reason why their dependence upon drugs should cause such people to become the depraved, vicious criminals described by Anslinger and others.

As so often before in the history of medicine, the new treatment (methadone maintenance) gained immediate and uncritical acceptance by many doctors and politicians because it gave the illusion of solving the drug addiction problem. The supporters of this new treatment were soon proclaiming that its effectiveness had been proved beyond any doubt. One textbook of psychiatry cited success rates of between 70 and 90 per cent in the treatment of drug addiction. In view of the usual limited success rates for such treatments, these optimistic assessments were startling. Unfortunately, as with other instant solutions to the problem of addiction, methadone maintenance failed to live up to its promises. Methadone did not turn criminal addicts into law-abiding citizens; addicts on methadone did not necessarily abandon the junkie subculture for the straight world. In some cases it did not even prevent addicts from using black-market heroin in addition to their prescribed methadone. Few addicts were under any misapprehension about the new drug treatment. William Burroughs wrote: 'If the addicts lose their desire for heroin it is because the methadone dosage is stronger than the diluted heroin they receive from the pushers' (*The Soft Machine*, 1961).

This is not to say that methadone maintenance does not have a role to play. The provision of a free, pharmaceutically pure drug, especially when it is supplied in conjunction with the appropriate support systems (including psychological and social counselling, and health care) can help many addicts to escape from the immediate demands of hustling to obtain money for drugs and all the other pressures of the addict lifestyle.

The study of methadone maintenance carried out by John Ball and Alan Ross (1991) looked beyond the simple issue of giving methadone to addicts and into the specifics of the treatment processes surrounding the provision of the drug. This provided good evidence that methadone maintenance can help many opiate addicts to reduce their illicit use of heroin and some other drugs. Maintenance also helped many addicts to cut down their involvement in criminal activities.

In the AIDS era, great interest has been shown in the possibilities that maintenance can help addicts to cut down their injection of drugs. However, it is important to be realistic about the levels of improvement. In the Ball and Ross study, although some methadone programmes obtained reductions in injecting and needle sharing, this varied between programmes, and the overall reduction was not significant. When interviewed, as many as 30 per cent of the drug users in this study continued to inject drugs while on the maintenance programme and, even more worryingly, maintenance had little effect on the percentage of patients who shared injecting equipment (with about 20 per cent sharing needles during treatment).

This study showed that the methadone programmes which had effective leadership, which provided psychosocial counselling and which had a strong orientation towards rehabilitation, were the most effective. A World Health Organization survey of methadone maintenance programmes in six countries found great variation in ways in which methadone programmes are structured. This variation will have a strong impact upon the effectiveness of maintenance programmes. The effectiveness of these programmes is strongly influenced by treatment effects other than the drug itself and it is a mistake to regard methadone (or heroin) maintenance treatments primarily as pharmacological interventions.

Finally, it is also important to note that the treatment gains were usually restricted to those who continued to receive the methadone maintenance intervention. When addicts left the programme they were typically found to relapse to prior drug-taking patterns. Many extravagant claims have been made for methadone maintenance. First, it was claimed that methadone provided a 'cure' for the metabolic disease of addiction. More recently, it has been claimed that methadone provides a sure and certain treatment which will prevent the transmission of HIV and the increase in AIDS. It would be a pity if these claims were allowed to draw attention away from the useful, if limited, role that methadone or other drugs can play in the management of drug addiction problems.

There undoubtedly are occasions on which it is useful to prescribe maintenance drugs (possibly including heroin) to addicts. Many drug takers can make impressive changes in their drug-taking patterns and in their social lives when supported by maintenance drugs. However, not all addicts will show such benefits and some may even be damaged, becoming trapped by replacing their chaotic street world of drug taking with the safer but institutionalized world of maintained drug taking. For some addicts, as well as some doctors, 'Methadone itself has turned out to be another illusion providing a spurious belief that one was accomplishing something by not using heroin' (Sharples, 1975).

Chapter 12

Doors in the Wall

Mankind has always sought doors in the wall of reality. In *The Doors of Perception*, Aldous Huxley wrote that 'Most men and women lead lives at the worst so painful, at the best so monotonous, poor and limited that the urge to escape, the longing to transcend themselves if only for a few moments, is and always has been one of the principal appetites of the soul.' Whether or not Huxley is correct in this pessimistic analysis of the reasons why people need such diversions, the longing for escape remains, and the ways in which different people have sought their own doors in the wall are infinitely varied. Drugs may be the most conspicuous way of producing altered states of consciousness, but they are far from being the only way. There are many other activities which do not involve drugs at all that produce powerful changes in the individual's state of consciousness. Art, literature, music, fantasy, dancing, religion, sport and holidays can all serve as escape routes from the ordinariness of reality, and some of these will be discussed later in this chapter. But there are still a few remaining drugs that deserve mention. Man's longing for altered states of consciousness has led him to try all manner of strange potions, a positive A to Z of chemical oddities, from 'angel dust' to ZNA.

New drugs, or discoveries of the potential to use existing substances as drugs, is a continuing theme in the history of drug taking. One recent development is the appearance of the 'designer drugs'. Designer drugs are synthetic versions of commonly misused drugs: they are manufactured illegally, often in kitchen laboratories. Because they have been made by producing subtle changes in the molecular structure of drug types, they have often evaded the drugs laws (at least in the US). Some of the designer drugs have been of truly awesome potency. Some have carried equally awesome health risks.

In 1980, the first wave of problems linked to what became known as 'designer drugs' turned up on the West Coast of the US. A new 'synthetic heroin' was leading to fatal overdoses. The drug turned out to be an analog of fentanyl, a powerful, short-acting, opiate type drug. It has since been estimated that there are about 1,400 analog combinations in this family group – easy to synthesize, highly potent, and more likely to produce fatal overdoses than heroin.

In 1982, another designer drug based upon pethidine (again an opiate-type drug) appeared in California. Because of a basic error in the manufacturing process of the new drug (known for short as M3P), many users developed an incurable syndrome similar to Parkinson's disease. Symptoms included severe damage to the brain and central nervous system, with almost complete paralysis. In some users, the side effects were so rapid that they were found paralysed with the needle still in their arms. Many other users suffered severe but less immediate forms of damage to their nervous systems, with arthritis-like symptoms including stiffness, tremors and seizures appearing two to 10 days after use.

Designer drugs are now available in all manner of shapes and forms but mainly they have heroin-like sedative effects, or hallucinogenic effects. Probably the best advice to users is to be extremely wary of them. Drugs have always been dangerous enough in the first place. The use of untried and illegally manufactured drugs raises the existing risks to a new and unpredictable level.

The history of drug taking sometimes appears to be little more than a catalogue of statements that this or that drug is the most dangerous known to man. The latest to receive this title is angel dust (a veterinary anaesthetic otherwise known as PCP or phencyclidine). In 1978, it was described by a coroner as the most devastating drug available in the US, and by a congressman as 'a threat to national security'. It is certainly surrounded by a gruesome reputation. There are reports which tell such stories as how one user extracted all his teeth with a pair of pliers or how another shot his best friend while intoxicated on the drug. Some of these stories may be true, but many seem to be apocryphal. By their very nature, such bizarre accounts are readily repeated and embellished with repetition. Although the drug was first synthesized in 1926, it was not until the mid-1950s that its value as an anaesthetic began to be investigated. The early animal studies seemed promising; it produced anaesthesia without loss of consciousness (a considerable advantage in some surgical operations). But the later work with humans showed that it had many unwanted side effects. Some patients became agitated, others experienced severe disorientation, delirium and hallucinations, and further clinical investigations were abandoned.

Angel dust seems to have made its debut as a street drug in San Francisco during the hippie era, but it quickly developed a bad name because of its unpleasant side effects and came to be used less frequently. Its reappearance as a 'problem' during the late 1970s prompted a federal investigation of the drug. One of the best recent studies of it concluded that angel dust was used mainly by white adolescents looking for excitement to counter their feelings of boredom, and that most users had a fairly sophisticated understanding of the drug and its effects. Almost all of them recognized the risks involved in using such a powerful drug and developed ways of minimizing these risks. Despite the public image of angel dust causing berserk violence, this seemed to be a rare occurrence. The picture that emerged was largely one of early adolescent experimentation with drugs. At about the age of 16, most users found other satisfactions and other ways of demonstrating their bravery and competence. In this, angel dust resembles another problem that is currently causing much concern in the UK – glue sniffing.

Various substances originally intended for non-drug purposes have been used as drugs. Among them are certain industrial solvents, cleaning fluids, nail polish removers, petrol and glue. It is precisely when faced by such forms of drug taking that the deficiencies of any substance-based definition of drugs become most obvious:

in these cases it is clear that what defines a psychoactive drug are the uses to which it is put.

The first synthetic psychedelic or hallucinogenic drug to have any impact on Europe and America was probably nitrous oxide (otherwise known as laughing gas). This was discovered in the 18th century by Joseph Priestley, and has a long association with famous men. Humphry Davy carried out a thorough and enthusiastic exploration of its effects, about which he wrote at great length, and Coleridge described it as 'the most unmingled pleasure' that he had ever experienced; others who used it were Josiah Wedgwood and Peter Roget. It was nitrous oxide that first seems to have persuaded William James of the consciousness-expanding potential of drugs. For more than half a century after its discovery it remained an esoteric diversion for the cultural elite, until it was applied to dentistry during the 1840s. It is still used legitimately as an anaesthetic gas, and although it is not available as a street drug it is said to be used for the occasional amusement of medical and dental staff.

In some respects, ether has a similar history, having been used on both sides of the Atlantic as an occasional inebriant for many years after its discovery. After a doctors' gathering at Epsom in 1880, the ground was reported to have been littered with empty bottles of champagne and phials of ether. By the turn of the century, ether had descended the social scale and its use as a cheap intoxicant was causing concern throughout Europe, from Ireland to St Petersburg. In some countries it rivalled alcohol in its popularity as a drug, despite the fact that it is nauseating to the palate and difficult to swallow or to keep down. Its period of greatest popularity in the US was during the Prohibition era, when it was added to soft drinks.

Glue sniffing is a more recent phenomenon. (The phrase 'glue sniffing' is generally, though inaccurately, used to refer to the inhalation of a variety of different volatile solvents and other substances such as paints, petrol, thinners, aerosols and so on.) Although the origins of this form of drug taking are not clear, one of the first reported sightings seems to have occurred during the 1950s in California. It instantly received full television and newspaper coverage and was soon a widespread practice. The hysteria and over-reaction that greeted the identification of glue sniffing seems to have done more to popularize it than to deter young people from experimenting with it. Glue sniffing is typically a pastime of early adolescence, and is usually abandoned as alcohol or other more attractive alternatives become available. Those who become most seriously involved with glue sniffing tend to be isolated, psychologically disturbed individuals. Users have described visual distortions (colours changing, cracks appearing in walls), feelings of disorientation in time and space, and delusions of being strong and invulnerable. Sometimes there are unpleasant effects such as feelings of dizziness and nausea, which soon subside as the effects wear off. The period of intoxication may last from five minutes to half an hour. The more objective signs of glue sniffing are a 'chemical' smell on the breath, slurred speech and a red facial rash; heavy users may lose weight through lack of appetite.

The various substances that are sniffed for intoxication contain organic (carbon-based) solvents, which to a greater or lesser extent vaporize at normal temperatures

– like alcohol. Inhaling petrol fumes produces effects similar to those of glue, though the lead and other additives of petrol make this a more hazardous venture. Aerosols containing metallic paints have also been used in this way. Again there are considerable risks involved in the inhalation of vapours carrying copper, zinc and tin particles, since the toxic effects of these metals are known to include circulatory problems and damage to the kidneys and liver. The propellant gas in aerosols is refrigerated, and if it is sprayed directly into the mouth it can cause the larynx to go into spasm, blocking off the air supply to the lungs and causing asphyxiation. Among the other organic solvents that have been inhaled to produce intoxication are nail polish remover, antifreeze, chloroform, paint thinners, lighter fuel and cleaning fluids. It is important to be aware of the differences between these substances, since each carries different risks. Glue sniffing is probably the least dangerous because its vapours do not contain the complicated chlorine and fluorine compounds in some other products and it is free from lead and other metals.

The shelves of the pharmacist produce some of the most fruitful areas of exploration for the person seeking new sources of intoxication. Although the heyday of the patent medicine is now long past, there were once hundreds of pharmaceutical preparations offering various combinations of heroin, morphine, chloroform and alcohol. Few remain. One of them is chlorodyne – a potent syrup of opium, chloroform and alcohol. In the UK this can still be bought over the counter of the local chemist and it is advertised as a treatment for coughs, colds, diarrhoea, colic and bronchitis. It is known to most addicts as a last resort to avoid withdrawal sickness, though there is a small minority of users who seem to prefer hlorodyne as their drug of choice. Codeine-based cough syrups also have a small number of devotees. The effects of these drugs are broadly similar to those of most opiates. Chlorodyne seems to have added complications caused mainly by the chloroform. Asthma medicines are also occasionally used to produce some sort of altered psychological state. Isolated cases of people using asthma inhalers to get high have appeared in medical journals, and the abuse of ephedrine tablets is a more widely recognized phenomenon. Ephedrine has stimulant effects broadly similar to those of the amphetamines, though it can also cause tremor, palpitations of the heart, anxiety and nausea.

Many of these preparations are readily available and the impossibility of bringing under control all substances that can be used for their psychoactive effects should be clear from the way in which petrol, paint and glue can be used for such purposes. Other familiar domestic substances that have been adopted for intoxicating purposes are the spices nutmeg and mace (see also Chapter 8). These contain psychoactive chemicals that are structurally similar to the amphetamines and mescaline. Those who have taken large doses of nutmeg or mace have reported a wide range of reactions, from euphoria and elation to anxiety, agitation and panic. Nutmeg intoxication also seems to carry a powerful hangover, with weakness and aching joints. Because of the unsatisfactory nature of the experience induced by these drugs, they have typically been used only by people who are denied access to other psychoactive drugs: for instance, nutmeg abuse has been reported among prisoners. At the beginning of the

20th century there was serious concern about the possible adverse effects of nutmeg. Doses of up to 5 milligrams (about the equivalent of one nutmeg) were said to cause stomach pains, vomiting, delirium and acute anxiety attacks, with these symptoms usually disappearing after about 24 hours, though there have also been reports of fatal cases of nutmeg poisoning. The first experimental investigation of nutmeg reported that it could cause fatty degeneration of the liver and kidney damage, though the amount required to produce such effects is probably way above what would ever be normally consumed. Nutmeg poisoning is rarely seen, but it has been reported as a consequence of attempting to use the drug to induce an abortion. This use of nutmeg is both unreliable and hazardous.

During the hippie era there emerged a popular rumour that dried banana skins could be smoked to achieve a cannabis-like state of intoxication. Federal authorities declared this to be a hoax, though there may have been a basis for the effect. Banana peel contains serotonin, a substance which is converted by heat to bufotenine, and bufotenine has effects similar to those produced by hallucinogenic drugs. However, the mild, drowsy mental state reported after inhaling banana smoke does not sound like the more powerful toxic effects of bufotenine and is more likely to be a product of the hopes and expectations of the user. The fact that it soon fell out of favour is perhaps the most telling evidence that it produced no satisfactory results. Other, even more bizarre, concoctions are reputed to have been used. A mixture of aspirin and Coca-Cola has occasionally been used by adolescents too young to have access to the adult mysteries of alcohol and other drugs, though any pleasurable effects must be ascribed to the placebo effect or to the social rewards that go with it. At most it might produce dizziness and a sensation of ringing in the ears, but the amount of aspirin required to produce such minimal effects would be dangerously near to an overdose. At the end of this alphabet of oddities, again used only rarely and by those lacking access to better alternatives, is ZNA, another refugee from the kitchen. ZNA is a mixture of dill and monosodium glutamate which is smoked for its alleged hallucinogenic effects.

There is a vast number of chemicals intended to put us to sleep, wake us up, calm us down, increase our concentration, intoxicate us or stimulate perceptual alterations and hallucinations. When we take into consideration those substances intended for other purposes but used as drugs, the range is truly enormous. However, a casual visitor from another planet could be forgiven for believing that our propensity for drug taking was even greater than it is. They could hardly fail to notice that vast numbers of people are avid consumers of a certain white crystalline substance. They take it several times every day without fail, often in amounts large enough to have physically damaging effects, and when temporarily deprived of it they seek out new supplies and become upset if none are available; when asked to give it up they become agitated, and offer such rationalizations as that they need it because it gives them energy. For the dependent heavy-dose user, few things could be more distressing than to be deprived of their 'fix'. (One of the surest ways of identifying drug dependence is through the craving that the user shows when they cannot obtain their drug.)

Sugar is a quite extraordinary substance. People buy and consume huge amounts of refined sugar (sucrose), yet there is absolutely no physiological need for it. For the average American, it may contribute up to one-fifth of the total calories in their diet. Coca-Cola (that most American of products) and most other soft drinks contain large amounts of sugar; about one-quarter of all the sugar consumed in the US reaches American stomachs in this form. Such drinks are virtually the staple food of school children, and a casual inspection of the ingredients listed on the tins of food available in any supermarket will confirm how entrenched this need for sugar really is.

Some readers (especially the sugar junkies) may be tempted to dismiss this analogy as far-fetched. After all, they might argue, sugar differs from drugs in several important respects. It does not have psychoactive effects and it does not harm your health in the same way that drugs do. Both of these assertions are questionable and probably incorrect.

There are neurochemical similarities in the ways in which both drugs and sugar affect the brain. Just as most drugs increase the release of specific neurotransmitters in the brain, so does sugar. Sugar and morphine appear to activate similar pathways in the forebrain. Sugar is a powerful reinforcer and can lead to bingeing and to addictive behaviours in the same way as drugs. Also, quite apart from the contentious issue that not all forms of drug taking damage the health of the user, there is an increasing medical evidence that has identified damage to health associated with sugar. Virtually everyone now accepts that sugar contributes massively to dental decay. In the UK, where the average person may consume as much as 120lbs of sugar a year, more than one-third of the adult population have had every single tooth extracted. A letter to the *British Dental Journal* described the case of a sweet addict, a 13-year-old boy whose need for sweets was so great that he would faint if deprived of them. Not surprisingly, the boy's teeth were in a terrible condition, and his dentist put him on a maintenance regime of sugar-substitute sweets and drinks (much like drug maintenance for opiate addicts), during which no new dental decay appeared.

Sugar is also related to more serious diseases. Coronary thrombosis, one of the greatest killers in the US, is the result of a complex interaction of different factors, but sugar certainly plays a contributory role as a cause of heart disease. As the consumption of sugar goes up, so does the incidence of coronary heart disease. Even among people who are physically active and who do not smoke cigarettes (inactivity and smoking have both been implicated as contributory factors in heart disease), those who consume large amounts of sugar run a high risk of suffering a coronary thrombosis.

Experiments have also shown that a sugar-rich diet can alter the body's secretion of hormones, produce an enlarged and fatty liver and enlarged kidneys, and result in a shorter life span. If these results were obtained in experiments with any illegal drug, they would certainly be used to justify the most severe forms of retribution against those unfortunate enough to be caught in possession of such a dangerous substance.

Eating habits can be just as compulsive as any drug addiction, just as physically and psychologically destructive to the individual and just as difficult to give up. Almost invariably, it is the sweet and starchy foods that are irresistibly attractive to compulsive eaters. It is significant that the phrases that have been used by doctors to describe compulsive eaters and obese patients are often the same ones used for drug addicts: they are difficult, they reject the patient role, they do not want to change, they lie to the doctor, they do not keep appointments. And the techniques that have been used to control and treat obesity are as bizarre as those that have been applied to the drug addictions. People have even gone to such extreme lengths as to have their jaws wired together, or to undergo surgery to bypass the small intestine and the stomach in order to lose weight. It is ironic that, whereas the illicit possession of amphetamines can lead to a compulsory high-carbohydrate prison diet, these drugs were once the most popular medically sanctioned treatment for obesity.

Just as some people use alcohol, heroin or Valium for the psychological reassurance they promise, so others relieve their nagging feelings of anxiety, guilt, insecurity and unworthiness by filling themselves with food. But, as if in answer to some archetypal memory of the days when gluttony was a sin, for many binge eaters their over-indulgence merely intensifies the very feelings that they sought to forget through their eating. If the exchange of morality for medicine has given us obesity where once we had gluttony, we also have anorexia where we once had fasting. Fasting was primarily a method of self-purification, a penance, but its psychological effects are not merely symbolic. It produces many alterations in the body's biochemistry and physiology, and there is no doubt that it can produce a light-headed euphoric state of mind.

A quite different sort of deprivation involves reducing the level (or, more precisely, reducing the variability) of sensory stimulation. This can also produce interesting psychological effects. Whether or not these changes in consciousness are regarded as pleasurable depends upon the conditions in which they take place, upon the personality of the person who experiences them and on what they mean to that person. For some people the experience of sensory deprivation is unpleasant. Conditions involving reduced levels of sensory stimulation have long been used as a punishment (as in solitary confinement) and more recently they have been systematically used as part of 'brainwashing' procedures (for instance, during the Korean War). One series of experiments that were carried out into sensory deprivation involved volunteers lying quietly on beds in lightproof, soundproof rooms. A few people find these conditions extremely unpleasant and ask to be let out fairly quickly; others are able to endure them for quite long periods (in one experiment the average time was 39 hours); and a further group seem to be able to tolerate and even enjoy more extended periods of sensory deprivation.

Most of the people who have taken part in sensory deprivation experiments had elaborate and vivid daydreams, and their capacity for rational, logical thinking was somewhat impaired. More strikingly, almost everyone reported unusual visual experiences. Often these were merely perceptions of simple geometric patterns, but some people 'saw' more complex patterns and a few saw complex scenes similar to a cartoon film. Auditory hallucinations were rare, though there were a few isolated reports of such phenomena. The most enthusiastic accounts of the experience have been given by John Lilly (1972), a medical researcher and psychoanalyst who conducted a series of trials using a more profound technique of sensory deprivation in which the subject floats motionless in a tank of water heated to body temperature, in a darkened room, wearing a breathing mask.

Lilly spoke of his initial experiences in terms of heightened awareness and increased sensory experiences in the absence of external stimulation, and denied that sensory deprivation need be either stressful or aversive. He suggested that such responses were due to the negative expectations of the experimenter and subjects, and emphasized the beneficial and enjoyable aspects of the experience. After 10 hours or so in the immersion tank, he described moving into 'dream-like states, trance-like states, mystical states', and had hallucinatory experiences in which he saw and heard other people. On later occasions Lilly took LSD while in the immersion tank, and his book, *The Centre of the Cyclone*, provides a full account of his strange experiences and his attempts to explain them. Other people have also been powerfully convinced that some significant qualitative change in their perceptions of reality occurred while in the immersion tank, and have described feelings of mellowness, total relaxation and being in harmony with the universe.

There are more prosaic claims that immersion can facilitate creative thinking, relaxation and reflection, and can help to alleviate pain. Immersion tanks are now commercially available in the US where it is possible to hire time in them, or even, as hundreds of people have done, to build your own. As with almost every other device that people can use to alter their states of consciousness, the immersion tank has provoked the standard warnings, among them that it can precipitate a psychotic breakdown in unstable users and that it has led to the breakdown of marriages.

It is far from clear how to interpret the validity of any of these claims, though it is interesting that extreme solitude and isolation have played a part in many important religious revelations. The founders of four of the world's greatest religions, Moses, Jesus, Mohammed and the Buddha, all achieved insight that led to their ministry while isolated in the wilderness. Many thousands of mystics have maintained that transcendental experiences are best sought in solitude – whether in the highest mountains, jungles, the desert, or within an enclosed order, and the emphasis upon stimulus reduction is common to many of the practices of yoga, Zen, Tao, Sufism and Christian monasticism. All forms of meditation shut out the external world to a greater or lesser extent.

Music and rhythmic stimulation undoubtedly have the power to produce altered states of consciousness. Music has been used successfully as a substitute for anaesthetic drugs in certain operations, notably in dental extractions, and music therapy and dance therapy have both been used in psychiatric hospitals to help change mood and emotional states. Rhythmic repetition has been used for many centuries to produce trance-like states: for instance, by the Dervishes and certain Hindu groups as well as by Christian sects such as the Shakers and the Holy Rollers. It can also be used as an aid to more reflective states of mind: there is a form of 'moving meditation' which involves repetitive body movements. The effectiveness of this technique is thought to be due largely to the soothing, monotonous quality of the repetition, but other techniques (chanting and singing hymns, for instance), if persisted with for long periods, can produce a feeling of light-headedness through the alteration of oxygen levels in the blood.

Religious and quasi-religious groups can operate in ways which for their followers can produce drug-like effects and can lead to dependence. Individuals who are otherwise apparently normal become changed by their involvement with cults and sects in ways that are perceived by their family and friends to be 'as if they were drugged'. The Heaven's Gate, Jonestown and Aum Shinrikyu experiences show how intelligent, superficially ordinary people can be induced to commit murder and mass suicide without apparent compunction or compassion. As with dependence-forming drugs, the individual within the sect can have seriously impaired control over their thoughts and behaviour; they become compulsive consumers of the group experience and experience distress or panic at the thought of being deprived of contact; they become distanced from their other lives and the wider social reality; their interests become narrowed so that participation within the sect takes precedence over everything else; and when removed from the sect, they show 'withdrawal' symptoms of anxiety, agitation and depression. Sect leaders quickly develop an understanding of how most effectively to generate and reinforce these feeling of dependence in order to enlist and retain their followers.

Many children know that over-breathing (hyperventilation) can induce altered states of consciousness. This was an occasional playground game among 10-year-olds when I was at school, and it is documented in Andrew Weil's 1973 book, *The Natural Mind*. There can be few children who have not been delighted by the altered mental states produced by whirling themselves around (or, better still, getting an adult to spin them round) until they fall to the floor in a dizzy, giggling euphoria. Somewhat later in life, as adolescents, they may seek the same effect from listening to deafeningly loud rock music while nodding their heads or jumping up and down to the beat. The current enthusiasm for rave dancing and ecstasy manages to combine loud repetitive music, vigorous dancing and drugs all at the same time. And at a time when marathon running is enjoying a certain vogue, it is intriguing that long-distance runners sometimes find that the physiological changes and the repetitive, rhythmic stimulation of running produce a trance-like 'high'.

There are other routes to altered states of consciousness which involve changes in the body's internally produced chemicals. Sex is the most obvious of these. It should be no secret that sex can be intensely pleasurable or that it can be used like a drug; the analogy between orgasm and intravenous injection has been drawn many times. And as with drugs, there are also people who become compulsive consumers of sex. A good deal of sexual activity, particularly of the single-handed variety, involves elaborate fantasies which both help to intensify the experience and to distance it from ordinary states of reality. Sexual fantasies often conjure up perverse or forbidden versions of sex which increase the sense of excitement through the complex emotional mixture of pleasure and fear that they provoke.

Like all human emotions, fear is more complicated than it might seem. In terms of our subjective experience, it seems unmistakeably different from excitement and euphoria, but they are closely related; they share the same components of physiological arousal, and psychologically, too, the line dividing fear from excitement is hard to define. It depends upon the social circumstances in which the arousing event occurs and on what the event means to the person experiencing it. Fear is not always an unpleasant feeling, as is shown by the popularity of fairground rides, horror stories and films. Provided that it does not go beyond a certain level, most people can enjoy being frightened, though it must be said that this level varies widely, depending upon the personality of the individual. For some, the thrill of the detective novel is enough. Others need a more pronounced element of danger to get their internal jolt of adrenaline.

Crime can provide this thrill. Petty theft such as shoplifting is more often stimulated by the need for the rush of adrenaline that accompanies the act than by simple economic necessity, and gambling too holds out a similar promise of risk and excitement. Both can produce an addiction as pronounced and as destructive as any drug. Skiing, hang-gliding, rock climbing, free-fall parachuting and pot-holing all provide opportunities for risk, fear and excitement, and all are capable of producing the same single-minded devotion that the addict reserves for their drugs.

Among that peculiar brand of person aiming for the world speed record on skis, attitudes towards speed are indistinguishable from those towards drugs. The 'sport' involves skiing down a 45° track of polished ice. Skiers wear shiny rubberized suits and bizarre fishhead helmets to reduce wind resistance. After setting the women's record of 187.5 kph (117 mph) Stella Sylvester said, 'It's like a balloon bursting. It's like sex, only more peaceful.' Another woman, after a 112 mph descent, said, 'You do three runs a day, and you're walking on air for a week. I'm hooked.' Between runs, the world record holder, Franz Weber, also ski dives: 'I'm not suicidal … but it extends my boundaries of fear.'

In its most extreme form, mountain climbing combines danger with perceptual changes due to sensory deprivation, metabolic changes due to food deprivation, and the rigours of extreme cold and oxygen starvation. When climbing the south-east ridge of Dunagiri in the Himalayas, Joe Tasker had the hallucination that another group of climbers was watching him and criticizing the slowness of his progress. Such hallucinations are not uncommon. Tasker described having had three or four such experiences, and another climber, Alan Rouse, described how on the ascent of the north face of Nuptse, at nearly 26,000 feet, he had the illusion of leaving his body and watching himself climbing. Neither Tasker nor Rouse felt that these experiences were frightening, though neither found them in any way exciting. After being buried by an avalanche close to the summit of K2 (the world's second highest mountain), Joe Tasker says that, after he had escaped, he felt as if he were high on a drug; he felt privileged to be alive, and his impression of everything seemed to be intensified. Such states of euphoria were rare. Even reaching the summit of a mountain was often something of an anti-climax. Any feelings of euphoria were lessened by the extreme tiredness, lack of oxygen, and weakness produced by the climb and by the climber's need to maintain his focus of concentration upon the details of the climb itself. Tasker said that he could not allow himself to relax enough to enjoy any such indulgence until he had completed the climb. The thrill is produced, not by the danger, but by controlling it.[1]

James Hunt, the 1976 World Champion Formula One racing driver, spoke to me of maintaining this delicate balancing act on the edge of disaster where the overriding need is for control and mastery. The penalties of taking undue liberties while racing a Formula One car are both obvious and severe. But the capacity for coping with danger does not rule out an inclination towards such sources of exhilaration. The late Patrick Depailler seems to have had a pronounced taste for dangerous pursuits, having injured himself badly in a motor-cycle crash and later a hang-gliding accident, before he was killed in a practice session at the Hockenheim circuit in 1980.

Although very different in many ways from the volatile Depailler, James Hunt was also rebellious and extremely competitive. After retiring from Formula One racing Hunt seriously injured his knee while skiing ('I always ski too fast'). During the earlier stages of his racing career he admitted that he would often be physically sick prior to a race and that 'there is a definite kick involved in frightening yourself'. Hunt felt that being under stress had a positive effect upon his driving: 'To me the surge of adrenaline felt like pressure to do better'.

Some indication of the intensity of the stress of Formula One racing can be gauged from the measures taken during the Monaco Grand Prix of the heart rate of one of the drivers (Didier Pironi). Pironi's resting pulse rate is between 60 and 70 beats per minute. This rose to 125 as he arrived in the pit lane but dropped to 73 as he sat in the car. During the race itself, which lasted for almost two hours, it rarely fell below 190 and shot up to a peak of 207 when his car touched another while overtaking. Pironi's Ferrari finished the race in fourth place.

During the 1970s, Formula One racing was at its most dangerous. There was at least one fatality during every season (9 during the decade) and either a death or a serious injury in one out every 10 accidents (the ratio now is about one in 300). It was in 1976, the year of James' championship, that he and Niki Lauda both started from the front row of the grid at the terrifying Nürburgring which had already claimed

---

1   The tragic footnote to this story is that Joe Tasker and Alan Rouse subsequently died on the world's two highest mountains. Joe Tasker's final climb ended in Tibet, on the north-east ridge of Everest. He and Peter Boardman, another British climber, were last seen climbing above 26,800 feet at 9pm on 17 May 1982. Their bodies were never found. Alan Rouse was the first Briton to climb K2, the mountain on which he died. He was last seen alive on 10 August 1986 at Camp 4 (at 26,000 feet). He is presumed to have died of severe mountain sickness.

130 lives. After two laps, Lauda's Ferrari had a mechanical failure, crashed, and burst into flames. With Lauda trapped in the wreckage, two other cars ploughed into the burning car. By the time Lauda was pulled from the flames, he was so terribly burned that he was given the last rites. James subsequently won the race by half a minute. One incident which did as much as anything to persuade James to retire from racing was the death of his friend Ronnie Peterson who was trapped in his burning car during the 1978 Italian Grand Prix at Monza.

There are other darker and more obscure avenues by which men have approached danger and excitement. Men are attracted to warfare for many reasons, though for most of the survivors the experience leaves a vile and sour taste. In many cases, it has proved useful to the general staff to provide the front-line soldier with chemical props to help ease the burden of combat. The rum ration has long been an invaluable aid to the British Navy. In the First World War, the massively potent and treacly SRD (service rum diluted) was distributed to British soldiers in the trenches and was guarded and protected with the very greatest care. Its effects were often to turn a sullen and cursing group of men into a whistling, cheerful band in a matter of minutes. Such rations were most reliably issued immediately prior to attacks. During the Battle of Stalingrad, the defending Soviet troops would fall silent when the vodka ration was distributed, and the strain of this awful battle was such that there was never enough alcohol to deaden the fear. Out on the steppe, or where the vodka was not available, troops would seek out surgical spirit, industrial alcohol, antifreeze which was filtered through the carbon filter of a gas mask, or various toxic preparations of home distilled spirits. On one occasion, the commander, second-in-command and 18 soldiers of a company became casualties after drinking captured German antifreeze. Three died and the remainder were sent to a field hospital in 'a serious condition'.

For a few men, war is detestable but has a fascination that goes to work on them. For some combat soldiers in Vietnam, the experience of killing came to combine feelings of calmness and tranquillity while zeroing in on a target with an exhilarating 'adrenaline rush' at the completion of the kill. For one Vietnam veteran, 'The more I killed, the more I liked it. It's the best high I ever had.'

The ranks of the war junkies also include a sizeable number of non-combatants, one of the most extravagant of them being Tim Page, a young Englishman who drifted into the role of war photographer in Vietnam because 'he would go places for pictures that very few other photographers were going'.[2] Page was wounded on several occasions, the first time by shrapnel in the legs and stomach, the second time, again by shrapnel, in the head, back and arms. Later, a boat in which he was travelling was blown out of the water by US aircraft under the misapprehension that it was a Viet Cong vessel: Page sustained more than 200 individual wounds and floated in the water for hours before being rescued. He left Vietnam for a while but was drawn back after the disasters of the Tet Offensive in 1968. Finally,

---

2   Cited in Michael Herr's excellent book about the Vietnam War.

… a helicopter in which he was riding was ordered to land to pick up some wounded men. Page and a sergeant ran out to help; the sergeant stepped on a mine which blew his legs off and sent a two-inch piece of shrapnel through Page's forehead and into the base of his brain.

The doctors predicted that he would be permanently paralysed down his left side. While convalescing, he received a letter from a publisher asking him to prepare some work for a book to be called *Through with War*, and which would be intended to take the glamour out of war. For Page the idea was preposterous: 'Page couldn't get over it, "Take the glamour out of war! I mean, how the bloody hell can you do *that*? It's like trying to take the glamour out of sex …" [Page] was speechless "… it just *can't be done*!" ' In the same way that drugs speak to the innermost needs of the drug addict, so for the terminal adrenaline addict war whispers things that echo loudly within him and the whisper proves irresistibly fascinating.

The desire to experience some altered state of consciousness seems to be an intrinsic part of the human condition, and the persistence that people have shown in pursuit of this goal is as remarkable as the diversity of ways in which they have sought such altered states. This same diversity is shown in the range of different types of drug taking. Whether taken alone or in company, for relaxation or stimulation, to satisfy some personal need or to comply with social pressures, we are surrounded by drugs, some more visible than others – the cups of coffee and tea, the glasses of beer, wine and whisky, the cigarettes, the snorts of cocaine, the joints, the tablets of acid, the fixes of heroin, and the ubiquitous tranquillizers and sleeping pills. It may be that every drug-induced state has its counterpart in a state of mind arrived at without drugs, but drug taking still remains one of the easiest and most immediate ways of altering psychological states; for some people, the ease and immediacy with which drugs achieve their effects proves particularly seductive. So long as there are drug takers there will be drug casualties. No form of drug taking is without its dangers, but the quest to eliminate drug taking has proved to be the search for a chimera. Drug taking is here to stay and one way or another we must all learn to live with drugs.

Selected Bibliography

The following books are useful general sources of information about drugs and drug taking.

Brecher, E.M. (1972), *The Consumers Union Report on Licit and Illicit Drugs*, New York: Consumers Union.

Goode, E. (1972), *Drugs in American Society*, New York: Knopf.

Gossop, M. (2003), *Drug Addiction and its Treatment*, Oxford University Press: Oxford.

Inglis, B. (1975), *The Forbidden Game*, London: Hodder & Stoughton.

Johnston, J.F.W. (1879), *The Chemistry of Common Life*, London: Blackwood.

Lewin, L. (1931), *Phantastica, Narcotic and Stimulating Drugs*, London: Kegan Paul, Trench, Trubner.

Malcolm, A.I. (1971), *The Pursuit of Intoxication*, Toronto: ARF.

Orford, J. (1985), *Excessive Appetites: A Psychological View of the Addictions*, New York: Wiley.

Schultes, R.E. and Hofmann, A. (1979), *Plants of the Gods*, London: Hutchinson.

Strang, J. and Gossop, M. (1994), *Heroin Addiction and the British System. Volumes 1 and 2*, London and New York: Routledge.

West, R. (2006), *Theory of Addiction*, Oxford: Blackwell.

The remainder of the references provide a more detailed background to some of the issues raised in this book.

Anslinger, H.J. and Tompkins, W.F. (1953), *The Traffic in Narcotics*, New York: Funk & Wagnalls.

Arendt, M., Rosenberg, R., Foldager, L., Perto, G. and Munk-Jørgensen, P. (2005), 'Cannabis-induced psychosis and subsequent schizophrenia-spectrum disorders: follow-up study of 535 incident cases', *British Journal of Psychiatry*, 187, 510–515.

Ashley, R. (1975), *Cocaine: Its History, Uses and Effects*, New York: St Martin's Press.

Ball, J.C. and Ross, A. (1991), *The Effectiveness of Methadone Maintenance Treatment*, New York: Springer.

Beattie, R.T. (1968), 'Nutmeg as a psychoactive agent', *British Journal of Addiction*, 63, 105–9.

Becker, H. (1953), 'Becoming a marihuana user', *American Journal of Sociology*, 59, 235–42.

Beecher, H.K. (1955), 'The powerful placebo', *Journal of the American Medical Association*, 159, 1602–6.

Berridge, V. (1979), 'Opium in the Fens in nineteenth-century England', *Journal of the History of Medicine and Allied Sciences*, 34, 293–313.

Brady, M. (1992), *Heavy Metal: The Social Meaning of Petrol Sniffing in Australia*, Canberra: Aboriginal Studies Press.

Brain Committee Report (1965), *Drug Addiction: Second Report of the Interdepartmental Committee*, London: HMSO.

British Medical Association (1997), *Therapeutic Uses of Cannabis*, Amsterdam: Harwood Academic.

Burroughs, W. (1968), *The Naked Lunch*, London: Corgi.

Cameron, H.M. and McGoogan, E. (1981), 'A prospective study of 1152 hospital autopsies. I and II', *Journal of Pathology*, 133, 273–83 and 285–300.

Campbell, A.M., Evans, M., Thomson, J.L. and Williams, M.J. (1971), 'Cerebral atrophy in young cannabis smokers', *The Lancet*, 4 December, 1219–24.

Carter, W. (ed.) (1980), *Cannabis in Costa Rica*, Philadelphia PA: ISHI.

Cederlöf, R., Friberg, L. and Lundman, T. (1977), *The Interactions of Smoking, Environment and Heredity*, Stockholm: Gotab.

Claridge, G. (1970), *Drugs and Human Behaviour*, London: Allen Lane.

Cocteau, J. (1957), *Opium: The Diary of a Cure*, London: Owen.

Cohen, M.M. and Marinello, M.J. (1967), 'Chromosomal damage on human leukocytes induced by lysergic acid diethylamide', *Science*, 155, 1417–19.

Cohen, M.M., Hirschhorn, K. and Frosch, W.A. (1967), 'In vivo and in vitro chromosomal damage induced by LSD-25', *New England Journal of Medicine*, 277, 1043–9.

Cohen, S. and Taylor, L. (1976), *Escape Attempts*, London: Allen Lane.

Connell, K.H. (1965), 'Ether drinking in Ulster', *Quarterly Journal of Studies on Alcohol*, 26, 629–53.

Connell, P.H. (1958), *Amphetamine Psychosis*, London: Oxford University Press.

Corti, C. (1932), *A History of Smoking*, New York: Harcourt Brace.

Crowley, A. (1922*), Diary of a Drug Fiend*, London: Collins.

Davies, D.L. (1962), 'Normal drinking in recovered alcohol addicts', *Quarterly Journal of Studies on Alcohol*, 23, 94–104.

DeWet, C., Reed, L., Glasper, A., Moran, P., Bearn, J., Gossop, M. (2004), 'Benzodiazepine codependence exacerbates the opiate withdrawal syndrome', *Drug and Alcohol Dependence*, 76, 31–35.

Dishotsky, N.I., Loughman, W.D., Mogar, R.E. and Lipscomb, W.R. (1971), 'LSD and genetic damage', *Science*, 172, 431–40.

Doll, R. (1971), 'The age distribution of cancer: implications for models of carcinogenesis', *Journal of the Royal Statistical Society*, 134, 133–55.

Doll, R. and Peto, R. (1976), 'Mortality in relation to smoking: twenty years' observations on male British doctors', *British Medical Journal*, 2, 1525–36.

Du Toit, B.M. (1977), *Drugs, Rituals and Altered States of Consciousness*, Rotterdam: Balkema.

Edwards, G. (1979), 'British policies on opiate addiction', *British Journal of Psychiatry*, 134, 1–13.

Edwards, G. and Grant, M. (1977), *Alcoholism, New Knowledge and New Response*, London: Croom Helm.

Engelsman, E. (1990), 'Dutch policy on the management of drug-related problems', in H. Ghodse and R. Mann (eds), *Drug Misuse and Dependence*, Carnforth: Parthenon.

Erickson, P. (1981), *Cannabis Criminals: The Social Effects of Punishment on Drug Users*, Toronto: ARF.

Everingham, R. and Woodward, S. (1991), *Tobacco Litigation: The Case Against Passive Smoking*, Sydney: Legal Books.

Ewing, J.A. and Rouse, B.A. (1978), *Drinking: Alcohol in American Society*, Chicago IL: Nelson-Hall.

Eysenck, H.J. (1967), *The Biological Basis of Personality*, Springfield IL: Charles C. Thomas.

Farkas, C. (1979), 'Caffeine intake and potential effect on health of a segment of Northern Canadian indigenous people', *International Journal of the Addictions*, 14, 27–43.

Feldman, H.W., Agar, M.H. and Beschner, G.M. (1979), *Angel Dust*, Lexington: Lexington Books.

Fields, A. and Tararin, P. (1970), 'Opium in China', *British Journal of Addiction*, 64, 371–82.

Fisher, R.A. (1959), *Smoking. The Cancer Controversy*, Edinburgh: Oliver & Boyd.

Fletcher, D. (1940), *The Amazing Story of Repeal*, Chicago IL: Willett, Clark & Co.

Frankenhaeuser, M., Post, B., Hagdal, R. and Wrangsjoe, B. (1964), 'Effects of a depressant drug as modified by experimentally induced expectation', *Perceptual and Motor Skills*, 18, 513–22.

Furst, P.T. (1972), *Flesh of the Gods. The Ritual Use of Hallucinogens*, New York: Praeger.

Gay, G., Sheppard, C. and Inaba, D. (1973), 'An old girl: flyin' low, dyin' slow, blinded by snow: cocaine in perspective', *International Journal of the Addictions*, 8, 1027–42.

Gertler, R , Ferneau, F. and Raynes, A. (1973), 'Attitudes towards death and dying on a drug addiction unit', *International Journal of the Addictions*, 8, 265–72.

Goldstein, A., Kaizer, S. and Whitby, O. (1969), 'Psychotropic effects of caffeine in man. IV. Quantitative and qualitative differences associated with habituation to coffee', *Clinical Pharmacology and Therapeutics*, 10, 489–97.

Goodman, J. (1993), *Tobacco in History*, London: Routledge.

Gossop, M. (1989a), 'The detoxification of high dose heroin addicts in Pakistan', *Drug and Alcohol Dependence*, 24, 143–50.

Gossop, M. (1989b), *Relapse and Addictive Behaviour*, London: Routledge.
Gossop, M. and Grant, M. (1990), *The Content and Structure of Methadone Treatment Programmes: A Study in Six Countries*, Geneva: World Health Organization, WHO/PSA/90.3.
Gossop, M., Marsden, J. and Stewart, D. (1998), *NTORS at One Year*, London: Department of Health.
Gossop, M., Marsden, J., Stewart, D. and Kidd, T. (2003), 'The National Treatment Outcome Research Study (NTORS): 4–5 year follow-up results', *Addiction*, 98, 291–303.
Gossop, M., Griffiths, P., Powis, B. and Strang, J. (1992), 'Severity of dependence and route of administration of heroin, cocaine and amphetamines', *British Journal of Addiction*, 87, 1527–36.
Gossop, M., Griffiths, P., Powis, B., Williamson, S. and Strang, J. (1996), 'Frequency of non-fatal overdose', *British Medical Journal*, 313, 402.
Graham, J.D.P. (1977), *Cannabis Now*, Aylesbury: H.M. & M. Publishers.
Gregory, R.J., Gregory, J.E. and Peck, J.G. (1981), 'Kava and prohibition in Tanna, Vanuatu', *British Journal of Addiction*, 76, 299–313.
Griffiths, P., Gossop, M., Wickenden, S., Dunworth, J., Harris, K. and Lloyd, C. (1997), 'A transcultural pattern of drug use: qat (khat) in the UK', *British Journal of Psychiatry*, 170, 281–4.
Grinspoon, L. and Bakalar, J.B. (1979), *Psychedelic Drugs Reconsidered*, New York: Basic Books.
Grinspoon, L. and Hedblom, P. (1975), *The Speed Culture*, Cambridge MA: Harvard University Press.
Heather, N. and Robertson, I. (1989), *Problem Drinking*, Oxford: Oxford University Press.
Herr, M. (1979), *Dispatches*, London: Pan Books.
Hirayama, T. (1981), 'Non-smoking wives of heavy smokers have a higher risk of lung cancer: a study from Japan', *British Medical Journal*, 282, 183–5.
Huxley, A. (1961), *The Devils of Loudun*, London: Chatto & Windus.
Huxley, A. (1969), *The Doors of Perception and Heaven and Hell*, Harmondsworth: Penguin.
Indian Hemp Drugs Commission (1894), *Report*, Simla: Government Printing Office.
James, W. (1942), *The Varieties of Religious Experience*, London: Longmans.
Jellinek, E.M. (1960), *The Disease Concept of Alcoholism*, New Haven CT: College & University Press.
Jones, R.T. (1971), 'Marihuana-induced "high": influence of expectation, setting and previous drug experience', *Pharmacological Review*, 23, 359–69.
Journal of the American Medical Association (1955), 159, 'Placebos' (editorial), 780.
Journal of the American Medical Association (1971), 216, 'Cannabis and educational performance' (medical news), 1701–10.

Keller, M. (1970), 'The great Jewish drink mystery', *British Journal of Addiction*, 64, 287–96.

Kelly, J. and Amirkhanian,Y. (2003) 'The newest epidemic: a review of HIV/AIDS in central and eastern Europe', *International Journal of STD & AIDS*, 14, 361–71.

Kingsley, C. (1970), *Alton Locke*, London: Dent, reprint.

Kissin, B. and Begleiter, H. (eds) (1971–6), *The Biology of Alcoholism*, New York: Plenum: *Vol. 1, Biochemistry*, 1971; *Vol. 2, Physiology and Behaviour*, 1972; *Vol. 3, Clinical Pathology*, 1974; *Vol. 4, Social Aspects*, 1976.

Kumar, R., Cooke, E.C., Lader, M.H. and Russell, M.A.H. (1978), 'Is tobacco smoking a form of nicotine dependence?', in R.E. Thornton (ed.), *Smoking Behaviour*, Edinburgh: Churchill Livingstone.

Lader, M.H. (1978), 'Benzodiazepines – the opium of the masses?', *Neuroscience*, 3, 159–65.

LaGuardia Committee (1944), *The Marihuana Problem in the City of New York: Sociological, Medical, Psychological and Pharmacological Studies*, Lancaster PA: Jacques Cattell.

The Lancet, 21 April 1973, 'Unreasonable profit' (editorial), 867.

The Lancet, 21 April 1973, 'Chlordiazepoxide and diazepam prices' (editorial), 876.

The Lancet, 12 May 1973, 'Price of tranquillizers' (editorial), 1069.

The Lancet, 19 May 1973, 'Benzodiazepines: use, overuse, misuse, abuse?' (editorial), 1101–2.

The Lancet, 14 July 1973, 'Price of tranquillizers' (editorial), 108.

Le Dain Report (1971), *Interim Report of the Canadian Government Commission of Inquiry*, Harmondsworth: Penguin.

Le Dain Report (1972), *Cannabis. A Report of the Commission of Inquiry into the Non-Medical Use of Drugs*, Ottawa: Information Canada.

Lefebure, M. (1974), *Samuel Taylor Coleridge: A Bondage of Opium*, London: Gollancz.

Lennard, H.L., Epstein, L.J., Bernstein, A. and Ransom, D.C. (1971), *Mystification and Drug Misuse*, San Francisco: Jossey-Bass.

Lewis, S.A., Oswald, I., Evans, J.I., Akindele, M.O. and Tompsett, S.L. (1970), 'Heroin and sleep', *Electroencephalography and Clinical Neurophysiology*, 28, 374–81.

Lilly, J.C. (1972), *The Centre of the Cyclone*, New York: Julian Press.

Logan, F. (ed.) (1979), *Cannabis: Options for Control*, Sunbury, Middlesex: Quartermaine House.

MacCoun, R. and Reuter, P. (1997), 'Interpreting Dutch cannabis policy', *Science*, 278, 47–52.

Mapes, R. (ed.) (1980), *Prescribing Practice and Drug Usage*, London: Croom Helm.

Marks, J. (1979), *The Search for the 'Manchurian Candidate'*, London: Allen Lane.

Masters, R.E.L. and Houston, J. (1973), *The Varieties of Psychedelic Experience*, London: Turnstone.

Mendelson, W.B. (1980), *The Use and Misuse of Sleeping Pills*, New York: Plenum.

Mikuriya, T.H. (1968), 'Physical, mental and moral effects of marihuana: the Indian Hemp Drugs Commission Report', *International Journal of the Addictions*, 3, 253–70.

Musto, D.F. (1973), *The American Disease*, New Haven CT: Yale University Press.

Nyswander, M. (1956), *The Drug Addict as a Patient*, New York: Grune & Stratton.

O'Donnell, J. and Jones, J. (1970), 'Diffusion of the intravenous technique among narcotic addicts', reprinted in J. Ball and C. Chambers (eds), *The Epidemiology of Opiate Addiction in the United States*, Springfield IL: Charles C. Thomas.

Pahnke, W.N. et al. (1970), 'Psychedelic therapy utilizing LSD with cancer patients', *Journal of Psychedelic Drugs*, 3, 63–75.

Patrick, C.H. (1952), *Alcohol, Culture and Society*, Durham NC: Duke University Press.

Powis, B., Strang, J., Griffiths, P., Taylor, C., Williamson, S., Fountain, J. and Gossop, M. (1999), 'Self-reported overdose among injecting drug users in London: extent and nature of the problem', *Addiction*, 94, 471–8.

Preventative Medicine Report, Vol. 1. First report from the Expenditure Committee, House of Commons, 17 February 1977, pp. 88–9.

Proctor, R.N. (1999), *The Nazi War on Cancer*, Princeton NJ: Princeton University Press.

Reuter, P., MacCoun, R. Murphy, P. (1990), *Money from Crime: A Study of the Economics of Drug Dealing in Washington, D.C.*, Santa Monica CA: RAND.

Robins, L.N. (1974), *The Vietnam Drug User Returns*, Washington: US Government Printing Office.

Robinson, J.T., Chitham, R.G., Greenwood, R.M. and Taylor, J.W. (1974), 'Chromosomal aberrations and LSD', *British Journal of Psychiatry*, 125, 238–44.

Royal College of Physicians (1971), *Smoking and Health Now*, London: Pitman Medical.

Royal College of Physicians (1977), *Smoking or Health*, London: Pitman Medical.

Royal College of Psychiatrists (1979), *Alcohol and Alcoholism*, London: Tavistock.

Saper, A. (1974), 'The making of policy through myth, fantasy and historical accident: the making of America's narcotics laws', *British Journal of Addiction*, 69, 183–93.

Schachter, S. and Singer, J. (1962), 'Cognitive, social and physiological determinants of emotional state', *Psychological Review*, 69, 379–99.

Select Committee of the House of Lords on Science and Technology (1998), *Cannabis, The Scientific and Medical Evidence*, London: HMSO.

Seltzer, C.C. (1968), 'Coronary heart disease and smoking', *Journal of the American Medical Association*, 203, 193–200.

Seltzer, C.C. (1972), 'Critique of the Royal College of Physicians report', *The Lancet*, vol. 1, 243–8.

Shafer Report (1972), *Marihuana: A Signal of Misunderstanding*, Washington: US Government Printing Office.

Sharples, A. (1975), *The Scorpion's Tail*, London: Elek.

Snyder, C.R. (1958), *Alcohol and the Jews*, Glencoe IL: Free Press.

Stafford, P. (1977), *Psychedelics Encyclopedia*, Berkeley CA: And/Or Press.

Strang, J. and Farrell, M. (1991), *Hepatitis*, London: ISDD.

Strang, J. and Stimson, G. (eds) (1990), *AIDS and Drug Misuse*, London: Routledge.

Strang, J., Griffiths, P., Abbey, J. and Gossop, M. (1994), 'Survey of injected benzodiazepines among drug users in Britain', *British Medical Journal*, 308, 1082.

Strang, J., Griffiths, P., Powis, B. and Gossop, M. (1992), 'First use of heroin: changes in route of administration over time', *British Medical Journal*, 304, 1222–3.

Strang, J., Griffiths, P., Powis, B., Abbey, J. and Gossop, M. (1997), 'How constant is an individual's route of heroin administration?', *Drug and Alcohol Dependence*, 46, 115–118.

Suedfeld, P. (1980), *Restricted Environmental Stimulation: Research and Clinical Applications*, New York: Wiley.

Szasz, T. (1975), *Ceremonial Chemistry*, London: Routledge & Kegan Paul.

Tjio, J.H., Pahnke, W.N. and Kurland, A.A. (1969), 'LSD and chromosomes: a controlled experiment', *Journal of the American Medical Association*, 210, 849–56.

Trethowan, W.H. (1975), 'Pills for personal problems', *British Medical Journal*, 2, 749–51.

Trocchi, A. (1960), *Cain's Book*, London: Calder.

United Nations Conference on Trade and Development (1978), *Marketing and Distribution of Tobacco*, United Nations.

Wagstaff, A. (1989), 'Economic aspects of illicit drug markets and drug enforcement policies', *British Journal of Addiction*, 84, 1173–82.

Waldorf, D., Reinarman, C. and Murphy, S. (1991), *Cocaine Changes: The Experience of Using and Quitting*, Philadelphia PA: Temple University Press.

Weil, A. (1973), *The Natural Mind*, London: Cape.

Wenger, J. and Einstein, S. (1970), 'The use and misuse of aspirin', *International Journal of the Addictions*, 5, 757–75.

Wikler, A. (1980), *Opioid Dependence*, New York: Plenum.

Willis, P. (1978), *Profane Culture*, London: Routledge & Kegan Paul.

Wolfe, T. (1969), *The Electric Kool-Aid Acid Test*, New York: Bantam.

Wootton Committee (1968), *Cannabis: Report by the Advisory Committee on Drug Dependence*, London: HMSO.

Yablonsky, L. (1968), *The Hippie Trip*, New York: Pegasus.

Young, J. (1971), *The Drugtakers*, London: Paladin.

Yudkin, J. (1972), *Pure, White and Deadly: The Problem of Sugar*, London: Davis-Poynter.
Zinberg, N. (1984), *Drug, Set and Setting*, New Haven CT: Yale University Press.

Index

see also hallucinogens
psychology of drug taker and reaction to
    drug, 23–4
psychotherapy, 59, 126, 128
psychotomimetic drugs, 117
    see also hallucinogens
pushers, myths about, 185–7

Quaalude, 156

Rabelais, François, 99
Rajastan, 172
religion
    alcohol, 35–6
    cannabis, 37
    drug-like effects of and dependence on,
        203
    Ethiopian Zion Coptic Church (EZCC),
        37
    guidelines about use of drugs, 35
    kava, 37
    and LSD, 38–40
    and magic mushrooms, 36–7
    and mescaline, 36
    peyote, use of by Native Americans and
        Aztecs, 36
    solitude and isolation, 202
    see also cults
Reynolds, J.R., 109
rhythmic stimulation, 202–3
rights of the individual, 175–6
Ritalin
    compared to amphetamines, 150n
    treatment for hyperactive children, 15,
        152
Robins, Lee, 184–5
Roget, Peter, 197
Rohypnol, 53–4
Ross, Alan, 192
Rouse, Alan, 204, 205n
routes of administration, 26, 133–5
Royal Commission into the Non-Medical
        Use of Drugs (South Australia), 114
rules and rituals of drug-taking, 43–4
Runciman Report, 170
running, long-distance, 203

sailors, 68

Saturnalia, 35–6
Schachter, Stanley, 16
schizophrenia and cannabis, 105–6
scopolamine, 6, 22
sects, 203
sedatives and introverts/extroverts, 15
self-medication, misuse of prescribed drugs,
        57–9
sensory deprivation, 201–2
serotonin, 6, 49, 129, 199
sex, 203–4
sexual transmission of HIV among drug
        users, 141
Shafer Report, 113
Sharples, Anthony, 184
Shiva, 37, 99
Singer, Jerome, 16
skiing, 204
sleeping tablets, 16, 50
    see also barbiturates
sleeplessness, barbiturates as treatment for,
        155–6
smoking
    bans in workplaces and public places,
        93–4, 95
    carbon monoxide, effects of, 92
    as cause of illness, 87–92
    coronary heart disease, 90–1
    difference between the sexes, 82–3, 89
    health warnings, 92–3
    inaccuracies in diagnosis of illness, 88
    and lung cancer, 88–90
    and the Nazis, 151
    passive, risks of, 94–5
    prevalence in films, 34–5
    respiratory disorders, 91–2
    as stress inducing, 91
    study of identical twins, 90–1
    see also cigarettes; tobacco
smuggling, 82, 135, 173, 177
social context, effect on drug taking
    availability of drugs, 33–4
    centrality of, 31–4
    khat, 35
    rules and rituals, 43–4
    smoking in films, 34–5
    street culture, 45–6